Walking the Cathedral Cities of Western England

Walking the Cathedral Cities of Western England

ROWLAND MEAD

TWENTY-EIGHT ORIGINAL WALKS
AND TOURS AROUND THE
CATHEDRALS AND CATHEDRAL CITIES
OF WESTERN ENGLAND

First published in 2001 by
New Holland Publishers (UK) Ltd
London • Cape Town • Sydney • Auckland

24 Nutford Place
London W1H 6DQ
United Kingdom

80 McKenzie Street
Cape Town 8001
South Africa

14 Aquatic Drive
Frenchs Forest, NSW 2086
Australia

218 Lake Road
Northcote
Auckland
New Zealand

ISBN 1 85974 519 9

Publishing Manager: Jo Hemmings
Editors: Paul Barnett, Pete Duncan, Jo Cleere
Cartographer: William Smuts
Designer: Alan Marshall
Indexer: Janet Dudley

Reproduction by Pica Colour Separation Overseas (Pte) Ltd, Singapore
Printed and bound in Singapore by Kyodo Printing Co (Singapore) Pte Ltd

Photographic Acknowledgements
All photographs by the author with the exception of the following:
Life File/Emma Lee plate 17; Life File/Mike Maidment plate 1; Life File/Andrew Ward
plate 25; Life File/Jeremy Hoare plate 32; James Morris/Axiom plate 20; Photobank/Peter
Baker plates 2, 6, 13, 15; Photobank/Gary Goodwin plate 19; PictureBank plates 5, 9, 18,
21; Travel Ink/Ken Gibson plate 14; Travel Ink/Christopher Nicholson plate 4; Travel
Ink/Tony Page plate 12; Travel Ink/David Toase plates 30, 31

Front cover: Wells Cathedral across the moat of the Bishop's Palace,
photographed by Jeanetta Baker, Photobank.
Back cover: The Sheldonian Theatre, Oxford, photographed by Ted Edwards, Travel Ink

Contents

Acknowledgements

This book and the earlier volume derived from an enthusiastically accepted early retirement and the wish to use the increased leisure time in a constructive way by visiting the ancient cathedrals of England. After I had studied several cathedrals in detail, it occurred to me there was a need for a book which provided information for a day out in a cathedral city, combining a tour of the cathedral, an agreeable lunch and a walk around the historic core of the city.

I set about writing the first regional guide and toted the idea around various publishers. No luck! Just when I was beginning to despair, the publishing firm of New Holland received my ideas with enthusiasm. I must therefore record my thanks to New Holland's former Publishing Director, Charlotte Parry-Crooke, and former Publishing Manager, Tim Jollands, for their encouragement and advice. I would also like to thank Pete Duncan for the calm and professional way he has dealt with the editing work.

When I set out on the research, I determined to avoid contacting cathedral authorities in a formal way, so that I could I could give a totally unbiased view. Nevertheless, I spoke to a vast number of cathedral staff and guides, who often revealed some gems of information which would not normally appear in the official brochures. My thanks to all who unwittingly helped. The same comments apply to the staff of the cities' Tourist Information Offices. They were invariably cooperative and helpful, despite the fact that I often caught them at times when they were busy and harassed.

Last but not least, my thanks to my wife for her encouragement and valuable theological knowledge. She uncomplainingly tested out all the tours in what often turned out to be vile weather. I could not have wished for a better companion to visit our wonderful cathedral cities.

Rowland Mead
Leighton Buzzard

Introduction

For many people, English cathedrals have a special fascination. They are undoubtedly the supreme expression of English architecture. In terms of enclosed space they were, until Victorian times, the largest buildings in the country. They are also extremely varied, both individually and in comparison with each other, lacking as they do the strict symmetry of the Classical style. Furthermore, English cathedrals often have as near neighbours the remains of their associated abbeys, and are usually surrounded by their host city's historic core, full of engrossing domestic architecture, ancient defensive walls and other sites of interest.

Numerous books have been written about the English cathedral, some emphasizing the architectural aspects and others of a more spiritual context. Most city authorities have produced a 'town trail' describing a route through the centre. This volume aims to combine these aspects on a regional basis. Each section begins by looking at the historical background of the cathedral and city. This is followed a guided tour of the cathedral itself (with a plan for easy reference), concentrating on not just the architecture but also on relevant odd quirks and historical relics. Then there is a walking tour, beginning and ending at the cathedral, of the historic core of the city (again with a map). Options and alternative routes are supplied to suit the energy of the visitor and the time available. Possibilities for refreshment en route are suggested, with particular attention to historic pubs and old coaching inns, essential features of the English cathedral city.

This, the second of two regional guides, deals with fourteen cathedrals and their cities in western England. An earlier volume covers the eastern part of the country.

English Cathedrals – An Introduction

A cathedral is a place of Christian worship that contains a *cathedra* – that is, a bishop's seat or throne. The *cathedra* was the bishop's symbol of authority; should the *cathedra* be moved, the cathedral building would have to be redesignated.

In medieval times, if a cathedral was attached to a monastery (a Norman innovation), the bishop had the further title of abbot, although the effective head of the monastery was its prior – an arrangement which often led to friction. Of the seventeen cathedrals in medieval England, eight were monastic, usually Benedictine (e.g., Canterbury, Ely and Winchester). Such cathedrals had a range of adjoining monastic buildings, usually on the south side, including a chapter house, dormitory, refectory, infirmary, hospital (or guest hall) and cloisters.

The other cathedrals were served by canons. There were two types of these: secular canons and canons regular, the latter working to fixed rules. The most important canons regular were the Augustinians, followers of the writings of St Augustine (d604); their liberal approach to life meant they had a much more workable relationship with the townspeople than did the monks.

The secular canons, on the other hand, were unhampered by rules and were generally free to live where they liked. They depended on a prebend or endowment (usually from a wealthy landowner), and were thus often known as prebendaries. This was, for example, the situation at Southwell, where many of the large houses around the cathedral were those provided for the prebendaries. The canons' function was to run the cathedral and its services, a role fulfilled by the dean and chapter today.

Newer Cathedrals

The cathedrals run by secular canons were collectively known after the Reformation as the Old Foundation. The five new sees created by Henry VIII – Oxford, Peterborough, Chester, Gloucester and Bristol – plus the surviving monastic cathedrals were the New Foundation. Confusingly, many of the secular cathedrals (e.g., Lincoln) have cloisters, although these were largely ornamental rather than practical.

During the Industrial Revolution people flocked from the land to the growing cities based on the coalfields in the Midlands and the north. This flow of population necessitated the setting up of a number of additional sees. New cathedrals were created, usually by upgrading existing parish churches – as at Manchester, Liverpool, Wakefield and elsewhere – but also from scratch, as at Truro. After World War II, some modern cathedrals were constructed: the one at Coventry replaced a building destroyed by enemy bombs, while that at Guildford was the product of an architectural competition.

Architectural Styles

The majority of English cathedrals are Gothic in style, but none has the purity of one specific period – indeed, it is often possible to find elements of Norman, Early English, Decorated and Perpendicular styles within a single cathedral.

It is frequently thought that English cathedral architecture originated in France and was brought over by the Normans, but this is an oversimplification: the Anglo-Saxons had imported the Norman style before the Conquest. Thereafter, English masons developed their own styles – for example, the Perpendicular, a style not seen among the French, who were then still experimenting with the Flamboyant, a development of the earlier Decorated style. Shape and form also differ between English and French cathedrals. The naves of French cathedrals soar to great heights, while English cathedrals tend to be long and low, with height gained by towers and spires. The extra length of English naves has two explanations. First, in monastic cathedrals the monks and townspeople were kept apart: the congregation occupied the nave and the monks the choir and presbytery, the two areas being separated by a *pulpitum* (screen). Second, the nave often had a non-religious use, such as the collection of tithes or the administration of justice, requiring a sizeable area. Another difference between English and French cathedrals can be found at the east ends. The French buildings are noted for their apse, a semi-circular structure within which was an ambulatory or processional way, often for pilgrims to pass by shrines. English cathedrals, on the other hand, are more likely to have a stepped or cliff-like east end, perhaps marked by a Lady Chapel.

Although one finds the occasional example of Anglo-Saxon work (such as Ripon's crypt), for convenience we can divide the medieval architectural styles into four.

Norman

The Norman style actually appeared (in parts of Westminster Abbey) during the reign of Edward the Confessor, but for simplicity's sake the start can be dated as 1066, at the beginning of the Norman Conquest. It lasted until approximately 1190. Known properly as Romanesque, it was common throughout Europe.

In English cathedrals much of the Norman work has been replaced, but sufficient remains in buildings such as Durham, Ely, Gloucester and many others to recognise the essential elements. It was during the Norman period that the idea of three horizontal layers was introduced – the main arcade, the triforium (or tribune) and the clerestory – and their relative proportions are a key to the aesthetic appearance of the interior. The piers or pillars tend to be massive and cylindrical, with engaged shafts and occasionally, as at Durham, etched or chevron decoration. Arches are invariably rounded, sometimes with zigzag or dog-tooth mouldings. Sometimes, as at Ely, the arches interlock. Windows are small and narrow and splayed only on the inside. Roofs were initially wooden and highly decorated, although vaulting put in an appearance towards the end of the period, particularly in the aisles. Few Norman towers survive – they dropped like ninepins and were

Norman: Nave, Chichester

Early English: North Transept, Salisbury

often replaced in later periods. Sculptural decoration was minimal, although exceptions are the west door at Rochester, the Prior's Door at Ely and the capitals in the crypt at Canterbury.

Early English

The Early English style marked the start of Gothic architecture and began in England around 1175, overlapping the end of the Norman period. It was to last until 1265. (It is interesting to note that the term 'Gothic' did not appear in the literature until the late 17th century). The Early English style had a lighter and more elegant appearance than the Norman. Pointed arches appeared and windows were tall and narrow, known as lancets after the surgeon's knife. Trefoils and plate tracery were used for the first time. Piers were often formed of columns with detached shafts (often of Purbeck Marble), united at the capitals, which frequently had stiff-leaved foliage. The Early English style probably first appeared in the choir at Lincoln and there are particularly fine examples to be seen at Exeter, Wells, the south Transept at York, Southwell and Peterborough.

Undoubtedly the most comprehensively Early English construction is at Salisbury, the English cathedral that comes nearest to having a single style; building started in 1220 and was more or less completed 38 years later.

Decorated

A further period of transition came with the Decorated style, which appeared *c*1250 and reached its zenith in the middle of the following century. (Architectural historians often divide the Decorated period into Geometrical or Early Decorated and Flowing or Late Decorated.) The style takes its name from the window tracery, which became extremely complex. The moulded stone mullions in the upper part of the windows formed graceful circles and other intricate designs. Piers came to have closely joined shafts, not detached as before, while capitals, bosses and other stonework were ornately carved with free-flowing foliage, animals and heads. All this work was expensive and labour-intensive, but this was no problem: it was a prosperous time and the Church was receiving considerable income from the land it owned. Examples of the Decorated style are plentiful in our cathedrals; there are particularly fine examples in the chapter houses at Southwell, Wells and Salisbury, in many parts of York Minster, in the Angel Choir at Lincoln and in the nave at Lichfield.

Decorated: Lady Chapel, Exeter

Perpendicular

The final stage of the Gothic, the Perpendicular, lasted 200 years, from 1350 to *c*1550. The Perpendicular, which has been described as the 'architecture of vertical lines', is best observed in window tracery, where the mullions carry straight on up to the head of the framework. The areas of glass became larger and the rectilinear spaces became more suitable for stained-glass renditions of stories and parables. Pillars were more elegant and led up to superb fan vaulting or the astonishing *pendant lierne* vault, such as that at Oxford. Rose windows appeared, usually in the transepts. Shallow panels in the solid masonry of walls were another hallmark of the period.

Perpendicular: Lady Chapel, Gloucester

The earliest extant Perpendicular cathedral window is probably that in the choir at Gloucester, but Southwell, Winchester and others have some striking west windows in this style. The crowning glory of the Perpendicular is to be found in Henry VII's Chapel at Westminster Abbey.

The subsequent Renaissance period saw a revival of the Classical and Roman styles of architecture. During this period – the 16th and 17th centuries – there was very little cathedral (or church) building in England, so the styles are little represented, the remarkable exception being St Paul's Cathedral. The huge Old St Paul's, a Gothic edifice, was destroyed in the Great Fire of 1666. The replacement – designed by Sir Christopher Wren (1632–1723) – with its massive dome, is totally unlike any other English cathedral.

The Gothic influence, however, would not go away. There was a strong revival of Neo-Gothic during Victorian times, often with unfortunate results; the replacement west front at St Albans is one example.

Early Cathedral Life

The medieval English cathedral was a very different place from what we witness today. Before the Reformation the cathedral was often a very wealthy establishment, particularly if it had an important shrine and thus attracted pilgrims. It would be a riot of colour, with abundant statuary, a bejewelled and gilded altar, rich tapestries and paintings.

Life in a medieval monastery or cathedral might seem very harsh to us, but by comparison with the lot of most of the common folk of the time it was fairly comfortable. Each day a monk would have to spend about four hours in public worship, about four in study or private prayer and perhaps another six engaged in work for the benefit of the monastic community – cooking, perhaps, or the tending of vegetables. The abbot's rule was supreme within the community: he could be as totalitarian as any despot if he wished, although most abbots had more sense.

The day was divided up by acts of worship. With Matins immediately after midnight, Prime at sunrise, Terce at about 9am, High Mass at about 10am, Sext at noon, None in midafternoon, Vespers in the early evening and Compline at sunset – with other services thrown in on special occasions – the monks were not left much time for such activities as sleeping! In fact, they retired to their dormitories to sleep twice each night, between Compline and Matins and between Matins and Prime.

While some monks would live, grow old and die within a single monastery – this was the life of the Benedictines (followers of St Benedict of Nursia (*c*480–*c*547)) – members of many orders would frequently move from one to the next, preaching in towns and villages en route, helping the poor and needy, and living off alms. Such was the practice of, for example, the Dominicans (adherents of St Dominic (*c*1170–1221); called the Black Friars because of their garb), the Carmelites (gaining their name from Mount Carmel, France, where the order was founded; the White Friars) and the Franciscans (adherents of St Francis of Assisi (1181–1226); the Grey Friars). Members of military orders, such as the Knights Templar, were likewise unbound to a single monastery.

At the Reformation, Henry VIII's men plundered the sacred shrines of orders such as the Benedictines, smashed the statues and removed much of the plate, jewels and hangings. The monasteries were closed down and their stonework was often stolen by townspeople for building purposes. Further vandalism occurred during the Civil War, with soldiers often using cathedrals as barracks. Then followed ages of neglect. The Victorians strove to rectify this, not always happily. Nevertheless, our cathedrals still retain much of their ancient beauty and charm and few of us can remain unmoved by them.

Life Today in England's Cathedrals

Life in today's – Church of England – cathedrals is in some ways not so dissimilar from that of the medieval monastery. Although such activities as the tilling of fields have been superseded by their modern counterparts, the priests nevertheless still divide their time between religious and pastoral concerns – typically there are five services on a Sunday and two or three on each of the other days. Choral music remains an important aspect of cathedral life, with various first-rate choir schools attached to cathedrals.

Also unchanged since early times is the need to raise funds for the upkeep of the cathedral and other expenses involved in running it on a day-to-day basis. While large-scale benefactors play their part in this, the dean and chapter are also heavily reliant on contributions from the general public; thus, while it may grate on the sensibilities to be asked on visiting a cathedral for either an admission fee or a 'recommended donation' – which is very much the same thing – do bear in mind that without such measures the cathedral would very soon decline into the kind of rack and ruin that was probably its condition for centuries before the Victorian era.

With their many visitors, their shops, their information desks, their audiovisual displays and so forth, it might seem that today's cathedrals lack the stillness and tranquillity – the space for contemplation – that one might expect in a house of God. To a great extent this can be true, especially in such popular venues as St Paul's and Westminster Abbey. Yet even in such places, as one gazes in awe at a stained-glass window or steps for a moment into the cool silence of a side chapel, one can discover the transcendent peace that lies at the core of us all.

English Cathedrals in Historical Context

Rulers of England and the UK		Cathedral History	
Edwy	955-959	600-1000	Many English cathedrals, e.g. Canterbury and Winchester, had their foundation in Saxon times, often attached to monasteries.
Edgar	959-975		
Edward the Martyr	975-979		
Ethelred the Unready	979-1016		
Edmund Ironside	1016	1066	Norman Conquest. Many Saxon cathedrals demolished or rebuilt.
Canute	1016-1035		
Harold I	1035-1040	*c*1066-1190	Norman or Romanesque style of architecture, well exemplified in Durham and Ely cathedrals.
Hardicanute	1040-1042		
Edward the Confessor	1042-1066		
Harold II	1066		
William I (the Conqueror)	1066-1087	1170	Archbishop Thomas à Becket murdered in Canterbury Cathedral.
William II	1087-1100		
Henry I	1100-1135	*c*1190-1300	Early English style of architecture, seen, for instance, at Wells and Lincoln.
Stephen	1135-1154		
Henry II	1154-1189		
Richard I	1189-1199	*c*1250-1380	Decorated Gothic style of architecture, typified by Exeter and York.
John	1199-1216		
Henry III	1216-1272		
Edward I	1272-1307	*c*1350-1550	Perpendicular Gothic style of architecture, as seen at Gloucester.
Edward II	1307-1327		
Edward III	1327-1377	1532	Henry VIII begins the Reformation in England, separating the English church from Rome. Many statues and stained glass windows destroyed in the cathedrals.
Richard II	1377-1399		
Henry IV	1399-1413		
Henry V	1413-1422		
Henry VI	1422-1461		
Edward IV	1461-1483		
Edward V	1483		
Richard III	1483-1485	1536-1540	Dissolution of the Monasteries by Henry VIII. Many were refounded as cathedrals.
Henry VII	1485-1509		
Henry VIII	1509-1547		
Edward VI	1547-1553	1642-1650	English Civil War. Troops used cathedrals as barracks, causing considerable damage.
Mary I	1553-1558		
Elizabeth I	1558-1603		
James I of England and IV of Scotland	1603-1625	1666	Old St Paul's Cathedral burnt down in the Great Fire of London.
Charles I	1625-1649		
Oliver Cromwell, Lord Protector	1653-1685	17th century	English Renaissance style of architecture.
Richard Cromwell	1658-1659	1675-1710	St Paul's Cathedral rebuilt in Classical style
Charles II	1660-1685		
James II	1658-1688	18th century	Period of decay for most English cathedrals
William III and Mary II (Mary died 1694)	1689-1702		
Anne	1702-1714	19th century	Victorian times saw English cathedrals heavily restored, often badly.
George I	1714-1727		
George II	1727-1760		
George III	1760-1820	Late 19th century	Gothic revival. New cathedral built at Truro in this style.
George IV	1820-1830		
William IV	1830-1837	1914-1918	World War I. English cathedrals largely unscathed.
Victoria	1837-1901		
Edward VII	1901-1910	1939-45	World War II. Many English cathedrals damaged in air raids, but only Coventry destroyed.
George V	1910-1936		
Edward VIII	1936		
George VI	1936-1952	1955-1962	Coventry Cathedral rebuilt in modern style.
Elizabeth II	1952-		

Cathedral Architecture – Glossary of Terms

APSE. A polygonal or semi-circular end to a cathedral chapel. It is usually vaulted.

ARCADE. A row of arches, usually between the nave and the aisles, supporting the main wall.

BALUSTER. A carved column supporting a handrail. A series of balusters is known as a balustrade.

BALL FLOWER. Stone ornament consisting of a globe shaped design with folded back petals, typical of the Decorated period.

BOSS. Located at the intersection of ribs in a vaulted roof. Usually carved with foliage or figures, it may be gilded or coloured.

BUTTRESS. A vertical area of stonework supporting a wall. An exterior buttress containing an arch is known as a 'flying buttress'.

CAPITAL. The moulded or carved block on the top of a column on which the superstructure rests. Often richly ornamented.

CHANTRY. A small chapel within a cathedral, in which prayers were 'chanted'. Usually named after a donor.

CHAPTER HOUSE. An assembly room for meetings of the chapter, who are the governing body of the cathedral.

CHOIR. The part of the cathedral east of the screen and west of the presbytery, in which the service is sung.

CLERESTORY An upper range of windows, below the eaves and above the aisled roof. Sometimes known as the 'clear storey' as distinct from the triforium or 'blind storey'.

CORBEL. A stone block projecting from a wall to provide horizontal support to various features. Often grotesquely carved.

CROSSING. The square space at the intersection of the nave and transepts, usually beneath the tower.

CRYPT. An underground chamber, usually vaulted, beneath the chancel. May contain an altar.

CHANCEL. The part of the cathedral east of the crossing.

DIOCESE. The area under the jurisdiction of a bishop.

FAN VAULTING. A type of vault in which the ribs (which are decorative rather than structural) are of equal length and curvature. Typical of the Perpendicular period.

GALILEE. A chapel or porch at the west end of a cathedral, usually included in the processional route.

GARTH. The area enclosed by cloisters.

HAMMER BEAM. A horizontal beam projecting at right angles from the top of a wall providing support for a wooden roof.

LADY CHAPEL. A chapel dedicated to the Virgin Mary, usually located at the east end of the cathedral.

LANCET. A tall, narrow window with a pointed head and no tracery. Typical of the Early English period.

LANTERN. A tower with windows designed to give light to the crossing beneath.

LIERNE. Short vault ribs, which are purely decorative. Typical of the Perpendicular and Late Decorated periods.

MISERICORD. A bracket beneath a hinged seat in the choir stalls. When the seat was tipped up it gave some support during lengthy periods of standing. Often engagingly carved.

MULLION. A vertical stone bar sub-dividing a window into 'lights'

NAVE. The main body and western arm of a cathedral. May have aisles.

OGEE. A double S-curve found on arches and typical of the Late Decorated period.

PIER. A solid stone vertical support. May be carved or moulded.

PRESBYTERY. The area east of the choir where the high altar is located.

PULPITUM. A screen dividing the choir from the nave. The gallery or loft supported by the pulpitum often provided the location for the organ.

REBUS. A pictorial play on words often linked with the name of the bishop.

RETROCHOIR. In the eastern arm of the cathedral behind the high altar, but not including the lady chapel.

ROOD SCREEN. A screen, usually just west of the pulpitum and generally made of wood.

ROSE WINDOW. A circular window in which the tracery resembles a rose.

SANCTUARY. The area of the cathedral containing the high altar. Synonymous with the presbytery. In medieval times, fugitives from justice could shelter here after using the sanctuary knocker.

SEDILLA. A row of 3 canopied seats for the clergy on the south side of the chancel.

SPANDREL. The roughly triangular space between the outer curve of an arch and the mouldings enclosing it. Usually elaborately carved with, for example, foliage.

TIERCERON. A type of vaulting where minor ribs spring from the main rib and lead to the ridge rib.

TRACERY. Slender stone ornamental ribwork on the upper part of gothic windows. Also found on walls and screens.

TRANSEPT. The short arms running north–south in a cruciform church or cathedral.

TRIBUNE. A gallery extending along the roof of an aisle.

TRIFORIUM. An arcaded or walled passage at the intermediate level between the main arcade and the clerestory. Often known as the 'blind storey' because of its lack of windows and light. If there are windows, the term 'tribune' is preferable.

VAULT. Ceilings or roofs with load-bearing arches.

Key to Maps

Each of the cathedral tours and city walks in this book is accompanied by a detailed map on which the route is shown in purple. Places of interest along the walks – such as churches, pubs and historic houses – are clearly identified. Opening times are listed chapter by chapter at the back of the book, starting on page 166.

The following is a key to symbols and abbreviations used on the maps:

Symbols

▬◄▬	route of walk
▬▬▬	railway line
▮	major building
†	church
🏻	public toilets
🌳	park
⇌	railway station

Abbreviations

APP	Approach	PH	Public House
AVE	Avenue		(Pub)
CLO	Close	PK	Park
COTTS	Cottages	PL	Place
CT	Court	RD	Road
DRI	Drive	S	South
E	East	SQ	Square
GDNS	Gardens	ST	Street
GRN	Green	STN	Station
GRO	Grove	TER	Terrace
HO	House	UPR	Upper
LA	Lane	VW	View
LWR	Lower	W	West
MS	Mews	WD	Wood
MT	Mount	WHF	Wharf
N	North	WLK	Walk
PAS	Passage	WY	Way
PDE	Parade		

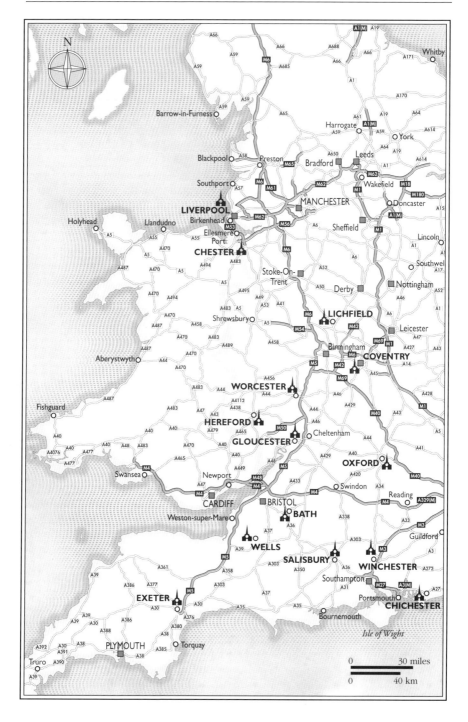

Exeter

Access: The days when Exeter was out on a limb and a full day's drive from London and the Midlands are now fortunately over. The improved motorway and trunk road system ensures that Exeter can be reached from Birmingham via the M5 and from London via the M4 and M5 in about three hours. Coach services make full use of this accessibility: the National Express 501 Rapide service, for example, runs eight times a day to and from London. Exeter also has good train services connecting with London, the Midlands and the North; during the week there are 20 trains a day (including overnight sleepers) from London. Exeter Airport, some six miles (10km) to the east of the city, operates scheduled air services to cities including Belfast, Dublin, and Manchester.

Exeter has a long and fascinating history. The city was occupied by the Romans for almost four centuries, the most obvious reminder of those days being the city wall, probably built *c*AD200 and still largely intact today. The Romans named the settlement Isca Dumnoniorum. Excavations have revealed a mosaic pavement, a basilica and (in the cathedral close) a legionary bathhouse. The Romans eventually withdrew their legions in the 5th century.

It seems the first Christian community at Exeter dates back to the 7th century: St Boniface (680–755), the Saxon missionary to the Germans, received part of his education at a monastery here, and excavations have revealed the possible position of this building. Later a Saxon church stood to the west of the present cathedral. It was destroyed by the Danes in 1003 but rebuilt by King Canute (*c*995–1035) in 1019. Bishop Leofric, whose jurisdiction covered the whole of Devon and Cornwall, decided to move his seat from Crediton to Exeter in 1050, so this small Saxon church became a cathedral. King Edward the Confessor came in person to enthrone Leofric as the first Bishop of Exeter.

The Saxons here, as in many parts of Britain, resisted the Norman Conquest. The citizens of Exeter were under siege from William the Conqueror for nearly three weeks in 1068 before an honourable surrender was negotiated. The Normans then built Rougemont Castle to deter further Saxon insurrection. The 3rd Bishop of Exeter, William Warelwast (in office 1107–37), a nephew of the Conqueror, started to build the new cathedral of St Peter. This Norman work survives in the tower and in the base of the nave walls. Further development came at the end of the 13th century when, spurred on by news of the new cathedral at Salisbury, Bishop Bronescombe began a rebuilding in the Decorated style, adding a Lady Chapel (where he was buried) and the presbytery. His successors carried on the work into the quire and nave, the work being completed by the time of Bishop John Grandisson (1292–1369), probably by 1350.

During medieval times the city of Exeter developed as an important ecclesiastic centre. Within the city walls there were, in addition to the cathedral, 32 parish churches plus chapels and monasteries. Wealth at this time was largely based on the wool industry. Guilds flourished and were both numerous and powerful. The Guildhall and Tuckers' Hall date from this period.

At the cathedral, minor additions and developments continued, with the reconstruction of the chapter house and the building of various chantry chapels. Exeter suffered less than most cathedrals during the Reformation, but its cloisters were destroyed in the mid-17th century. At this time the cathedral was divided into two sections by a brick wall built over the Great Screen, with the Independents worshipping on one side and the Presbyterians on the other.

During the Tudor period Exeter was the sixth largest city in England, and it developed as an important trading centre. Many examples of Tudor domestic architecture can still be seen around the central area of the city, with the most famous illustration being Mol's Coffee House in the Cathedral Close. Famous sea captains like Hawkins, Drake, Frobisher and Raleigh were frequently seen around the city, which provided three ships to fight the Spanish Armada.

During the Civil War Exeter's loyalties were divided, and both Royalists and Parliamentarians occupied the city at various times, with more than one siege taking place. After the war the city soon recovered and prosperity resumed. In Georgian times development was largely outside the city walls and many distinguished crescents and terraces were built to house the burgeoning middle classes.

Lacking coal deposits, Exeter experienced a relative decline during the Industrial Revolution, but the Victorian era saw the expansion of the canal trade, the coming of the railways and the advent of horse-drawn trams. By 1860 the population had reached 50,000 and industries such as brewing, papermaking and printing had become established.

The cathedral had meanwhile been suffering from two centuries of neglect. The architect Sir George Gilbert Scott (1811–1878) began a major restoration in 1870. The stonework was cleaned, the Bishop's Throne was restored and the quire was transformed to match it. The outer bays of the organ screen were removed, as were the side walls of the quire, allowing a view into the quire from the nave.

The two world wars had little effect on Exeter until the night of May 3, 1942, when a German air raid, said to be in retaliation for an RAF raid on Lübeck, devastated the central part of the city: 156 people were killed, over 500 were injured and more than 1500 houses, many of historical and architectural importance, were completely destroyed. At the outbreak of World War II some of the cathedral's most valued treasures had been taken to a place of safety, and this precaution paid off when the cathedral received a direct hit during the Blitz. Luckily, although there was a considerable amount of damage, particularly to the quire, the main structure was unaffected. Recent years have seen a concentration on the cleaning of the stonework and the recolouring of the sculptures and monuments, so that the general impression today is of a cared-for and efficiently maintained cathedral.

These days Exeter is a thriving regional centre. Its university is popular and respected, while business and commerce prosper. Tourism has become increasingly important, with the cathedral a major magnet, attracting over 400,000 visitors annually.

TOUR OF THE CATHEDRAL

Start: The west front.
Finish: The chapter house.

The **West Front (1)** dates from the mid-14th century and is designed on three levels. The lower part consists of a screen of sculptured figures which make a fascinating study, although in many cases the statues are badly weathered; they are currently under restoration, along with the front as a whole. The second and third levels consist of windows in Decorated style with interesting tracery, but each in turn is partly obscured by the level below.

If the initial exterior view is a little disappointing, the interior more than compensates. The **Nave (2)** is one of the delights of English cathedral architecture. Proportion is the key. The arcades have shafted pillars of unpolished Purbeck Marble that support moulded arches of Beer Limestone (from a quarry owned by the Dean and Chapter). Above is a narrow triforium, followed by a clerestory in which each bay is filled with a single large window containing complex tracery and which is largely responsible for the overall impression of light in the whole of the nave. Capping everything is the magnificent tierceron vaulting, probably the finest in Europe. Complementing this rich stonework are well coloured and gilded bosses and corbels.

At the nave entrance we find the first two of many chapels. To the left, in the northwest corner, is the Chapel of St Edmund, which has links with the Devonshire Regiment. To the right is the Chapel of Bishop Grandisson, who completed the 14th-century redevelopments.

Now move to the **Font (3)**, which is made of Sicilian marble dating from 1687. The oak cover has eight inlaid figures of the apostles. The stem is modern. From the font there is a fine view of the **Minstrels' Gallery (4)**, the front of which contains angel figures playing medieval musical instruments; from left to right these are citole, bagpipes, recorder, fiddle, harp, trumpet, portative organ, gittern, shawm, tambourine and cymbals. The gallery is still used on occasions.

Sedilia, south side of Lady Chapel

20

An Astronomical Clock

You now arrive at the **Great Screen (5)**, which was completed in 1325. It supports the organ, built by John Loosemore (*c*1613–1681) in 1665, and divides the nave from the quire. Along the top of the screen you can see a series of 17th-century paintings, while under the two side arches are the altars dedicated to St Mary and St Nicholas. Stepping into the **North Transept (6)** you find, dominating it, the orrery clock, probably dating from the late 15th century, although the dial at the top that records the minutes was added in 1760.

Walk along the north quire aisle and into the **Lady Chapel (7)**. Begun by Bishop Bronescombe around 1270, it has some splendid vaulting and a fine Decorated window. For a while it served as a library, but it was restored for worship in 1820 and is now used for daily services and private prayer. Don't miss the sedilia (tiered seats for the clergy) on the south side, or the dominating and beautifully gilded effigies of bishops Bronescombe and Stafford on either side of the entrance.

The Lady Chapel is flanked by two smaller chapels: to its north the Chapel of St Gabriel and to its south the Chapel of St Saviour (or Bishop Oldham's Chantry), which has a nice rebus (pictorial play on words) involving owls and dams.

From Quire to Chapter House

Move halfway down the south quire aisle and turn right into the **Quire (8)**, which is dominated by the Bishop's Throne, which is huge. This was made in 1312 using oak from the bishop's estates, and is considered one of the finest of its kind. It was dismantled during World War II and taken to safety, being returned during the

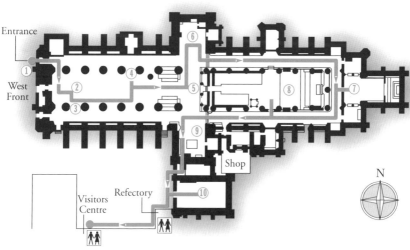

Key

1. West Front
2. Nave
3. Font
4. Minstrels' Gallery

5. Great Screen
6. North Transept
7. Lady Chapel
8. Quire

9. South Transept
10. Chapter House

postwar repairs. Next to the throne is the lectern, made of latten and probably dating from the early 16th century. The current quire stalls date from Sir George Gilbert Scott's renovations of 1870–77, but some of the old misericords were maintained. At the end of the quire is the Great East Window, one of the few examples of Perpendicular architecture in the cathedral; it replaced an earlier window whose stonework had decayed, but much of the original glass was retained.

Returning to the south quire aisle, note the Chapel of St James and St Thomas, destroyed by a bomb in 1942 and afterwards completely rebuilt.

Finally walk into the **South Transept (9)**. On your left is the Chapel of St John the Baptist. Next to the south wall is a monument to Sir John Gilbert, half-brother to Sir Walter Raleigh (1552–1618). Above the south transept is one of two Norman towers that contain the cathedral's bells – forming, it is claimed, the second heaviest ringing peal in England.

A door in the corner of the south transept leads to the **Chapter House (10)**. This was built in 1224 and underwent reconstruction in 1412. There was a further major renovation in 1969, enabling it to be used not only as the traditional meeting place for the clergy but also as an assembly room available to the public for concerts and other functions.

Leaving via the chapter house door you find yourself in a courtyard, crossing which you can make your way back to the Cathedral Green.

WALKING TOUR FROM EXETER CATHEDRAL

This figure-of-eight walk looks at most of the historic features of Exeter's city centre, including parts of the old walls, the castle – which is built on Roman foundations – some old sandstone churches, historic inns, part of the riverside area and the postwar shopping centre, rebuilt after the 1942 Blitz.

Start and finish: The west front of the cathedral.
Length: 2½ miles (4km).
Time: 1½ hours, but longer if you visit the museum and churches.
Refreshments: A number of historic pubs and old coaching inns provide lunchtime sustenance. The following, all on the walking route, are of particular interest: the Ship Inn in St Martin's Lane, reputed to be a favourite of Drake; the Bishop Blaize Inn, the Prospect Inn and On the Waterfront, all close to the quayside; the White Hart Inn, Exeter's most famous coaching inn and full of atmosphere; and the Turk's Head in the High Street, where Dickens was a regular visitor. The cathedral's own refectory is highly recommended.

The cathedral stands by the **Cathedral Close (1)** amid a grassy area which was opened up by the demolition, in 1971, of the Church of St Mary Major. Look in the middle of the lawns for the **Statue of Richard Hooker (2)**; Hooker (*c*1554–1600) was a 16th-century ecclesiastical scholar.

The Cathedral Close is bordered by a collection of historic buildings in a variety of styles. On the west side, next to the former Broadgate, is a building known as **Tinley's (3)**; once a hostel for travelling priests, it was a tearoom for decades until recently being made into a restaurant.

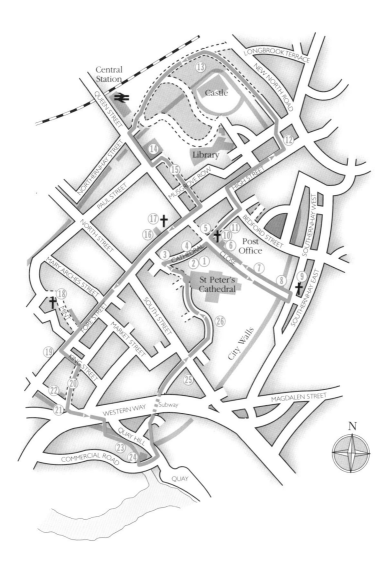

Key

1. Cathedral Close
2. Statue of Richard Hooker
3. Tinley's
4. Royal Clarence Hotel
5. Ship Inn
6. Mol's Coffee House
7. Bishop of Crediton's House
8. Burnet Patch Bridge
9. Southernhay

10. St Martin's Church
11. Ruins
12. Underground Passages
13. Northernhay Gardens
14. Royal Albert Museum
15. Gandy Street
16. Guildhall
17. Church of St Pancras
18. St Nicholas' Priory

19. Tuckers' Hall
20. Stepcote Hill
21. The House That Moved
22. St Marys Steps
23. Bishop Blaize Inn
24. Custom House
25. White Hart Inn
26. Bishop's Palace

Moving to the right along the close you come to the **Royal Clarence Hotel (4)**. Dating from 1769 and built in Georgian style, it gained its name from the Duchess of Clarence (later the wife of William IV), who stayed here on more than one occasion. Next to the Clarence is a narrow pedestrian alley, St Martin's Lane, in which stands the **Ship Inn (5)**. Claimed to have been a favourite watering-hole of Sir Francis Drake (*c*1540–1596), it also boasts a resident ghost.

A Historic Meeting Place

Move now to the north side of the close, to perhaps its most striking building (and certainly its most photographed), **Mol's Coffee House (6)**. This is a stark black-and-white example of Tudor domestic architecture, bearing the date 1596; the top storey, with its Dutch gable, was added around 1885. The building gained its name from an Italian, Thomas Mol, who once lived here. In all probability it has never been a coffee house, but certainly it was a gentlemen's meeting place for the famous Devon sea dogs, among others; today the premises are occupied by a jeweller.

There follows a series of half-timbered and red sandstone buildings, now mainly offices. The most striking is the **Bishop of Crediton's House (7)**, notable for its magnificent carved oak doorway.

Carry on parallel to the cathedral until you reach the old city walls and pass under the **Burnet Patch Bridge (8)**; made of cast iron, this was built by Mayor Burnet Patch in 1814 to aid the regular inspection of the city walls.

You now reach **Southernhay (9)**, one of many elegant Georgian terraces in the central part of Exeter. The word `hay', found as a suffix in several Exonian place-names, means `enclosure', and refers to developments outside the old city walls.

A Haven

Return now to the Cathedral Close. Keeping to the pavement, pass Mol's Coffee House on your right and leave the close at the northwest corner via Catherine Street, an alley between the SPCK Bookshop and **St Martin's Church (10)**. In medieval times there were as many as 32 parish churches in Exeter, and a number of these survive today. Built like most of the others in the local red sandstone, St Martin's dates from 1065, but was rebuilt in the 15th century. Should it be open, go inside: after the glories of the cathedral this much smaller, simpler church is a welcome oasis of tranquillity. Look for the chancel arch, the font, the Jacobean altar rails and the oak wagon roof. Externally, there is a fine Perpendicular window.

Proceeding along Catherine Street, note on the right a complex of **Ruins (11)**. These were once almshouses, in the middle of which was a small chapel. Excavations in 1987–8 revealed an early Roman fortress in the area and a house occupied by the cathedral's canons in medieval times; at Exeter the canons, whose work was to serve in the chantry chapels, were known as annuellars. The whole site was demolished by German bombers in 1942. A board recounts much of this history

Ancient Water Supplies

You are now entering a part of the city that was rebuilt after World War II. Turn left at Bedford Street and then right into the pedestrianized (except for minibuses) High Street. At the side of Boots, turn down a small arcade.

After a few yards you'll find on the right what looks like a normal shop front but is in fact the entrance to the unique **Underground Passages (12)**, the city's most unusual attraction. These were built during the 14th century to carry fresh water from the springs of St Sidwella in two distinct systems, one serving the cathedral precincts and the other the nearby town. Visitors with claustrophobic tendencies might wish to give this diversion a miss, because the passages are extraordinarily cramped, but for anyone else the experience is a fascinating one.

Back Above Ground

After the underground passages you may well be in the mood for some fresh air! So what better than a stroll around **Northernhay Gardens (13)**. These well laid-out gardens, claimed to be the oldest in Britain, follow the line of the Roman walls and the ditch of Rougemont Castle. Little remains of the castle, which was erected by William the Conqueror and is now the site of the Crown Court, built in 1774 in the inner bailey.

Leave the gardens at the far end of Queen Street and turn left along the Victorian Gothic façade of the **Royal Albert Museum (14)**. Built between 1865 and 1869, this has a good collection of historical, ethnographic and industrial exhibits, plus silver, glass and china. There is also a small collection of the work of Devon artists.

Now take the road at the side of the museum into **Gandy Street (15).** Once a dingy back lane, this has become revitalized in recent years, with thriving bistros, boutiques and specialist shops.

The far end of Gandy Street brings you back to the High Street. Turn right. A number of Tudor-aged buildings survived the Blitz, such as those occupied by Laura Ashley, Thornes (the chocolate makers), the Abbey National and the Turk's Head Inn. Next to the latter is the celebrated **Guildhall (16)**, believed to be the oldest municipal building in the country. Much of the present edifice dates from 1330, but there was almost certainly a Saxon building on the site. The Purbeck Stone portico is Tudor, and the attractive single-span wooden roof was installed around 1468. The imposing interior has been used for centuries as a meeting place and for civic ceremonies, as well as to house the municipal treasures.

At the rear of the Guildhall is a modern shopping centre; in the middle of all the concrete and glass is the tiny red sandstone **Church of St Pancras (17).** Once derelict, it has now been restored and it has become fashionable for the mayor to adopt it as his or her parish church.

Down Fore Street

Return to the High Street and pass by yet another sandstone church, St Petrock's, to the traffic lights where Exeter's four main historic roads meet: High Street (which you're on), South Street (to your left), North Street (now a minor opening, to your right) and Fore Street (straight ahead). Go on down Fore Street and after 100yd (100m) or so turn right along a small alley called The Mint. At the end of this alley is **St Nicholas' Priory (18)**, founded in 1070 as a Benedictine daughter house of Battle Abbey in Sussex. In medieval times it is said to have entertained King John and other noble guests. Following the Dissolution of the Monasteries in 1536 only the guest wing survived. This was sold to the Mallet family, who were rich Elizabethan merchants. The city council purchased it for £850 in 1913 and has gradually restored it. Today the Priory is a museum where visitors can view the 17th-century furnishings, bells, clocks, tapestries and the pillars and vaulting of the Norman cellar.

Return to Fore Street, turn right and continue down the hill. After 50yd (50m) or so on the right you find the **Tuckers' Hall (19)**, an imposing sandstone building dating from 1471. This was the hall of the most powerful guild – the Company of Weavers, Fullers and Shearmen – when the city was an important centre for the production of woollen goods. Fullers, known also as Tuckers, had the job of removing the grease from the wool and there were many fulling mills along the River Exe. The Hall fell into disrepair during the 19th century, but has now been fully restored. It has some fine panelling and carving, plus a collection of weapons surviving from the days when the guild played its part in the defence of the city.

The House That Moved

Now cross Fore Street and proceed into King Street. A little way along, turn right into an unnamed road which becomes **Stepcote Hill (20)**. The hill has over 100 steps on each side for pedestrians, with a cobbled packhorse track in the centre. Its name derives from the Old English word for 'steep'. The West Gate to the city stood here until demolished in 1815. William of Orange marched his men through this gate when he entered the city in 1688.

At the foot of Stepcote Hill is an interesting collection of Tudor houses, with half-timbered work and jettied walls. The most famous of these is **The House That Moved (21)**. Once a merchant's house and reputed to be one of the oldest timber-framed houses in Europe, this was moved on rollers to its present site when a new inner relief road was built in 1961.

Among the Tudor houses is yet another small sandstone church, **St Mary Steps (22)**, founded in the 12th century and rebuilt in the 15th. When nearby St Mary Major was demolished its wooden screen was re-erected at St Mary Steps. The attractive east window is modern, but the font is almost certainly Norman. The church's main claim to fame, however, is its clock, sometimes known as the Matthew the Miller Clock after the central figure, although an alternative theory suggests this figure is actually Henry VIII. The clock, believed to have been erected in the 16th century, was restored in 1980. The figures 'perform' on the hour.

On the Waterfront

From Stepcote Hill, cross the inner relief road (Western Way) by the pedestrian crossing, turn left and, after a few yards, turn down some steps with blue railings. This route takes you over the city wall and down to the level of the quay. On the right is the **Bishop Blaize Inn (23)**, the first inn to be built (1327) outside the city walls. A plaque at the front of the inn tells the visitor that Blaize was a bishop who was martyred in the 4th century, having had his flesh torn with woolcombers' rakes; for this reason he was adopted as the patron saint of weavers.

Turn left and head for the waterside. The whole area, once a dangerous slum, has been redeveloped over the past couple of decades as a leisure and residential complex, mainly in a sympathetic way. Where buildings have historic or architectural interest they have been carefully preserved, even though their use may have changed (note the bonded warehouses which are now discos and nightclubs!). The most impressive building is the **Custom House (24)**, an indication of Exeter's former maritime importance. Erected in 1681, it was one of the first brick buildings in the city. The arches over the ground-floor windows indicate there was once a colonnade here. A royal coat-of-arms in the roof pediment probably dates to the early 19th century. The two handsome cannon outside the Custom House came from a batch impounded in 1819 for non-payment of dues, having originally been bound for the Wellington Monument in Somerset.

Other buildings here include the tiny Wharfinger's Office, the Prospect Inn (excellent for lunches) and two huge five-storey warehouses (one in red sandstone, the other in white limestone) built in 1835. In one of the warehouses is On the Waterfront, an surprisingly good pizza restaurant with additional outside seating where you can watch boats, ducks, swans and moorhens pass by as you eat, all framed by an extremely pretty modern footbridge. Regrettably, the popular Maritime Museum on the far side of the river closed in the mid-1990s, although there are still boats you can explore; cross the river using either the footbridge or, for fun, the little hand-operated ferry.

To leave the waterside area, take the narrow lane opposite the Custom House and turn almost immediately right up a zigzag path by the multi-storey carpark and through a pedestrian tunnel (which bears one of several modern murals you'll have spotted around Exeter) under Western Way to emerge into Coombe Street. Pass behind the **White Hart Inn (25)**, the most famous of Exeter's coaching inns, to emerge on South Street.

Cross South Street and walk up the hill into Palace Gate. Ahead, through a gap in the stone wall, you can catch a glimpse of the **Bishop's Palace (26)**, where the cathedral library is located. This elegant building contrasts with the Cathedral Choir School on the other side of the road, which has a strong Victorian custodial look about it.

This brings you back to the Cathedral Close and the end of your walk.

The House That Moved

Wells

Access: Despite being at the centre of a network of roads, Wells is rather remote from the main lines of communication. The nearest motorway is the M5, some 15 miles (25km) to the west, linking Wells with the Southwest and the Midlands. Some 20 miles (32km) to the north is the M4, which most visitors will use if driving from London. The nearest railway stations are at Frome and Bridgwater, while the closest international airport is at Bristol.

Set close to the rolling Mendip Hills, Wells is England's smallest cathedral city. It gained its name from the springs which rise near to the Bishop's Palace and which for centuries provided the town's inhabitants with reliable drinking water. A religious site developed close to these springs and Roman and Saxon burial places have been found nearby. Excavations in 1978 confirmed that a Saxon church was founded here by Aldhelm, Bishop of Sherborne, around AD705. In AD909 the diocese of Wells was set up and the church became the Cathedral of St Andrew. In 1088 the bishopric was moved to Bath and the Saxon cathedral was left to decay. The building was restored and enlarged by a later bishop, Robert of Lewes.

Robert's successor, Reginald de Bohun, decided to build a new church at Wells, and work started in 1180. The building was constructed in a cream-coloured limestone – the Inferior Oolite from Doulting, some eight miles (13km) from Wells. Work began on the quire and progressed along the nave. By 1239 enough had been completed for the building to be dedicated. Meanwhile, attempts were made to have the cathedral status restored and success came in 1245, when Bishop Roger became the Bishop of Bath and Wells, a title which remains to this day. Bath and Wells were joint cathedrals until Bath Abbey was dissolved during the Reformation. The town of Wells had by that time been granted its royal charter, King John giving it the status of a free borough.

The octagonal chapter house of the cathedral was completed in 1306, and later the quire was extended eastwards to join the Lady Chapel, which had begun life as a separate structure. Also in the 14th century there were elaborate plans to build a spectacular central tower and spire, but these were aborted when it was clear the foundations could not support the additional weight. The solution came in 1338–48 when master mason William Joy constructed the remarkable scissor arches to support the tower on three sides. The bells were removed, later in the century being installed in the purpose-built southwest tower.

Although Wells is not a monastic cathedral, it has a fine set of cloisters. These were the last part of the cathedral to be built, being completed in 1508 in Perpendicular style. The east cloister is the traditional entrance to the cathedral for the bishop from his palace. Built by Bishop Jocelyn in the 13th century, the palace has had numerous additions, including the Great Hall and chapel. Relations between the bishop and the townspeople were not always cordial and eventually a protective moat was built around the palace, with a drawbridge over the main gate. In an effort to appease the local people, Bishop Bekynton used the palace wells to provide a public water supply. Other bishops, such as Nicholas Bubwith (d1424) in the 15th century, provided almshouses for the poorer people in the town.

By the 14th century Wells was the largest town in Somerset, its wealth based on the textile industry. Unfortunately, during the Industrial Revolution industries such as this moved to the coalfields, and clothmaking collapsed. The up-side of this was that Wells was untouched by the grimier aspects of the Industrial Revolution. It survived as a market and ecclesiastical centre, attracting genteel society. Today it is a small regional centre with a growing tourist industry based around the cathedral, which in the view of many is the most attractive in the country.

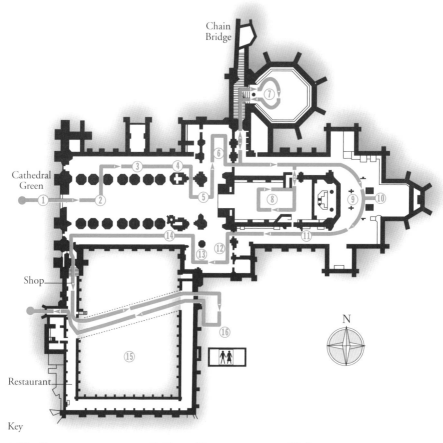

Key

1. West Front
2. Nave
3. North Porch
4. Bubwith Chantry Chapel
5. Strainer Arches
6. North Transept
7. Chapter House
8. Quire
9. Retrochoir
10. Lady Chapel
11. Bekynton Chantry Chapel
12. South Transept
13. Font
14. Sugar Chantry Chapel
15. Cloisters
16. Camery Gardens

TOUR OF THE CATHEDRAL
Start: The west front.
Finish: The cloisters.

The **West Front (1)** is best viewed from back across Cathedral Green. This is undoubtedly the finest west front in England. It is 147ft (44m) wide, so that it is as broad as it is high, and it resembles a huge and elaborate altar screen, complete with nearly 400 statues and three clearly defined horizontal architectural zones. Its buttresses and arcades cast strong shadows, so it does not have the flat appearance of other cathedral fronts such as those at Southwell and Winchester.

The sculptures represent a complete theological theme. The lowest zone (with many statues missing) concerns prophets and angels. Above this are biblical scenes. The central zone has martyred monarchs, saints and bishops, and then comes the Resurrection of the Dead. If you look next at the stepped gable in the centre, you can see that the lowest part shows the Nine Orders of Angels with, above this, the apostles. Finally, at the top, is Christ in Majesty, flanked by seraphim, dating from 1985 and replacing the rather battered medieval original. During recent restoration work, traces of medieval painting and gilding have been noted, so the west front must have once been even more impressive than it is today.

Step through the unremarkable west door and enter the cathedral. You are now in the **Nave (2)**. The vista in this part of the building is dominated by the massive strainer or scissor arches, but ignore these for now and concentrate on the main features of the nave. This was the earliest extant medieval building in England to have pointed arches used throughout. The scale here is modest, with the height from floor to vault only 67ft (20m), but the proportions are satisfying. Alec Clifton Taylor has described the piers as the most beautiful in England, and few would quarrel with this. Each pier is covered with some 24 slender shafts, while the stiff-leaved capitals and corbels are boldly presented, particularly towards the crossing, with heads and grotesques.

At the upper levels the nave is less impressive, with an arcade consisting of an unbroken line of small lancets below a rather plain clerestory. The simple vaulting reflects the curve of the strainer arches, and there is some recent painting of a delicate nature between the ribs.

Move across into the north aisle, pausing by the **North Porch (3)**. Dating from *c*1215, this is the main processional entrance into the cathedral and connects with the canons' quarters on the north side of Cathedral Green. Continue eastwards along the aisle until you reach, on your right, the first chantry chapel, the **Bubwith Chantry Chapel (4)**, dating from 1425. Bishop Nicholas Bubwith left his personal fortune to build the library over the east cloister and also set up almshouses in the town.

The Arches and the Chapter House
We now arrive at the crossing, which is dominated by the massive **Scissor (Strainer) Arches (5)**. The original central bell tower had a spire added in the early 14th century, but the foundations could not support this additional weight and the spire began to lean and crack. William Joy, the master mason at the time, devised a solution which is unique in English cathedrals. The scissor arches were built on three sides of the crossing, thereby bracing the tower. From the engineering point of view

they were a great success, but aesthetically they might be considered an ugly intrusion. It is difficult to be neutral about them: you must decide for yourself.

Now enter the **North Transept (6)**, one of the oldest parts of the cathedral. The astronomical clock you see here is the most ancient of any English cathedral, being first mentioned in 1392, and is the second oldest working clock in the country.

Climb the well worn sloping stairs towards the **Chapter House (7)**; the flight actually continues through to the Chain Bridge, but this section is rarely open. Pause to look at the stained glass, which is the oldest in the cathedral. Turn right into the chapter house itself, completed in 1319. Although unusual in being above ground level, it has the normal octagonal shape. The windows, with some excellent stained glass, are in Geometric Decorated style; and below them is an arcade with 51 stalls containing richly decorated canopies. An elegant central pillar leads up to some wonderful tierceron vaulting with carved foliage bosses. From the architectural point of view this is arguably the most beautiful of the English cathedral chapter houses.

The Cathedra and the Lady Chapel

Leave the chapter house and descend the steps back to the north transept and the crossing. Turn left here into the north quire aisle. Walk east and then turn right into the **Quire (8)**. This was the first part of the new cathedral to be built. Note that there is no triforium here, but the slender shafts give an impression of height. Also notice the unusual lierne vaulting, like a spider's web with lozenge-shaped intersections. The eastern aspect is dominated by the Decorated-style Jesse Window, dating from *c*1340 and sometimes called the Golden Window because of its colouring. At the east end of the quire is a `Father' Willis organ, built in 1857. The wooden choir stalls go back to 1330 and have a fine collection of misericords – three of these have been mounted on the wall of the retrochoir. The *cathedra*, or Bishop's Throne, on the south side of the quire is of similar age to the stalls; it is unusual for its heavy stone door.

Return to the north quire aisle and turn right to the **Retrochoir (9)**. This part of the cathedral was completed in 1340 to link the quire with the Lady Chapel. Most experts feel this difficult task was sympathetically achieved. There are four chapels in this area – from north to south, Corpus Christi, St Stephen's, St John the Baptist's and St Katherine's – but none need detain you long. Spend your time instead looking at the **Lady Chapel (10)**. Originally octagonal in shape, this was separate from the main building until the retrochoir was built. The windows of the Lady Chapel have Reticulated Decorated tracery and their upper parts still have some of the original early-14th-century glass. The lower areas have a kaleidoscopic jumble of glass, broken during the Civil War. Don't miss the intricate `starburst' lierne vaulting, which has some delicate modern decoration.

Leave the east end of the cathedral via the south quire aisle. Almost immediately on your right is the **Chantry Chapel of Bishop Bekynton (11)**. Built 15 years before his death and now surrounded by iron railings, the chapel contains Bekynton's Tomb, with two effigies, the upper one of the bishop in full regalia and the lower one of his cadaver. Bekynton, Bishop of Bath and Wells 1443–65, was also secretary to Henry VI and Lord Privy Seal. This important benefactor to both the cathedral and the town built the Chain Bridge, provided houses in the Market Place and supplied fresh water from St Andrew's Well for the populace.

The South Transept and the Cloisters

Turn left into the **South Transept (12)**. There are two more chapels on the east side, those of St Martin and St Calixtus, but the main item of interest is the Saxon **Font (13)**, the only item remaining from the Saxon building and the oldest feature of the present cathedral. Its rounded arches, now bare, once contained carvings of saints. The gilded oak cover of the font dates from *c*1635.

Before you leave the south transept take a look at the capitals on some of the pillars. These strong carvings have narrative themes. One shows a man with toothache – a recurring subject in the days when there were no real dentists! – while another depicts thieves taking fruit and being apprehended by the owner, who is seen delivering a hefty blow to one man's head.

Leave the transept and turn into the south nave aisle. On the right the beautifully carved **Bishop Sugar Chantry Chapel (14)** incorporates the pulpit. Both chapel and pulpit date from the 15th century.

At the end of the aisle, turn left through the shop into the **Cloisters (15)**. Built in the 13th century, they were enlarged two centuries later.

The Font at Wells

They enclose the Palm Churchyard and the entrance to Bishop Bekynton's conduit.

Cross the grass to the east cloister. Above this is the Cathedral Library, paid for by Bishop Bubwith; looking back across the cloisters you can see, above the west cloister, the Choir School set up by Bishop Bekynton around 1460.

Pass through the door in the east cloister and out into the **Camery Gardens (16)**. Here an information board shows where you can view the foundations of the Saxon Cathedral buildings; the Lady Chapel, Stillington's Chapel and much of the old cathedral can be clearly picked out.

Return through the cloisters and out onto Cathedral Green.

WALKING TOUR FROM WELLS CATHEDRAL

This circular walking tour takes a comprehensive look at the historic core of the city of Wells. It passes the ancient buildings around the cathedral close, including the Bishop's Palace and a number of gateways. The tour also looks at some of the city's old coaching inns, one of the most fascinating parish churches in the country and a wide range of domestic architecture.

Start: The west front of the cathedral.
Finish: The cathedral cloisters.
Length: 1½ miles (2km).

Time: About 1hr, but allow extra time if you want to visit the museum, parish church or Bishop's Palace.

Refreshments: There is a wonderful selection of old coaching inns which are full of character and offer lunchtime bar meals. There are three in Sadler Street – the Ancient Gate House, the Swan and the White Hart. In the High Street the best bet is the Star, while in the Market Place consider the 15th-century Crown Inn. Also recommended is the City Arms, once the town gaol, in Queen Street. All but the City Arms offer accommodation.

From the west front of the cathedral, head southwest to Market Place through **Penniless Porch (1)**, one of a number of ancient gateways leading to Cathedral Green. The porch was built in the time of Bishop Bekynton – his rebus may be seen on the north side – and got its name from beggars who congregated here, seeking alms from churchgoers. *Plus ça change* – today Penniless Porch is a favourite spot for buskers.

Continue along the north side of Market Place. On the pavement is a plaque measuring 22 feet 2½ inches (6.765m), the distance jumped by a local resident, Mary Bignall Rand, when she won the gold medal in the 1964 Olympic Games.

Turn right into **Sadler Street (2)**, which has a number of old coaching inns. The Swan goes back in the city's records to 1422, and was once the banqueting hall of the mayor; the present frontage is more modern. On the same side of the road is the half-timbered White Hart, while opposite is the Ancient Gatehouse Inn, both likewise dating from the 15th century. The latter incorporates **Brown's Gate (3)**, which was used by vehicular traffic as late as 1965.

Step through Brown's Gate to Cathedral Green, which is an excellent spot from which to photograph the west front of the cathedral. Follow the road which runs along the north side of Cathedral Green; this road was once the main route through Wells for the stage coaches running from London to Exeter via Bath. On the left-hand side is a row of historic buildings, starting with the **Old Deanery (4)**, parts of which go back to the 15th century. The Dean now lives elsewhere and the building is used as the offices of the diocese. Some of its windows are believed to have been designed by Christopher Wren (1632–1723).

The next building is the **Wells Museum (5)**, which has displays on traditional lines, including sections on local archaeology and geology and the Local History Reference Library. The most bizarre exhibit is a stuffed swan, claimed to be the first of these birds to learn to ring the moat bell for food.

Vicars Choral

You now approach the **Chain Gate and Bridge (6)**, built in the mid-15th century by Bishop Bekynton. The idea was to link the quarters of the Vicars Choral with the chapter house stairs, thereby keeping the choristers away from the temptations of the town. The gate probably gained its name from chains which at one time closed the entrance. Just to the right, on the north wall of the cathedral, is the external face of the cathedral clock. It dates from 1495 and shows two knights in armour who strike the bells at quarter-hourly intervals.

After passing through the Chain Gate, turn immediately left through an archway into **Vicars' Close (7)**. This delightful little cul-de-sac was built in 1363 in the time of Bishop Ralph of Shrewsbury as accommodation for the Vicars Choral. There were originally 42 small dwellings here, but after the Reformation the gentleman choristers were allowed to marry, so many of the dwellings were amalgamated to provide accommodation for families. The small walled front gardens were not originally part of the design. It seems the close was once a quadrangle which, it is claimed, provided a model for England's ancient universities. At the far end of the close is the **Vicars' Chapel and Library (8)**. The chapel was built *c*1400, in the time of Bishop Bubwith, but unfortunately is rarely open to visitors.

Almshouses and a Fine Church

On the right-hand side of the chapel some steps lead up to the road called North Liberty. Turn left here, noting the large houses of character, most of which are used by the Cathedral School. At the end of North Liberty, fork left to the head of Sadler Street. Here turn right into Chamberlain Street, with its varied range of domestic architecture. You are now entering the part of the city noted for its **Almshouses (9)**. On the right-hand side of Chamberlain Street are Harper's Almshouses, built from a bequest by Archibald Harper in 1711 for 'five poor decayed woolcombers'. Just past the junction with Priest Row are Bubwith's

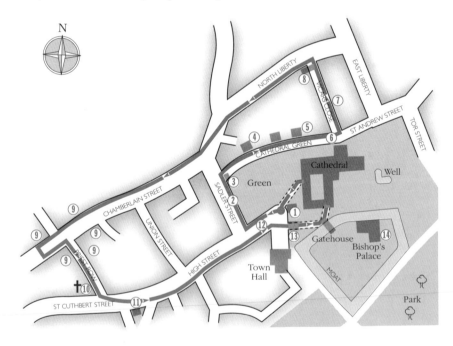

Key

1. Penniless Porch
2. Sadler Street
3. Brown's Gate
4. Old Deanery
5. Wells Museum
6. Chain Gate and Bridge
7. Vicars' Close
8. Vicars' Chapel and Library
9. Almshouses
10. St Cuthbert's Parish Church
11. City Arms
12. Market Place
13. Bishop's Eye Gateway
14. Bishop's Palace

Almshouses, provided in the early 15th century by Bishop Bubwith for poor men and women burgesses of the city. Turn down into Priest Row and on the left you find Llewellyn's Almshouses, which date from 1614. On the right is a complex of three further sets of almshouses, built at the bequests of Bishop Still, Bishop Wilkes and Walter Bricke, a wealthy draper.

At the end of Priest Row, on the right, is **St Cuthbert's Parish Church (10)**. The present building is almost certainly the fourth church to be built on the site. The original, probably a wooden Saxon church, was replaced by an 11th-century Norman building from which the piscina remains (in Tanner's Chapel in the south aisle). The third church was built in the middle of the 13th century in Early English style; several parts of it remain, such as the piers and arches in the present nave. Finally, a major renovation and extension took place in the 15th century in magnificent Perpendicular style. St Cuthbert's has some wonderful interior features, including a huge medieval door, a Jacobean pulpit, the Great Jesse Reredos, a marvellous 16th-century panelled ceiling in St Cuthbert's Chapel, some superb bosses and much more besides. Take time to appreciate this building – the largest parish church in Somerset.

Leave St Cuthbert's and swing round eastwards into the High Street, the main shopping thoroughfare. Immediately on your right, at the junction with Queen Street, is the **City Arms (11)**. This pink-washed stone-built pub was the city gaol from the time of Elizabeth I until the 19th century, and some of the cells still exist. Today a number of bars surround an attractive cobbled courtyard.

Proceeding up the High Street, note the water swilling down the gutters, part of the fresh-water system provided for the townsfolk from the wells near the Bishop's Palace.

The Market Place and Bishop's Palace

You now reach the **Market Place (12)**. This area is dominated by the Town Hall, which contains the Council Offices, the Law Courts and the Tourist Information Office. Note also the Gothic-style conduit, which in 1799 replaced an earlier one provided by Bishop Bekynton. Take a look at the two plaques on the wall of the Crown Hotel on the south side of the Market Place. One describes how an old Guildhall once stood in the Market Place and was the venue of the Bloody Assizes after the Monmouth Rebellion. The other marks the spot where William Penn (1644–1718), founder of Pennsylvania, preached to a crowd of 3000 in 1685.

Leave the Market Place via the **Bishop's Eye Gateway (13)**, to the right of the National Trust shop, one of four gateways built by Bishop Bekynton. This leads you to the **Bishop's Palace (14)**, the official residence of the Bishop of Bath and Wells. If it's open, do go in: this is the finest remaining example in England of a medieval bishop's palace. The building is surrounded by a sturdy wall and moat. Bishop Ralph of Shrewsbury built a gatehouse here with a drawbridge and portcullis, which were last used in 1831, when there were serious fears of riots over the Reform Bill. Look at the side of the gatehouse drawbridge, where there is a rope with a bell attached. Swans have learned to tug the rope when they wish to be fed. If time permits, take a stroll around the shady moat where a variety of waterfowl can be seen.

Leave the Bishop's Palace via the path opposite the gatehouse and follow the short route taken by countless bishops to their cathedral over the centuries until you reach a doorway giving access to the cathedral cloisters, where the tour concludes.

Bath

Access: There have always been important routeways west from London to the fashionable city of Bath. The A4 London–Bath road (the Great West Road) was a routeway even in pre-Roman times. Today motorists are more likely to use the fast M4, although speeds slow on the 12 miles (20km) from the motorway to the city. The nearby M5 provides links with the Southwest and the Midlands. The train from London's Paddington Station reaches Bath Spa Station in 1hr 10 minutes; the station is a short walk from the city centre. The nearest airport – at Bristol, west of Bath – deals mainly with charter flights; Heathrow Airport can be reached in about 2hr via the M4.

Bath owes its origins to the hot, mineral-rich springs that rise here. The first settlement may have been in Celtic times; legend has it that Prince Bladud cured his leprosy in the springs and perhaps gave the city its name. More historically certain is that there was an important Roman settlement here from AD43. The Romans built sophisticated hot baths, a temple to the goddess Minerva, numerous luxurious villas and formidable defensive walls. The Roman name for the town was Aquae Sulis.

When the Empire collapsed the baths went into decline, and the succeeding Saxon town centred instead on an important monastery, probably called St Peter's. It is known that King Offa (d796) of Mercia seized the monastery in 781. Interestingly, although Winchester had become the capital of the first united England, it was at Bath Abbey that Edgar the Peaceful (944–975) was crowned King of All England in 973.

After the Norman Conquest, John de Villula (d1122) was appointed bishop of nearby Wells, and two years later he transferred his seat to Bath. He immediately set about building a new cathedral. After de Villula's death the work continued, eventually being completed in 1170. This Norman building was almost twice the length of the present abbey. In 1244 it was decided that Bath and Wells should share cathedral status, and Roger of Salisbury became the first Bishop of Bath and Wells, a title which remains today. Later in the 13th century Bath's importance waned as subsequent bishops took up residence in Wells.

Meanwhile the monastery was going through hard times. The diminished number of monks found it impossible to maintain the cathedral, which gradually fell into ruins. Rescue came when in 1495 Oliver King was appointed Bishop of Bath and Wells. The story goes that he had a vision that left him in no doubt he should restore the abbey church. Work began in 1499, in the Perpendicular style. Magnificent though the new building was, it was on a relatively small scale – it could have fitted into the nave of the old cathedral. Within a few years the monastery had been dissolved in the Reformation, the see had been permanently relocated to Wells and the building had become Bath's parish church.

With the local wool trade languishing, Bath renewed its role as a spa town. This was stimulated in 1574 by a visit from Queen Elizabeth I, who granted the town a municipal charter. Later, Queen Anne was a frequent visitor, taking the waters to seek a cure for dropsy. As throughout history, society follows where royalty leads. Bath rapidly became a fashionable resort, its population increasing tenfold during the 18th century. The wealthy visitors expected more than health-giving waters, however. The Bath Improvement Act of 1789 provided the powers to redevelop the town. Three men led the move towards Bath's Golden Age: the city surveyor, Thomas Baldwin (1750–1820), the architect John Wood (1704–1754), later succeeded by his son, and the larger-than-life bon viveur Richard `Beau' Nash (1674–1762). Elegant terraces and crescents appeared, built in the local honey-coloured Bath Stone, along with hotels, hospitals, theatres and casinos. Everyone of importance came here, often not only for the season but to live. Horatio Nelson (1758–1805), William Pitt the Elder (1708–1778), Thomas Gainsborough (1727–1788) and Jane Austen (1775–1817) were among many who had properties in Bath. A glance at the memorial tablets and stones in Bath Abbey reflects the importance of these times. This brilliant period also spawned the Bath bun, the Bath chair, Bath Oliver biscuits and the Sally Lunn bun.

By the mid-19th century, however, Bath was losing its pre-eminence. The railways had made seaside towns attractive, and Bath gained the image of being a home for the elderly and the infirm; in response it did indeed develop into a genteel residential town, attractive to retirees. By the end of the 20th century, though, tourism was booming and visitors were attracted to the city again by its fine setting and beautifully preserved buildings. Many consider that it has the most complete set of Georgian domestic architecture to be seen in the country, and this has encouraged its designation as a World Heritage City. Meanwhile the abbey and the nearby Roman Baths are on every visitor's itinerary.

The central door on the West Front

37

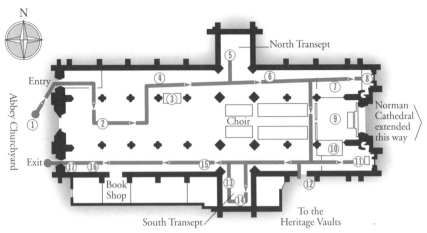

Key

1. West Front
2. Nave
3. Tomb of James Montagu
4. Memorial to Isaac Pitman
5. Organ Loft
6. Memorial to Admiral Arthur Philip
7. St Alphege Chapel

8. Edgar Window
9. Sanctuary
10. Chantry Chapel of Prior William Birde
11. Norman Chapel
12. Heritage Vaults
13. Waller Memorial
14. Jesse Window

15. Memorial tablet to Richard 'Beau' Nash
16. Memorial to William Bingham
17. Prior's Door

TOUR OF THE ABBEY

Start and finish: Abbey Churchyard, outside the abbey.

Stand outside the entrance to the Pump Room and the Roman Baths and look towards the abbey's **West Front (1)**. The view is dominated by the tall west window, built in Perpendicular style in the early years of the 16th century. On each side of the main window are 'ladders' on which angels ascend and descend, representing the dream experienced by Bishop Oliver King in which he was encouraged to build a new abbey church. Other details on the west front include the rebus of Oliver King (involving an olive tree and a crown), 16th-century statues of St Peter and St Paul and a late-19th-century effigy of Bishop King's patron, Henry VII.

The main central door on the west front, made of solid oak, contains the coats-of-arms of various members of the Montagu family. Enter the building, however, through the smaller northwest door. Proceed through a small foyer where you will be encouraged to pay a recommended entry fee. Move into the central aisle of the **Nave (2)**, where the character of the building can be appreciated. You will immediately be struck by the vast number of memorials – hardly a spare inch is not covered by a plaque or tablet. Of all England's cathedrals and abbeys, only Westminster can offer comparison. This position in the nave also gives good views of the almost identical east and west windows. The glass in both is Victorian, the west window depicting scenes from the Old Testament and the east window showing New Testament subjects.

Look next at the superb fan vaulting. In fact, only the vaulting in the east end is original. This was designed by the Vertue brothers, master masons to Henry VII. The vaulting in the nave is an accurate copy constructed as part of the Victorian restorations.

Memorials

Walk now into the north aisle, which is dominated by the **Tomb of James Montagu (3)**, Bishop of Bath and Wells 1608–16 and a great benefactor to the abbey. Montagu became bishop at a time when the abbey was in an appalling state of decay after the ravages of the Reformation. The story goes that on one particularly wet day he was in the roofless abbey with a friend, who complained about the lack of shelter: 'If it keeps us not safe from the waters above, how shall it save others from the fires beneath?' Montagu resolved to remedy the situation and spent £1000 of his own money to construct a wooden roof, which remained until the Victorians replaced wood with stone. Montagu went on to become Bishop of Winchester; his alabaster effigy shows the Blue Ribbon of the Garter, traditionally worn by holders of that post.

Among the many tablets on the wall of the aisle opposite the tomb is the **Memorial to Isaac Pitman (4)**. Pitman (1813–1897) did much to reform the spelling of the English language and, of course, invented Pitman Shorthand. Move into the north transept, where there is an audiovisual presentation on the life and work of the abbey. Note here the wooden spiral staircase to the **Organ Loft (5)**. The organ was rebuilt in 1996–7 by Klais of Bonn.

Proceed into the north choir aisle, where, immediately on the left, an Australian flag marks a tablet which is the **Memorial to Admiral Arthur Philip (6)**. Philip (1738–1814) founded the first penal settlement in Australia and was the first Governor of New South Wales. On retirement he lived in Bath until his death.

A Colourful Saint

Continue to the end of the aisle to reach the **St Alphege Chapel (7)**. Alphege or Aelfheah (954–1012) had a lively career. Born in Bath, he became a Benedictine monk here, eventually rising to be abbot. He went on to be Bishop of Winchester and then, in 1006, Archbishop of Canterbury. He was taken hostage by Danes at Greenwich and, when he refused to raise money for his release, was 'stoned' to death with ox bones. The chapel, a gift of the Friends of Bath Abbey, was dedicated in October 1997. Alphege's story is told in the embroidered triptych behind the altar. Note the cross made of copper from Zambia, denoting the link between the abbey and the church in that country. The font in the chapel dates from 1710. Look for the grating on the floor, through which there is a view of the floor and pillars of the old Norman cathedral.

At the end of the aisle is the **Edgar Window (8)**, the glass of which shows the crowning in Bath Abbey of King Edgar in 973. This ceremony joined Wessex and Mercia, so that Edgar became the first effective ruler of a united England. The ceremony, performed by the archbishops of Canterbury and York, remains the basis of coronation procedure to this day. Look for the nearby stone in the floor that marks the service attended by Queen Elizabeth II and Prince Philip in 1973 to celebrate the thousandth anniversary of Edgar's coronation.

Step round to the **Sanctuary (9)**. Above the high altar is the east window, whose Victorian glass was badly damaged during World War II. On either side of the window are some coats-of-arms from Stuart times. On the north side of the sanctuary is the large carved-oak chair occupied by the Bishop of Bath and Wells when he attends services in the abbey. Also on the north side is the **Chantry Chapel of Prior William Birde (10)**. After the death of Bishop Oliver King, Prior Birde completed the construction of the present abbey. Look for his rebus, often repeated among the detailed stonework, which involves a `W' and a bird. The chapel is today reserved for private prayer.

Relics of Previous Abbeys

Walk to the eastern end of the south choir aisle, to the **Norman Chapel (11)**, named for a Norman arch into which is set a Perpendicular window. The original arch led into the south transept of the old Norman cathedral, which gives you some indication of how far past the east end of the present abbey church the older building stretched. The Norman Chapel contains a Book of Remembrance with the names of civilians and members of the armed forces killed during the bombing of the city during World War II.

Return westwards along the south choir aisle. A door on the left leads out to the **Heritage Vaults (12)**, opened to the public in 1994. The structure of the vaults goes back to 1499, but some of the artefacts on display go back much further, to Saxon times, including a small 10th-century window which may have come from the original Saxon church. Other interesting features are a section of the floor of the monastery's cloisters and a scale model of the monastery and church as they were *c*1300. If open, the Vaults should not be missed.

Back in the abbey proper, continue along the south choir aisle and into the south transept, used for visiting exhibitions. Among the features of interest here is the **Waller Memorial (13)**, provided by Sir William Waller (*c*1597–1668) for his first wife Jane. Waller was a general on the Parliamentary side during the Civil War, and actually lost Bath to the Royalists (1643). His effigy was later damaged by Cavalier soldiers and was never repaired. He made provision to be buried here with his wife, but ended up in the Tothill Street Chapel in Westminster. Also of interest is the Victorian, but elegant, **Jesse Window (14)**, showing the descent of Our Lord from Jesse the father of David. Dating from 1872, it commemorates the return to health of the Prince of Wales, later Edward VII.

Turning into the south aisle, look immediately for the marble **Memorial Tablet to Richard `Beau' Nash (15)**, who lies buried beneath the floor nearby. The flamboyant Nash was the self-proclaimed King of 18th-century Bath and the master of ceremonies of the spa's social life. Just past the bookshop is another interesting and more elaborate monument, the **Memorial to William Bingham (16)**; William Bingham (1752–1804), an influential US senator and financier, died during a visit to Bath. In the southwest corner of the south aisle you can see the outline of the **Prior's Door (17)**. Before the Dissolution of the monastery in 1539 this was the door through which the prior would leave for his lodgings, which overlooked the cloisters.

Leave the abbey through the southwest door of the west front to reach Abbey Churchyard once more.

Plate 1: *The west front of Exeter Cathedral viewed from the Cathedral Close. The west front has three rows of sculptured figures, but many are badly eroded (see page 20).*

Plate 2: *The quire at Exeter dates from Scott's Victorian renovations, although some of the old misericords were retained. The Perpendicular east window dominates the background (see page 21).*

Plate 3: *Mol's Coffee House in the Cathedral Close at Exeter (see page 24). The building dates from 1596 and was named after an Italian, Thomas Mol. It was a favourite meeting place of the Devon 'sea dogs'.*

Plate 4: *Vicars' Close, Wells (see page 33). This was the traditional home of the choristers, who reached the cathedral via the Chain Bridge. It is claimed that the close provided the model for the quadrangles of Britain's ancient universities.*

Plate 5: *The magnificent west front at Wells seen from Cathedral Green (see page 29). Generally considered the finest west front in England, it is often compared to a huge altar screen.*

Plate 6: *The River Avon at Bath looking towards Pulteney Bridge (see page 41). The bridge was designed by Robert Adam (1728-1792) and was influenced by the Ponte Vecchio in Florence.*

Plate 7: *The nave of Bath Abbey, with its eloquent flying buttresses (see page 38).*

Plate 8: *Roman pipe work still supplies water to the Great Bath at Bath (see page 45).*

WALKING TOUR FROM BATH ABBEY

This circular walk around the centre of Bath concentrates on the city's role as a fashionable resort and spa from Roman times to the days of 'Beau' Nash. It covers some outstanding domestic architecture, including the terraces of the Georgian and Regency periods, and looks at features which developed from this time of affluence in Bath's history, such as the Theatre Royal, the Assembly Rooms, the Guildhall and Poulteney Bridge.

Start and finish: The west front of the abbey, in Abbey Churchyard.
Length: 2½ miles (4km).
Time: 2hr, but allow longer if you want to visit the museums and the Roman Baths.
Refreshments: Many visitors will wish to have a meal in Sally Lunn's, claimed to be Bath's oldest house. There are a number of old inns of character, but they can be difficult to find. Try the Crystal Palace in Church Street, the Garrick's Head by the Theatre Royal, the Pig and Fiddle in Saracen Street, or the Saracen's Head in Milsom Street, said to be a favourite of Dickens and more or less unchanged since it was built in 1713. There is also a vast array of restaurants, wine bars and bistros.

Leave the west door of the abbey and head south between the Roman Baths and the abbey, passing the Tourist Information Office on the left. Walk down narrow, cobbled Church Street, passing the Crystal Palace pub on the right, and head into the square known as **Abbey Green (1)**. Recent excavations under the Crystal Palace have unearthed a number of skeletons, suggesting that this area might have been the monks' burial ground in monastic times. The area has even older associations, however, as the same excavations also revealed a Roman mosaic. Today the square is flanked by attractive Stuart houses and graced by a London plane tree 200 years old.

Leave Abbey Green eastwards along North Parade Passage. On the left is **Sally Lunn's Restaurant (2)**, an ancient building that once was part of the monastic buildings. It dates from 1482; Sally herself lived there at the bakery around 1680, producing her famous buns, modern versions of which are still on sale today. The building makes an excellent lunchtime stop not only for good food and ambience, but because of the delightful little museum in the cellar. This shows baking artefacts and ovens, plus a series of stone foundations of Roman, Saxon, Norman and medieval age. Indeed, excavations carried out in the 1980s suggest that there was a Roman guest house on the site.

Walk to the end of North Parade Passage and turn left into Terrace Walk. Cross the road towards the balustrades which mark the riverside Parade Gardens. Look left at a tree-lined square, **Orange Gardens (3)**, dominated on the left by the east front of the abbey and on the right by the rather ugly building which was once the Empire Hotel. The square was named after William of Orange, in honour of whose visit to Bath in 1734 Beau Nash erected an obelisk. Today the area around the obelisk is called Alkmaar Gardens, to mark the twinning of Bath with the Dutch town.

Continue walking along the edge of Parade Gardens. The road, known as Grand Parade, swings right towards the River Avon. Across the river is Bath Rugby Ground. Ahead, just past an attractive weir, is **Pulteney Bridge (4)**, designed by Robert Adam (1728–1792) in 1770 (his only work in Bath) and commissioned by

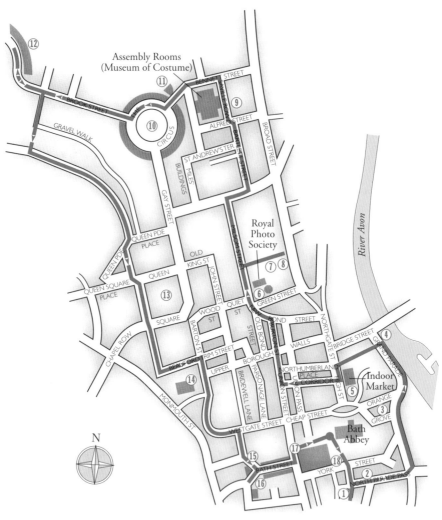

Key

1. Abbey Green
2. Sally Lunn's
3. Orange Gardens
4. Pulteney Bridge
5. Guildhall
6. Octagon

7. Shire's Yard
8. Postal Museum
9. Assembly Rooms
10. The Circus
11. Museum of East Asian Art
12. Royal Crescent

13. Queen Square
14. Theatre Royal
15. Cross Bath
16. Hot Bath
17. Pump Room
18. Roman Baths Museum

the wealthy Sir William Pulteney (1684–1764), who was later to become Earl of Bath. Adam was clearly influenced by the Ponte Vecchio in Florence, as the bridge was originally lined with shops on both sides. It replaced a ferry and was planned to open up the eastern side of the city, where Pulteney had a large estate.

Traders

Just before the bridge, cross Grand Parade and walk through the indoor market, built on the site of a medieval slaughterhouse. It has a twelve-sided dome and a pillar known as the Nail; legend has it this was the spot where business was concluded, leading to the saying 'to pay on the nail'.

Emerge from the indoor market at the High Street. Immediately to the left is the **Guildhall (5)**, built by Thomas Baldwin (1750–1820) in the Adam style in 1766 and extended in Victorian times. Its notable Banqueting Room has a minstrels' gallery, magnificent fireplaces, portraits by Joshua Reynolds of George III and Queen Charlotte, and graceful chandeliers which, it is claimed, contain over 15,000 pieces of glass.

Cross the High Street and proceed along an arcade called The Corridor. You are now in the heart of Bath's pedestrianized shopping centre. Carry on until you reach Union Street. Turn right and walk on to where New Bond Street swings left into Milsom Street. This was Bath's fashionable shopping street during its Golden Age, the 1800s. On the right is the **Octagon (6)**, a former chapel and now the headquarters of the Royal Photographic Society; it was here that Sir William Herschel (1738–1822) discovered the planet Uranus in 1781. A small museum has a Herschel exhibition, plus work by major photographers and classics from press photographs.

Next on the right is the entrance to **Shire's Yard (7)**, a development of over twenty shops on two levels around a courtyard. The area has changed little since the 1740s, when Alderman Walter Wiltshire ran a carting and carrying business from these premises, his carts taking 2½ days to reach London. One of Wiltshire's clients was Thomas Gainsborough, who lived in Bath at one time and who borrowed one his horses for his famous painting *The Harvest Wagon*, which he gave to Wiltshire as a gift. At the far end of Shire's Yard is access to the **Postal Museum (8)**. It was from this building in 1840 that the letter bearing the first Penny Black was posted. The museum has a good collection of postal memorabilia, plus a full-size reconstruction of a Victorian post office.

Architectural Grandeur

Back in Milsom Street, continue to the junction with George Street. Turn right here and then left into Bartlett Street. This is Bath's antique quarter, with over 200 dealers plus shops where craftsmen such as goldsmiths can be seen at work.

Continue across Alfred Street and into Saville Row, where, on the left, are the **Assembly Rooms (9)**. Often claimed to be the finest suite of rooms in Europe, these were designed by John Wood the Younger (1728–1781) and opened in 1771. They became the centre for social life in the town, with dazzling balls and much gambling. Later they were a concert venue. The Assembly Rooms were restored in 1938, but badly damaged during World War II. After another restoration they reopened in 1963. Today, they house the Museum of Costume, depicting 400 years of fashion – there are some 200 dressed figures in period settings. Modern fashion is not forgotten, with an annual 'dress of the year'.

Leave the Assembly Rooms and walk along Bennett Street to **The Circus (10)**, designed by John Wood the Elder (1704–1754) and the first circular plan in the history of British urban architecture. The architect died shortly after the first foundation stone was laid in 1754, but the work was continued by his son. The houses are laid out in three sets of 33, interspersed with three equally spaced roads. Each house has three Classical columns, with Doric on the ground floor, Ionic on the middle floor and Corinthian on the top floor. A frieze above the Doric layer has a number of mystic symbols. Houses in The Circus were rented out during the `season' and past residents (shown by wall plaques) have included William Pitt the Elder (1708–1778), David Livingstone (1813–1873), Robert Clive of India (1725–1774), William Makepeace Thackeray (1811–1863) and Thomas Gainsborough. In the early years of The Circus, the central space was occupied by a reservoir, which, being above the level of the basement kitchens, was able to provide a gravity-fed water supply. This area is now graced by a number of 200-year-old plane trees.

On the corner of The Circus and Bennett Street is the **Museum of East Asian Art (11)**, with artefacts from China, Japan, Korea and other countries, ranging in date from 5000BC to the 20th century. Leave The Circus from the west side, walking along Brock Street, where there are further examples of fine domestic architecture, with some interesting insurance company firemarks and ornate wrought-iron work.

You now reach one of England's most remarkable architectural features, **The Royal Crescent (12)**. Designed by John Wood the Elder and completed by his son between 1767 and 1775, the crescent comprises a semicircle of 30 houses with a frontage of Ionic columns, supporting a continuous cornice over 660ft (200m) long, all built in the honey-coloured Bath Stone. As in The Circus, the houses were often rented out for the `season'. They are now largely privately occupied, although no. 1, once occupied by George III's son the Duke of York, has been preserved as a museum of 18th-century life. Period background music gives a lived-in feeling. The grassy space in front of The Royal Crescent features a ha-ha – a ditch constructed to keep cattle away from the houses.

Leave The Royal Crescent and walk southwards across the grass until you reach Royal Avenue. Turn left here (eastwards) through Royal Victoria Park. A jink in the road through Queen's Parade (the centre of the sedan-chair trade until that was superseded by the Bath chair) brings us to **Queen Square (13)**. Again we have John Wood to thank for this development: he built the square privately between 1729 and 1736, after the city authorities had rejected his plans, and himself lived in it, at no. 24, until his death. The square was named after Queen Caroline, the wife of George II. Famous residents have included Jane Austen (1775–1817), who lodged at no. 13. The obelisk in the centre of the square was provided by Beau Nash to celebrate the visit of Prince Frederick and his wife in 1738.

The Performing Arts

Leave Queen Square via Princes Street in the southwest corner. Swing left into Beauford Square and then right into Barton Street. Almost the whole of this block is taken up with the **Theatre Royal (14)**. One of the country's oldest theatres, this has seen many famous names perform on its stage over the last 350 years. Backstage tours are available on certain days.

On the south corner of the theatre is a bust of the 18th-century actor David Garrick, and nearby is the Garrick's Head pub. This building and part of the theatre were once the palatial home of Beau Nash, who lived there with his first mistress,

Fanny Murray. Later he lived with his second mistress, Joanna Popjoy, in a more modest nearby house, now a restaurant.

Hot Baths

From the Garrick's Head continue south along Sawclose, which swings round to the left into Westgate Street, the location of one of the gates in the old city walls. Turn immediately right down a paved path, St Michael's Place, past the Little Theatre Cinema on the right, to reach the area where the hot baths are located. This is the part of the city where the socialites gathered in the 1700s and 1800s to take and drink the waters.

Occupying a small triangle of land is **Cross Bath (15)**, probably named after the cross erected to commemorate the fact that the previously infertile Queen Mary, the wife of James II, conceived after taking the waters here. Cross Bath was a favourite of the nobility; the ladies, serenaded by musicians, would bathe alongside floating wooden trays that bore their cosmetics. A grille on the south side of the building looks across a steaming pool, giving a good idea of the ambience of those times.

Walk across the road to the building which contains **Hot Bath (16)**, designed by John Wood the Younger and a popular place for visiting royalty. Today, however, there is little to see here.

Leave the area eastwards along the colonnaded Bath Street, constructed by Baldwin in 1791 (he afterwards went bankrupt) and designed to provide a sheltered walkway for socialites as they moved between the baths. This brings you to the pedestrianized Stall Street.

Ahead is the **Pump Room (17)**, built by Baldwin in 1790 to replace an earlier building. It overlooked the Royal Bath and was a rendezvous for all who took the waters. It has 16 fluted columns and is lit by a huge chandelier. Other attractions are a bust of Beau Nash, two original sedan chairs and a tall clock, 10ft (3m) high, dating from 1709. The Pump Room remains a popular venue today, and you can drink the waters and/or other beverages while eating to the strains of the Pump Room Trio. Note the plaque on the exterior of the Pump Room which identifies Bath as a World Heritage Site.

Now turn into Abbey Churchyard (where the tour began). On the right is the entrance to the **Roman Baths Museum (18)**. By anyone's standards, this is one of the best museums in the country, containing the most comprehensive collection of Roman remains in Britain. Concealed for over 1000 years, the baths were rediscovered and excavated in the 19th century. Although the pillars and some of the statues are Victorian, one can still see the bases of the columns which supported the original roof. The ruin of the Roman Temple to Sulis Minerva can be seen, along with much of the pipe-work that supplied the water to the baths. The Roman remains are about 20ft (6m) below the present street level. The main Great Bath is 70ft (22m) long, 30ft (9m) wide and 5ft (1.5m) deep, and is still fed by the original Roman plumbing. The museum section shows some of the Roman artefacts discovered on the site, such as jewellery, carved inscriptions and coins, many of which were thrown into the sacred spring.

The Roman Baths, highly recommended, represent the conclusion of the walking tour.

Salisbury

Access: Although not served by motorways, Salisbury is at the hub of a network of main roads. The A303, an important route from London to the West Country, runs just to the north (driving time from London about 2hr), while the A30, another key east–west link, passes through the city itself. Other main roads connect with Bath, Southampton, Portsmouth and Dorchester. Salisbury is a major stop on the London–West Country rail route from Waterloo. Regular coach services link with London, Southampton and Bristol. The nearest main international airports are at Gatwick and Heathrow, both of which can be reached by car and coach in under 2hr. There are ferry links from France through Southampton and Poole.

The story of Salisbury begins on a windswept hill known as Old Sarum, a couple of miles north of the present town. It was a hill fort in Iron Age times and later became the hub of a network of Roman roads; the Romans called the settlement Sorbiodunum. The Saxons in turn occupied the site, calling it Seares byrig; from the number of coins found it seems likely the Saxons had a mint here. William the Conqueror strengthened the defences of Old Sarum and built a military castle, and the Normans also united the dioceses of Sherborne and Ramsbury and built a new cathedral at Old Sarum, occupying a quarter of the space within the walls of the for-tifications. Completed in 1092 by Bishop Osmund, the cathedral was badly dam-aged by lightning only a few days after its consecration.

Osmund's successor, Bishop Roger, immediately started on a new building. The foundations of this second Norman cathedral show that it was 317ft (96.6m) in length. By the early 13th century, however, there were plans to move the cathedral to a lowland site. The reasons are obvious: the site was bleak and lacked fresh water, and relations between the military and the clergy were often acrimonious – on one occasion the bishop and his clerics returned in the evening to find the gates locked against them and had to spend an uncomfortable night out in the open. Enough was enough and eventually, in 1219, Bishop Richard Poore obtained permission from the Pope to build a new cathedral in the valley nearby.

The foundation stone was laid in 1220. Along with the new cathedral, houses were built in what is now the Close for not only the bishop but the canons, other clergy and workmen. Poore also laid out the street pattern of New Sarum, or Salisbury, which received its Royal Charter in 1227 – although it was to remain under the control of the cathedral for another four centuries.

The construction of the new cathedral began at the east end with the Lady Chapel (now known as Trinity Chapel), under the supervision of the master mason Nicholas of Ely, helped by one of the canons, Elias de Dereham; Elias was one of Henry III's courtiers and had been present in 1215 at the sealing of the Magna Carta, one of the four original copies of which can be seen in Salisbury today. The building stone used for the cathedral was a cream limestone from Chilmark, some 12 miles (19km) west and, as with many cathedrals of this era, the limestone was set off by thin dark shafts of Purbeck Marble. On completion of the Lady Chapel, the bodies of three former bishops were brought down from Old Sarum and re-interred; they included Bishop Osmund, who was later canonized and whose shrine soon attracted pilgrims in large numbers.

By 1258 the nave, choir and transepts of the cathedral had been completed and the building was consecrated. The west front was finished *c*1265 and an enormous detached bell tower was built on the southwest side of the cathedral. The architectural style throughout was Early English, making Salisbury a rarity among English cathedrals. Only St Paul's in London can claim such devotion to one particular style.

Just two major additions were to come. Between 1285 and 1310 the magnificent tower and spire were constructed, rising to a height of 404ft (123m) – the tallest in England. The foundations were never designed to support such a structure, so drastic measures had to be taken to provide additional strength. Buttresses were built into the clerestory walls, plus external flying buttresses coming from the main aisles to the tower, while strainer arches were built in the choir aisles. These measures seem to have worked, as neither the spire nor the supporting pillars have moved since Wren's survey in 1668. The second addition was the construction of the cloisters, between 1240 and 1270. These were the first to appear in an English cathedral and are arguably still the best. Cloisters are normally associated with monastical cathedrals, but Salisbury has always been a secular establishment, so its cloisters were clearly built for their aesthetic value alone. Each cloister stretches for 140ft (42m), and the style is Geometric Decorated. Leading off the cloisters and in similar architectural style is the chapter house, built between 1263 and 1284.

There was often friction between the clergy and the citizens of Salisbury, and in 1327 the dean and chapter obtained a licence from Edward III to build a protective wall around the close. Permission was given to use stone from the Old Sarum cathedral, by now derelict. With the river on two sides and the new wall on the other two sides, the close became secure. The gates were locked at night and one, the North (or High Street) Gate, had a portcullis which could be dropped whenever the townsfolk were being particularly obstreperous.

In the Civil War both Royalists and Parliamentarian troops occupied the close at various times while fighting for control of the city. During this period Parliament appropriated the bishop's estate, which was later bought by the city authorities: the clergy had to suffer the indignity of seeing the Bishop's Palace being used as an inn.

Things returned to normal for both Close and cathedral after the Restoration in 1660. This coincided with the reign (1667–89) of the able and learned Bishop Seth Ward, previously Professor of Astronomy at Oxford. Many intellectuals were attracted to Salisbury, including Samuel Johnson (1709–1784), James Boswell (1740–1795) and Joshua Reynolds (1723–1792), while Sir Christopher Wren (1632–1723) had an influence on many of the new buildings now appearing in the Close. The city of Salisbury had meanwhile become increasingly prosperous, its wealth based on wool. The twice-weekly markets attracted people from far and wide, stimulating the growth of inns, many later to specialize in coaching. The road system, previously focusing on Old Sarum, was reorganized, and new bridges were built across the rivers.

By the mid-1700s the cathedral was in urgent need of repairs. Shute Barrington (1734–1826), who became bishop in 1782, arranged for the architect James Wyatt (1746–1813) to undertake renovations. Wyatt, who had studied in Italy and become the fashionable architect of the time, made a disastrous foray into cathedral work. His appalling alterations to Lichfield are well known, and his work at Salisbury was equally vandalous. On the credit side, he levelled and drained the churchyard and removed the ugly bell tower, but inside the cathedral he removed a number of chapels, stripped away much of the medieval glass, broke up and moved around a number of tombs, covered the medieval paintwork with limewash and scrapped the pulpitum, replacing it with an inferior screen. This was not a happy period in the cathedral's history!

Victorian renovations in cathedrals are generally not highly regarded, but Sir George Gilbert Scott's work at Salisbury at least repaired some of Wyatt's damage. Scott (1811–1878) strengthened the tower with iron bracing, provided replacement statues for the west front and revamped the choir. Wyatt's screen was replaced by an open metal one (since removed) designed by Francis Skidmore (1816–1896), and a new Minton floor was laid in the choir. Glass was reintroduced to many of the windows. The limewash, alas, could not be removed, and was painted over with the old designs.

Repair and restoration have continued ever since. In the 1950s it was found that the spire needed urgent attention and the top 30ft (9m) had to be completely rebuilt at a cost of £6½ million – a sum which most visitors would consider well worth spending. Between 1978 and 1983 the 15th-century library over the eastern cloister was restored. The 1980s saw the appearance of two notable works of art. In 1980 the Prisoners of Conscience window was unveiled; designed by Gabriel Loire of Chartres, it is of Impressionist design but is coloured in 13th-century style. And in 1982 Elisabeth Frink's remarkable bronze statue *Walking Madonna* was placed outside the north porch.

The city of Salisbury was largely unaffected by the Industrial Revolution. Today it is a regional centre and market town with industries largely of an agricultural and technological nature. Tourism is a major money-earner, and the cathedral and its tranquil close are a magnet for the many visitors from home and abroad.

TOUR OF THE CATHEDRAL
Start: Cathedral Close, near the path leading to the north porch.
Finish: The refectory and bookshop.

The tour begins by the **Statue of the Walking Madonna (1)**, close to the path leading to the north porch, which is the cathedral's main ceremonial entrance. This bronze sculpture by Elisabeth Frink (1930-1994) was completed in 1981 and put in place a year later.

Walk around the west front of the building. At the time of writing this was covered with scaffolding and plastic sheeting. The work, which is likely to take several more years, is concentrated on the statuary, which is badly eroded. (It is worth remembering that the cathedral's stonework has suffered more atmospheric pollution during the last 150 years than in the rest of its history.) Plans are also underway to restore the main west porch to the colours of medieval times.

Enter the cathedral via the southwest door, next to the cloister wall. You are obliged to pay a 'donation', the amount of which is detailed on a notice board; to all intents and purposes this is an entrance fee, with concessions for students and pensioners.

Pass into the **Nave (2)**. Despite the fact that you can see the whole length of the building (the choir screen has been removed), the general impression is of height rather than length. Simplicity, some would say severity, is the keynote of the architecture. The cathedral is mainly built of Chilmark Limestone, a white oolitic rock, and there is a strong contrast between this and the almost black shafts of Purbeck Marble (widely used in Early English architecture). The arches and capitals of the arcade are plain, while the triforium is rather squat, with its arches divided by trefoils. Above, the clerestory windows have triple lancets. The light-and-shade effect is pleasing, but the nave suffers through lacking its medieval glass, removed by Wyatt in the late 18th century.

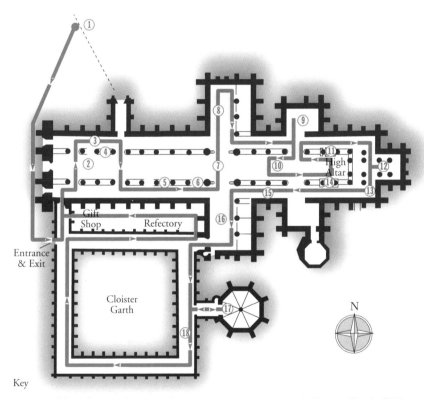

Key

1. Statue of the Walking Madonna
2. Nave
3. Medieval Clock
4. Tomb of William de Longespée the Younger
5. Tomb of St Osmund
6. Tomb of William de Longespée the Elder
7. Crossing
8. North Transept
9. Morning Chapel
10. Choir
11. Chantry Chapel of Edward Audley
12. Trinity Chapel
13. Tomb of the Earl of Hertford
14. Chantry Chapel of Walter, Lord Hungerford
15. Mompesson Tomb
16. South Transept
17. Chapter House
18. Cloisters

Walk across to the north aisle, where there is a **Medieval Clock (3)**. This was once positioned in the detached bell tower on the northwest side of the cathedral, but the tower was demolished by Wyatt in 1790. The clock, which has no face, dates from *c*1386 and is certainly the oldest working clock in England, if not the world.

Tombs and Monuments

The spaces between the arches of the nave are taken up with numerous tombs – some plain slabs, others with effigies, some of early bishops and brought from Old Sarum, others of local soldiers and statesmen. Unfortunately, most of the tombs were placed here by Wyatt, who in moving them from their previous positions in the cathedral apparently mixed up the effigies and put them on tombs to which they did not belong.

Three of the tombs are of particular interest. Close to the medieval clock is the **Tomb of William de Longespée (4)**. Son of the third Earl of Salisbury, de Longespée (*c*1212–1250), a general in the Crusades, was killed in the assault on Mansura. On the same slab is a small tomb, possibly of a `boy bishop' who died in office. (Choristers used to elect one of their number to bear the title of `bishop' from the Feast of St Nicholas on December 6 to the Feast of the Innocents on December 28). More probably it is an example of a heart burial, quite likely that of Richard Poore, bishop 1217–29 and founder of the cathedral.

Cross to the south aisle to find the **Tomb of St Osmund (5)**. St Osmund (d1099), second bishop of Old Sarum, was canonized in 1457. His remains were brought to the cathedral in 1226 and originally placed in a shrine in Trinity Chapel. The shrine was broken up in 1539 during the Reformation. The `tomb' we see in the nave today may be part of the shrine. Finally, next to the crossing is the **Tomb of William de Longespée the Elder (6)**. De Longespée (1196–1226), third Earl of Salisbury, was a half-brother to King John, a witness to the signing of the Magna Carta (1215) and present at the laying of the cathedral's foundation stone in 1220.

Proceed to the **Crossing (7)**. The tower and spire (said to have a combined weight of 6400 tons) are supported by four Purbeck Marble pillars which have a decided bend. Hardly surprising, considering there is only 3ft (1m) of foundations! The tower has been subsequently supported by strainer arches, flying buttresses and interior stone buttresses. The vaulting of the crossing dates from 1480; its paintwork shows the royal arms of the time plus the arms of various bishops.

Move left into the **North Transept (8)**, dominated by three levels of Early English lancet windows. The stained glass, by Hemmings, dates from 1895, although 13th-century in style. Of the numerous monuments the most impressive is that of John Blythe, bishop 1494–9 and at one time Chancellor of Cambridge University. Along the east side of the transept a modern wooden screen conceals the Chapel of St Edmund of Abingdon and St Thomas of Canterbury. The triptych and altar front date from the late 19th century and were originally in the Trinity Chapel.

Leave the north transept and walk along the north choir aisle, turning left into the **Morning Chapel (9)**. The most interesting feature here is the monument to the artist Rex Whistler (1905–1944), which takes the form of a revolving glass prism. Engraved by his brother Laurence, the prism is set in a blue-and-gold lantern resting on a corbel of Purbeck Marble (from the same quarries as most of the cathedral's 13th-century stone). Alongside the monument are the remains of the stone pulpitum removed from the choir by Wyatt in the 18th century.

Choir and Chantry Chapels

Cross the north choir aisle and enter the **Choir (10)** – the archaic term 'quire' is often used at Salisbury. While the architecture of the choir is similar to that of the nave, the fabric owes much to the Victorian renovations. The canons' stalls, some of which have misericords, are 13th-century, but the rest of the stalls were added in the 19th century and the canopies in 1913–25. Sir George Gilbert Scott (1811–1878) provided the Bishop's Throne and the Willis organ (this replaced George III's organ, which was given to St Thomas's Church in the city). Scott was responsible also for the repainting of the vaulting in the medieval style, after being unable to remove Wyatt's coating of whitewash. Two of Scott's introductions have not survived – the Minton floor and an open metal screen by Skidmore. The new high altar, introduced in 1984 and made from stone from Old Sarum, is notable for its superb modern altar frontals. Note also the wall plaque commemorating the distribution of the Maundy Money by Queen Elizabeth II in April 1974.

Return to the north choir aisle. On the right is the delightful little **Chantry Chapel of Edward Audley (11)**. Audley was bishop 1502–24. The chapel is in Perpendicular style and retains some of its original colouring. The painting of the Virgin and Child comes from Florence, while the altar fabrics are modern.

On reaching the end of the aisle turn right into the open-plan **Trinity Chapel (12)**, formerly known as the Lady Chapel. This is the oldest part of the cathedral, and was the scene of the initial consecration in 1225 – note the consecration crosses on the wall on either side of the altar. The superb Early English architecture is graced by slender pillars of Purbeck Marble, leaving narrow side aisles with blind arcading. Dominating the chapel is the Prisoners of Conscience Window (1980) by Gabriel Loire of Chartres. People's opinions on the window differ enormously: to judge it fairly, view it in the morning when the suns streams in from the east; a wet afternoon produces an entirely different effect. To the left of the altar is the Prisoner of Conscience Candle, festooned in barbed wire. Before leaving Trinity Chapel, look for the 14th-century wooden Madonna and Child on the north wall.

Move now into the south choir aisle. At the east end is the resplendent **Tomb of the Earl of Hertford (13)**. Born Edward Seymour (1539–1621), the earl was the nephew of Jane Seymour (1509–1537), Queen of England. Beside him lies the effigy of his wife, Lady Catherine Grey (*c*1538–1568), sister of Lady Jane Grey (1537–1554), Queen of England for nine days in 1553 before being imprisoned and beheaded. Further down the aisle on the right, framed with iron railings, is the **Chantry Chapel of Walter, Lord Hungerford (14)**, who died in 1449. The chapel was restored in 1778 by the Earl of Radnor and removed from the nave to this position to be used as the Radnor family pew – you can see a line of seats inside.

Next, on the left, is the sumptuous **Mompesson Tomb (15)**, repainted in its original colours in 1964. A curiosity here is that the figures of Sir Richard

Mompesson (d1624) and his wife, Lady Katherine, face west rather than the usual east. This is explained by the fact that the tomb was originally on the north side of the cathedral.

Step now into the **South Transept (16)**, structurally a replica of the north transept. There are three chapels here. In the Chapel of St Margaret of Scotland the altar frontal is a 17th-century Spanish embroidery with scenes of the life of St Theresa of Avila; this is one of the treasures of the cathedral. In the Chapel of St Laurence – a deacon *c*258 and said to have been martyred in Rome on a gridiron – the altar top is 13th-century and the oldest in the cathedral. And finally, in the Chapel of St Michael the Archangel are regimental colours and books of remembrance.

The Chapter House and Cloisters

Leave the south transept by the door in the southwest corner. Go along the north cloister and turn left into the **Chapter House (17)**. Built 1263–84, this was clearly closely modelled on that in Westminster Abbey. It is octagonal with a slim central pier of Purbeck Marble leading up to fine fan vaulting, somewhat spoiled by insipid painted decoration. The windows are Geometric Decorated in style (almost all the original glass has gone), and below is blind arcading with stone benches. Notice the capitals on the wall shafts, where the carved foliage also reveals occasional birds, heads and animals. The spandrels of the arcade have a medieval stone-carved frieze showing scenes from the Old Testament – the stewards can provide a detailed list of the subjects. The overall effect is perhaps ruined by the Minton tiled floor, which seems totally out of place. There are displays of silverware and religious documents, and the chapter house also contains one of the four surviving originals of the Magna Carta (1215), written in Latin on vellum and running to about 3500 words.

Leave the chapter house and return to the **Cloisters (18)**. Completed *c*1340, these are the largest and, with the possible exception of Gloucester, the finest in England. The style is Early Geometric Decorated, matching the chapter house, and there is simple quadripartite vaulting. Salisbury was never a monastic cathedral, so monks never walked in contemplation here. In the cloister garth are two magnificent cedar trees, planted in 1837 to commemorate Queen Victoria's accession to the throne; superb though the trees are, many visitors feel they detract from the simple lines of the cloisters. A library built over the eastern cloister in 1445 contains many ancient manuscripts and early printed books, but is not open to the public without a special permit.

The exit from the cathedral is, in true modern commercial fashion, via the refectory and bookshop.

WALKING TOUR FROM SALISBURY CATHEDRAL

The tour begins in the Cathedral Close, arguably the finest of any English cathedral city, with its superb late-18th-century buildings, including two museums. You then leave the close via one of the gates in the wall and move into the city centre, with its ancient coaching inns, vibrant market and St Thomas's Church, undoubtedly one of the most interesting parish churches in the country. A short stretch of the River Avon follows before you return through another gate to the Cathedral Close.

Start and finish: The west front of the cathedral.
Length: 1½ miles (2.4km).
Time: The walk is on level ground throughout, so can be comfortably completed in well under an hour. Allow extra time if visiting the museums and St Thomas's Church.

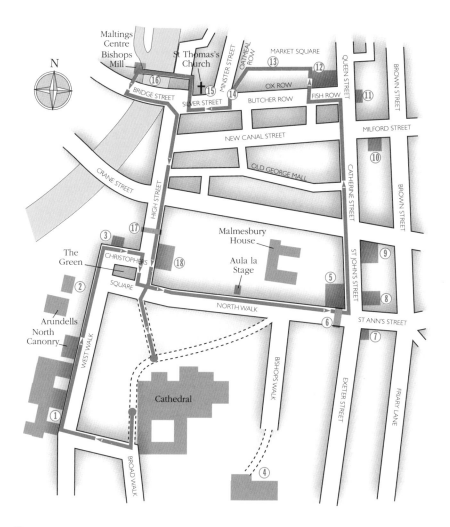

Key

1. The King's House
2. The Wardrobe
3. Mompesson House
4. Bishop's Palace
5. Malmesbury House
6. St Ann's Gate

7. The Old Bell Inn
8. The King's Arms
9. The White Hart
10. The Red Lion
11. House of John a'Porte
12. Guildhall

13. Market Place
14. Poultry Cross
15. St Thomas' Cross
16. City Mill
17. North (or High Street) Gate
18. Matrons' Collage

Refreshments: Light snacks are available in the cathedral refectory. There are no other food outlets in the close, except within the two museums. There is a wide selection of ancient inns on the walking route, many with coaching origins. These include: the Old Bell in St Ann's Street; the King's Arms and the White Hart Hotel in St John's Street; and the Red Lion Hotel in Milford Street. In summer the Bishop's Mill has some pleasant outdoor tables alongside the River Avon. Many of these hostelries offer accommodation.

The first part of the tour concentrates on the Cathedral Close, one of the most attractive in England. There are some superb examples of domestic architecture, particularly from the late 17th century. The size of the open space around the cathedral means that photographing England's tallest cathedral spire is not a problem.

The Cathedral Close
From the west front of the cathedral take the path south for about fifty yards until you reach Broad Walk. Turn right here and, the playing field to your left, stroll on another fifty yards until you arrive at West Walk. Turn right.

Immediately on your left now is **The King's House** (1), which has a long and interesting history. It was built by the Abbots of Sherbourne, but with the Dissolution of the Monasteries it fell into lay hands. The impressive oriel window was added in the

St Ann's Gate leading to the Cathedral Close

late 15th century. In the early 17th century the owners played host to King James I on a number of occasions – hence the building's name. In the 19th century it was a school and then became a Diocesan Training College for schoolmistresses; the two sisters of Thomas Hardy (1840–1928) were students at the college. In 1980 The King's House became the home of the Salisbury and South Wiltshire Museum, which has won several awards for its innovative presentation.

The next building on the left is the Old Deanery, which

has a medieval hall. Pass the North Canonry to Arundells, for many years the home of Sir Edward Heath (b1916), the former prime minister. Set back from West Walk is the **Wardrobe (2)**, originally a 13th-century canonry, although with many later additions. It may have gained its name through being some sort of storehouse for the bishops. It was then a hall of residence for the training college before becoming the Museum of the Royal Gloucestershire, Berkshire and Wiltshire Regiment.

Proceed now into Choristers Square, which runs round a grassy area known as The Green. The most important building here is **Mompesson House (3)**, located on the north side. Built in the late 17th century by Sir Thomas Mompesson, MP for Salisbury, it was used between 1942 and 1946 as the official residence of the Bishop of Salisbury. It is now owned by the National Trust.

Leave Choristers Square and turn left along North Walk. On the left is the flint end of the former canonry, known as Aula le Stage, parts of which date from the 13th century. Next on the left is the former Salisbury Theological College; this closed in 1994 but still holds courses for external students.

From outside the college, look south along Bishop's Walk and in the distance you can see the gates leading to the **Bishop's Palace (4)**. Parts of the building go back to the consecration of the cathedral in 1225. It received considerable damage during the Civil War, but was restored in the late 17th century by Bishop Seth Ward (1617–1689) with the help of Christopher Wren (1632–1723). In 1947 the bishop moved into smaller premises and the palace was taken over by the Cathedral School. The grounds are private and the building is not normally open to the public.

Continue along North Walk towards St Ann's Gate. On the right, the brick Georgian building is the sixth-form block of Bishop Wordsworth School. On the left just before the gate is **Malmesbury House (5)**, another 13th-century canonry. It was enlarged in the 14th century and leased to the Harris family, one of whose descendants became the first Earl of Malmesbury. The façade of the building was added by Wren. Charles II and George Frederick Handel (1685–1759) were among the more illustrious visitors to the house.

You are now approaching **St Ann's Gate (6)**. The gate was built in the early 14th century, although the Vicars Choral Chapel above the arch was added later. St Ann's, like the other gates to the close, is still locked at 23:00 (which must have been very frustrating for the lady students at the training college!). It is thought that Handel made his first public performance in England in the room above St Ann's Gate.

Inns of Character

Pass through the gate and turn left. Pause for a moment to inspect the wall, which displays some carved stonework which came from the first cathedral at Old Sarum.

Turn left into St John's Road, which runs parallel to the wall of the close. This street is notable for its number of inns of character, many of which offer possibilities for a lunch stop. Opposite St Ann's Gate, on the corner of St John's Road and St Ann's Road, is the **Old Bell Inn (7)**, which dates back to the 14th century. Heading into the city centre, you can see on the right of St John's Road the **King's Arms (8)**, a half-timbered coaching inn with a medieval atmosphere. Further along on the right, on the corner of Ivy Street and St John's Road, is the **White Hart Hotel (9)**; with its Classical façade, this was undoubtedly Salisbury's grandest coaching inn. Stagecoaches left for London at 22:00 nightly.

Carry on northwards as St John's Road merges into Catherine Street. A brief diversion to the right into Milford Street takes you to the **Red Lion Hotel (10)**, a half-timbered building of considerable character. The south wing was constructed between 1280 and 1320, reputedly to house men working on the cathedral. The main part of the Red Lion belongs to the 18th century, when it was a thriving coaching inn. From here a coach called the Salisbury Flying Machine left daily for London. Wander under the huge archway, designed to take the largest carriages, into the attractive courtyard with its models of red lions.

Return to Catherine Street and continue north into Queen Street. Immediately on the right is the **House of John a'Porte (11)** This magnificent half-timbered building with a double-jettied frontage was built in 1425 by John a'Porte, a wealthy wool merchant and several times Mayor of Salisbury. The ground floor is now a shop specializing in glass and china.

Cross the road and enter Fish Row. On the right is the **Guildhall (12)**, which houses the Tourist Information Office. In order to see the front of the building, turn down a small alleyway to the right, which brings you into the Market Place. The original Guildhall was burnt down in 1780 and the present building, with its Classical façade, was completed 15 years later. It was donated to the city by the Earl of Radnor.

The Market Place and St Thomas's Church

You now find yourself in the **Market Place (13)**. A market has been held here twice weekly since 1361, and this area has always been the hub of commercial activity in the city. Numerous inns lined the Market Place to provide accommodation for pilgrims visiting the Shrine of St Osmund; today only two of these inns remains, the rest having been converted to other uses.

Leave the Market Place in the southwest corner and come to the **Poultry Cross (14)**. The present Cross dates from the 15th century, replacing an earlier one which had stood on the site for over 200 years. It consists of six piers enclosing a central column. Above is a superstructure with flying buttresses surrounding a central spire topped with a cross. Farmers used to sell their wares beneath the Poultry Cross, which was also a popular venue for open-air sermons.

Leave the Poultry Cross westwards along Silver Street and turn right almost immediately along the alleyway leading to **St Thomas's Church (15)**. This must be one of the most fascinating parish churches in the country – it is an absolute gem and should not be missed. It dates back to *c*1220, but most of the building is 15th-century Perpendicular. There is a tremendous amount to see, including the Doom Painting over the chancel arch, a magnificent carved 'Somerset Angel' roof, a superb Lady Chapel with medieval murals, a Georgian organ presented to the cathedral by George III in 1792 and given to St Thomas's in 1877 – and much more. A small brochure giving full details of the church is well worth buying.

Leave St Thomas's Church and go straight ahead towards the Maltings Centre. After crossing the River Avon, turn immediately left under an arch and head towards the bridge, a few steps away. This gives you a superb view back towards the old **City Mill (16)**, which is mostly 17th-century in age, although the original mill is believed to be one of four Salisbury mills mentioned in the Domesday Book. It was used for grinding grain and for fulling cloth, while the associated buildings have at various times produced beer, tobacco and snuff. To the left is the Bishop's Mill, an old building which has been modernized and converted into a popular restaurant.

Walk back to Silver Street and turn right into High Street. Note on the left the modern Old George Shopping Mall, named after a coaching inn. Ahead is the **North Gate (17)** or High Street Gate, leading into the Cathedral Close. The North Gate, built 1327–42, is still locked between 23:00 and 06:00. For many years it had a portcullis which could be lowered if the townsfolk became rebellious, and the culprits could then be locked up in the small jail contained within the gate. Next to the gate is the porter's lodge – the job of porter was much sought after by royal servants in the Middle Ages.

Pass through the gate and immediately on the left is the **Matrons' College (18)**, founded in 1682 by Bishop Seth Ward to house ten widows of clergy – a function it still fulfils today. Note the coat-of-arms of Charles II above the main doorway.

You are now back in the Cathedral Close, where the tour concludes.

Most of St Thomas's is built in the Perpendicular style

Winchester

Access: Winchester is linked by road to London via the M25 and the M3 (junctions 9–11). The A34 provides access to the Midlands. There are frequent railway connections with London Waterloo. The nearest airport is Southampton International, which has scheduled services to a number of European and British cities.

The Romans formed a settlement at the place where Winchester now stands. Called Venta Belgarum, it in due course became probably the country's fifth largest city. There is no evidence of Christianity in Roman Winchester; this had to wait until Anglo-Saxon times. In 635 Cenwahl built the Old Minster, which three decades later became a cathedral when the ecclesiastical centre of Wessex was transferred from Dorchester-on-Thames. Excavation work in the 1960s revealed the foundations of the Old Minster and these have been marked out in brick on the north side of the present cathedral.

The Anglo-Saxon city, known as Wintancaestre, was notable for two men, King Alfred and Bishop Swithun (St Swithin). Alfred the Great (*c*848–899), who made Winchester his capital city, was a noted scholar and statesman, and performed heroic deeds in protecting the city from the invading Danes, rebuilt the city walls and laid out the present street plan. When he died in 899 he was buried in the Old Minster, but his tomb was later transferred to the New Minster built by his son Edward the Elder (d924). The Old Minster thereafter became a Benedictine monastery, while Alfred's widow Ealhswith founded a nunnery called Nunnaminster, which later became St Mary's Abbey. As a result of all this Winchester became one of the most important ecclesiastical centres in Europe. Bishop Swithun (d862), for his part, probably built the city's bridge over the River Itchen. When his bones were exhumed in 971, to be placed in a shrine, it rained heavily for a considerable time, leading to the popular saying that, if it rains on St Swithin's Day, it will rain for the next forty days.

The Norman period brought notable changes to Winchester. The city, still capital of England, surrendered to William the Conqueror in November 1066, and after he was crowned later in the year he ordered the construction of a castle on the city's west side which was to become the seat of the early Norman kings. Four years later William appointed a Norman bishop, Wakelin, whose task was to build a new cathedral. Work began in 1079 and by 1093, when the first dedication took place, the east end, transepts, central tower and part of the nave were complete. The Old Minster was then demolished so that the nave could be finished. The Norman cathedral, now measuring 535ft (164m) in length, was the longest in Europe at the time. The only parts of it remaining today are the transepts and crypt.

In the early 13th century the east end of the cathedral was extended by a large retrochoir built in Early English style. It was once thought this was done to house the remains of St Swithun, which were attracting hordes of pilgrims, but in fact these remains were located on a feretory platform behind the high altar until shortly before the Reformation. During the early 14th century, the choir – located, unusually, underneath the crossing – was constructed and the presbytery arches were rebuilt. Attention then turned to the nave. Rebuilding work was started by Bishop Eddington and completed by probably the most famous Bishop of Winchester of all, William of Wykeham or Wickham (1324–1404), who founded Winchester College and New College, Oxford. The work, in Perpendicular style, started at the west front and proceeded eastwards. The existing Norman piers were encased by new stone and the entire nave was revaulted. Many of Winchester's chantry chapels also date from this period. The final major work on the cathedral came around 1500, when the eastern end of the Lady Chapel was rebuilt.

Up to now the cathedral had been the monastery church of St Swithun's Priory, but in 1539 the priory was officially dissolved, along with the other monastic foundations and friaries in the city. At the same time St Swithun's Shrine was destroyed. The prior became the first bishop, with a chapter of twelve canons. Further disruption came during the Civil War: the cathedral was twice entered by Parliamentary soldiers, who inflicted considerable damage before riding through the city brandishing their spoils.

By now the city of Winchester had lost much of its importance, political power having moved to London and ecclesiastical influence to Canterbury. There was little industry in the city and, by the late 18th century, it had become a residential town for the gentry. The coming of the railways in the mid-19th century, however, led to a new expansion and also brought in tourists for the first time.

During the early years of the 20th century it was realized that the walls of the east end of the cathedral were in danger of collapse, as the foundations were subsiding into the marshy subsoil. Underpinning was obviously necessary. The work was carried out by a deep-sea diver named William Walker. Working six hours a day for five years in atrocious conditions, he eventually underpinned almost the whole cathedral by removing old logs and replacing them with sacks of cement concrete.

In 1993 a new Visitor Centre was opened by Her Majesty Queen Elizabeth II. It is located within an attractive walled garden and includes a restaurant and giftshop.

TOUR OF THE CATHEDRAL
Start and finish: The west door.

The **West Front (1)** is approached through an avenue of lime trees. Built in the time of Bishop Eddington, it is dominated by the elegant Perpendicular Window. Although it has been criticised by several architectural historians, you will probably be impressed by the window, particularly when you come to look at it from inside, where you'll be able to see that scraps of glass recovered after the vandalism of the Civil War have been used.

Step inside the building via the west door, to the left of which stairs lead to the treasury, housed in a Tudor gallery. Note here the 17th-century bronze statues of Charles I and James I.

Proceed to a position halfway down the **Nave (2)**. Largely built in the time of Bishop William of Wykeham, the nave is Perpendicular in style but, remarkably, was transformed from the original Norman without the latter being demolished: the pillars were simply encased in the later stonework, and much of the Norman masonry remains. The three storeys of the Norman nave were replaced by two storeys, enlarging the main arches and removing the triforium. The roof was completely revaulted in lierne style, with some superb bosses and corbels which you'll be able to see better if you've brought binoculars with you.

An Author's Tomb

Move into the north aisle and look for the simple slab on the floor marking the **Tomb of Jane Austen (3)**. Austen lived in the nearby village of Chawton, but died in the city at the age of 42; surprisingly, the inscription gives little indication that she was a writer! Close to her tomb is the Norman **Font (4)**. Made from black Tournai Marble, it is decorated with scenes and miracles from the life of St Nicholas, the Patron Saint of children. The end of the nave is terminated abruptly by the Victorian **Choir Screen (5)**, designed by Sir Gilbert Scott (1811–1878). Dark and spiky, it stands out irritatingly against the mellow cream-grey stonework of the nave. Turn now into the **North Transept (6)**, where you can see how the cathedral would have looked in Norman times. The transept was built between 1079 and 1093 out of limestone brought from the Isle of Wight. There are three equal levels, all with rounded arches – the main arcade, a triforium with each arch subdivided, and a clerestory. The flat wooden ceilings were added in Victorian times.

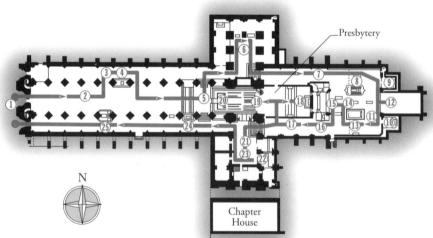

Key

1. West Front
2. Nave
3. Tomb of Jane Austen
4. Font
5. Choir Screen
6. North Transept
7. Bishop Gardiner's Chapel
8. Bishop Waynflete's Chapel
9. Guardian Angels Chapel
10. Bishop Langton's Chapel
11. Diver Statuette
12. Lady Chapel
13. Cardinal Beaufort's Chapel
14. Monument to St Swithun
15. Holy Hole
16. Bishop Fox's Chapel
17. Mortuary Chests
18. High Altar and Screen
19. Tomb of William Rufus
20. Choir
21. South Transept
22. Chapel of Prior Silkstede
23. Bishop Wilberforce's Memorial
24. Bishop Eddington's Chapel
25. William of Wykeham's Chapel

Chantry Chapels

Winchester is noted for its many chantry chapels, and you'll see the first examples in the north transept, with the Epiphany Chapel on the west side and the Holy Sepulchre Chapel, which has some interesting wall paintings, adjoining the choir.

Leave the transept and proceed into the north retrochoir aisle, passing the presbytery on your right. The retrochoir is the area of the cathedral where the more interesting chantry chapels are found. First on the right is **Bishop Gardiner's Chapel (7)**, showing a strange variety of styles. Next on the right is **Bishop Waynflete's Chapel (8)**; Waynflete was also a headmaster of Winchester College and founded Magdalen College, Oxford. At the east end of the cathedral the Lady Chapel is flanked by two more chapels. On the north side is the **Guardian Angels Chapel (9)**, named after the paintings of angels in the vaulting, and on the south side is **Bishop Langton's Chapel (10)**. Langton died of the plague in 1500, unfortunately just before he was to become Archbishop of Canterbury. Look for his rebus and note also the ceiling, which has been restored and painted to resemble its medieval appearance.

At the entrance to Bishop Langton's Chapel is the **Diver Statuette (11)**, made to commemorate the work of the deep-sea diver William Walker, who as we have seen saved the cathedral by underpinning the foundations. Unfortunately the statuette was modelled on the consultant engineer rather than on Walker himself!

The **Lady Chapel (12)** was built in two stages. The western end is 13th-century, and the chapel was extended eastwards around 1500 in Perpendicular style, a project funded by Elizabeth of York whose son, the unfortunate Prince Arthur (1486–1502), was christened here. Look for the rebuses in the vaulting of bishops Hunton and Silkstede. Murals from Silkstede's time show legends from the life of Our Lady.

Leave the East End and walk past **Cardinal Beaufort's Chantry Chapel (13)** – Beaufort was present at the trial of St Joan of Arc (*c*1412–1431), whose statue is outside the Lady Chapel, and is believed to have held the keys to her dungeon – and turn into the centre of the retrochoir, where there is a modern **Monument to St Swithun (14)** at the spot where his shrine finally stood. Earlier the saint's remains had been displayed on a feretory platform behind the high altar. Look for the **Holy Hole (15)** at the base of the rear of the altar which enabled pilgrims to crawl under the platform to get closer to the healing powers of the relics. This part of the retrochoir has some particularly fine 13th-century floor tiles.

Bones of Monarchs

Return to the south retrochoir aisle. Immediately to the left is **Bishop Fox's Chantry Chapel (16)**, beautifully carved in stone. His effigy is in the form of a cadaver; as the chapel was built before he died, there was plenty of time for him to be reminded of his own mortality! Further west, high on the screen, are the famous **Mortuary Chests (17)**, which contain the bones of many pre-Conquest bishops and monarchs, including possibly King Canute (*c*995–1035). Unfortunately, Cromwell's men rummaged through the chests, so the bones have become somewhat disordered.

Turn now into the presbytery, which dates from the 14th century and is the only part of the cathedral in Decorated style. Behind the **High Altar (18)** is the massive

15th-century Great Screen. The original statues on the screen were smashed during the Reformation, but the remains are on display in the Triforium Gallery Museum. The present statues were placed there in Victorian times. At the boundary of the presbytery and the choir is the so-styled **Tomb of William Rufus (19)**, although the ashes of this king are in fact among the bones in the mortuary chests. Son of William the Conqueror, the unpopular King William Rufus (c1087–1100) was killed by an arrow while hunting in the New Forest, possibly shot by his companion Walter Tirel.

The **Choir (20)**, which is located under the central tower, is distinguished by its early-14th-century stalls, with their superb carving. Look for the heads of monkeys and other animals, plus a Green Man. There are over 60 misericords. Note, too, the Jacobean choir pulpit, given by Prior Silkstede around 1500.

An Angler and a Philanthropist's Son

Leave the choir and walk via the south retrochoir aisle to the **South Transept (21)**, which like the north transept is in Norman style. There are two chapels here, the more interesting being the **Chapel of Prior Silkstede (22)**, which, although Norman, was restructured by Silkstede in the early 16th century. The chapel has some interesting murals, but the important feature is the grave of Isaak Walton (1593–1683), author of *The Compleat Angler*, who died in Winchester's Cathedral Close in 1683.

In the centre of the transept is **Bishop Wilberforce's Memorial (23)**. Samuel Wilberforce (1805–1873) was the son of William Wilberforce (1759–1833), the philanthropist who was prominent in abolishing the slave trade. The monument, which was designed by Sir George Gilbert Scott (1811–1878), shows the bishop's colourful effigy supported by six angels.

There are two more chantry chapels to see, and these are the oldest in the cathedral – fittingly they are named after the two men who between them remodelled the nave. At the eastern end of the south nave aisle is **Bishop Eddington's Chantry Chapel (24)**, which was meant to fit under the original Norman arcade, and **William of Wykeham's Chantry (25)**. Wykeham, in addition to his work as a bishop, founded Winchester College, whose former pupils are known as 'Wykehamists'.

From Wykeham's Chapel continue along the south nave aisle to the west door, where the tour concludes.

WALKING TOUR FROM WINCHESTER CATHEDRAL

The tour includes the Cathedral Close, parts of the pedestrianized shopping centre, some of the city's ancient monuments and a section of the Riverside Walk.

Start and finish: The west front of the cathedral.
Length: 1¾ miles (3.2km).
Time: 1½hr, though allow longer if you want to visit the museums and other buildings.
Refreshments: A number of ancient hostelries and coaching inns on or close to the walking route offer excellent pub lunches and bar meals. You might try: the Eclipse, on The Square, a half-timbered former rectory whose tables spill out onto the pavement in the summer; the Wykeham Arms, in Kingsgate Street, a pub close to Kingsgate and Winchester College and full of old school desks and other

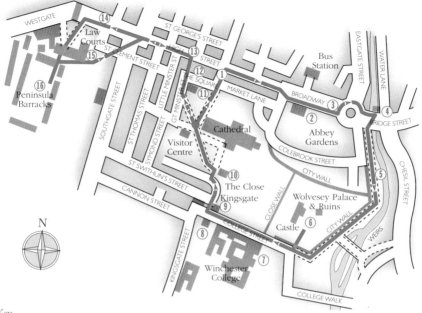

Key

1. High Street
2. Guildhall
3. Statue of King Alfred
4. City Mill
5. Riverside Walk
6. Wolvesey Castle

7. Winchester College
8. Jane Austen's House
9. Kingsgate
10. The Deanery
11. City Museum
12. The Eclipse

13. City Cross
14. Westgate
15. The Great Hall
16. Peninsula Barracks

memorabilia from the college; the Hotel du Vin and Bistro (formerly the Southgate Hotel), in Southgate Street, a Georgian building close to the law courts; and the Old Market Tavern, in Market Lane, a traditional pub overlooking the cathedral.

Leave the west front of the cathedral and turn right, crossing the Cathedral Close, to arrive at the gap between The Square and Market Street. Pass through this gap to reach the pedestrianized **High Street (1)** where, despite some modern shop fronts, many of the buildings retain their ancient features and character. Turn right and proceed down the gentle hill. The High Street now widens out into The Broadway. On the right is the Victorian **Guildhall (2)**, with its green-roofed clock tower a prominent local landmark. The Guildhall is now used as a conference centre and has an art gallery; it is also the home of the helpful Tourist Information Centre. Next door is the Abbey House, the official home of the Mayor of Winchester. Opposite the gardens of Abbey House is the imposing bronze **Statue of King Alfred (3)**. Standing on a plinth of Cornish granite, Alfred clasps a shield and raises his sword, staring resolutely up the High Street. The statue was erected in 1901 on the millennial of his death.

Along the Waterside

Continue past the statue until you reach the City Bridge. The first bridge here over the River Itchen was probably built by St Swithun; the present one dates from 1813. Cross the road carefully to the **City Mill (4)**, built in 1744 with the wheel restored in 1995. There were numerous mills along the River Itchen from medieval times onward. There is a speedy mill race to see, plus an attractive island garden. The City Mill is owned by the National Trust (which has a small giftshop on the premises), and part of the building acts as a Youth Hostel.

Leave the mill and return to the south side of City Bridge. Take the path between the river and the pub called Barringtons. You are now on the **Riverside Walk (5)**, locally called Weirs Walk, which leads to the water meadows of the River Itchen and eventually to the Hospital of St Cross. The tour takes you along only a few hundred yards of the walk, but it shows some of the leats and mills of pre-Industrial Revolution times. To your right is a stretch of the old city walls, parts of which may date back as far as Roman times. After an area of public gardens, you come to a large mill which has been converted into accommodation, and shortly after this you should turn right into College Street.

The Castle and College

Behind the wall to the right are the remains of **Wolvesey Castle (6)**. There was a building here in Anglo-Saxon times, but the present ruins are of a 12th-century fortified palace constructed by various bishops. It was a popular residence for visiting royalty, and Henry V is believed to have received the French ambassador here before the invasion prior to Agincourt. Wolvesey Castle was almost entirely destroyed in the Civil War, when parliamentary troops captured the city. A few years later, Bishop Morley began to build a new palace in Baroque style. One wing of this building remains and is the residence of the present Bishop of Winchester.

Proceed further along College Street. Almost the whole of the left-hand side is occupied by **Winchester College (7)**. Founded by Bishop William of Wykeham in 1382 and designed by William Wynford – who was also responsible for the cathedral nave – the college was set up to train seventy scholars for the church. Their education was to be completed at New College, Oxford, also founded by Wykeham. Winchester College expanded considerably during the 19th century and is now one of the country's foremost public schools. The highlight is the College Chapel, where there is the tomb-effigy of William of Wykeham. The chapel tower is believed to have been designed by Sir Christopher Wren (1632–1723) in the 1680s.

Further left along College Street is **Jane Austen's House (8)**. In fact, the novelist lived here for only a few weeks before her death. Her main residence was in the village of Chawston, a few miles outside the city, but she had come to live in this modest yellow brick house to be near her doctor. At the end of College Street, turn right under **Kingsgate (9)**, one of two surviving city gates. Above the gateway is the tiny Church of St Swithun, still in use as a place of worship.

Carry on and pass through Priory Gateway into the Cathedral Close. Immediately to the right is Cheyney Court, undoubtedly the most photographed house in the city. With yellow and black half-timbered work, it is partly built into the medieval walls and is festooned with wisteria in early summer. Once part of the Bishop of Winchester's courthouse, Cheyney Court was restored after damage in the Civil War.

Cheyney Court

Go left through the close. Ahead is **The Deanery (10)**, which was the Prior's House before the Dissolution of St Swithun's Priory. The 13th-century porch is distinctive, with three lancet-shaped arches. Attached is the 15th-century Prior's Hall, while to the southeast is the Pilgrims' Hall with one of the earliest surviving hammer-beam roofs.

Ancient and Modern

Take the pathway to the left of the Deanery, which leads to the south side of the cathedral. The grassy area here has a number of modern sculptures, mostly made of scrap iron.

You are now back at the west front of the Cathedral, where the second part of the walk starts. Take the path obliquely northwest across the grass through an avenue of lime trees to The Square. On the corner to the right is the **City Museum (11)**, a flint building with some interesting exhibits showing the archaeology and history of the Winchester area. Some fascinating Victorian shop interiors have also been recreated. Opposite the museum is a delightful little half-timbered pub, the **Eclipse (12)**, once the rectory of the old Church of St Lawrence.

Pass through the narrow end of Great Minster Street into the upper portion of the High Street. Immediately to the right is the **City Cross (13)**, also known as the Buttercross. Erected in the 15th century and restored in 1865, it is backed by ancient half-timbered houses with jettied walls and is roughly on the site of William the Conqueror's palace. Notice the nearby clock, jutting out over the High Street on an ornate wrought-iron frame; it was given to the city of Winchester in 1713.

State and Military History

Walk up the High Street to the **Westgate (14)**, one of four original gates in the city's walls. About six hundred years old, it stands on the site of an earlier Roman gateway and was well fortified in its time, with a portcullis (you can still see the grooves) and openings from where burning oil and missiles could be hurled at attackers. Note on the north side the two coats-of-arms – the royal arms and those of the City of Winchester. The Westgate became a debtors' prison in the 17th century. Today it houses a small museum displaying ancient weights and measures, plus a painted ceiling which came from Winchester College. There are superb views over the city from the roofwalk.

Pass through the Westgate's arch and turn immediately left into a large square surrounded by a complex of buildings, including the modern law courts. The most important building here is the **Great Hall (15)**, sometimes known as the Castle Hall because it is part of the complex of castle buildings built originally by the Conqueror – although the Great Hall itself in fact belongs to the rebuilding period of Henry III in the early 13th century. It is considered the finest medieval hall in the country after Westminster. Once a royal residence, it suffered from a serious fire in 1302, after which monarchs preferred to stay at nearby Wolvesey Castle. Following the Civil War the hall was used for the administration of justice: the infamous Judge George Jeffreys (1648–1689) often sat here, and Sir Walter Raleigh (1552–1618) was condemned to death here in 1602. It was a county court until the 1970s, when the new law courts were built.

The star exhibit in the Great Hall is the Round Table, which is mounted on the west wall. Measuring some 18ft (5.5m) across, the table shows King Arthur in Tudor clothing and has the names of his knights around the edge.

Behind the Great Hall is Queen Eleanor's Garden, said to be a faithful representation of a medieval garden. On the southeast side of the Great Hall are some excavations of William the Conqueror's castle, which have excellent viewing platforms and information panels.

College Street from Kingsgate

To the west of the Great Hall, and approached via Queen Eleanor's Garden, is the **Peninsula Barracks (16)**, the home of no fewer than five regimental museums including that of the Gurkhas. Winchester has always been a garrison town, and several centuries of military tradition are on display in the museums. Return to the Westgate and walk back down the High Street. Turn right at the City Cross through a narrow passageway past the City Museum, and return to the west front of the cathedral, where the tour concludes.

Chichester

Access: Chichester is some five miles (8km) from the coast (it is often claimed Chichester has the only English cathedral which can be seen from the sea). The A27, which becomes the M27 to the west of Chichester, is the main east–west coastal road in Southeast England. A number of other main roads lead to the city from the north and south. There are coach services to London. The main south coast railway line from Brighton to Southampton runs through the city, with the station located on the south side of the ring road. There are twice-hourly services to London Victoria and hourly services to London Waterloo. The nearest international airport is London Gatwick, with which Chichester is connected by coach. Ferry services from the continent arrive at Portsmouth, some 12 miles (19km) to the west.

Although there were certainly Bronze Age people living in the area, Chichester's history really begins with the Romans. Around AD40, the Romans established a strategic base at Fishbourne, near one of the arms of Chichester harbour. Within a few years they formed a settlement at Chichester itself, which they named Noviomagnus. Walls of earth and timber were built around the town and the cross-like street plan that survives to the present day was laid out. Roman roads radiated out from Noviomagnus, including Stane Street, which ran northeast to Londinium.

The Romans left around AD410 and there gradually followed a large-scale settlement of people from Lower Saxony. Among these immigrants was a chieftain whose son Cissa is believed to have given his name to the present-day town – `Chichester' can be parsed as `Cissa's fortified place'. The Saxons increasingly suffered from Viking raids, and in the 9th century the original Roman walls were rebuilt as part of King Alfred's scheme to construct a chain of fortified towns. The Saxons, under Saint Wilfrid or Wilfrith (634–709), a former Bishop of York in exile, built a small cathedral at Selsey to the south.

Following the Conquest, William I decreed that all bishoprics should be in large centres of population, so in 1075 the Selsey see was moved to Chichester. In 1100, work on a new cathedral began under Bishop Ralph de Luffa. Enough of the building was completed by 1108 for it to be consecrated. Despite delays caused by fires, much of the building had been completed (in Romanesque style) by 1123. In the 12th century another fire destroyed the wooden roof. Bishop Seffrid (in office 1180–1204) rebuilt it with stone vaulting and added a clerestory. The ubiquitous Purbeck Marble, in the form of shafts, was also introduced at this time, along with flying buttresses on the exterior.

The 13th century saw the addition of a number of chapels and porches, mainly in Early English style. This century was also important for the episcopate of Richard of Wych – later to become St Richard of Chichester. His shrine attracted pilgrims in large numbers. During the 14th century, the Lady Chapel was extended with three more bays and the quire was laid out in much the form we see today.

The 15th century was marked by the addition of the somewhat asymmetrical cloisters and the completion of the bell tower – the only remaining detached example among English cathedrals. John Arundel (in office 1459–78) was responsible for the stone quire screen or pulpitum.

The Reformation proved an eventful time for Chichester. The cathedral was perhaps fortunate in having as bishop Robert Sherburne (in office 1508–36), who had been secretary to Henry VII and was very much a 'political' bishop. He accepted Henry VIII's changes to the religious system and followed a practical and accommodating course. As a result Chichester did not suffer the damage which many other English cathedrals received during the Reformation, although the Shrine of St Richard was a notable casualty.

The city of Chichester had become a thriving market town meanwhile, its prosperity being based largely on the wool trade, with needlemaking another important local industry. During the Civil War most of the local traders and merchants supported the Parliamentarians, while the religious elements were staunchly Royalist. Parliamentarians besieged the city for several days in 1642 before the Royalists surrendered. At this time, street markets were held on Wednesdays and Saturdays, with livestock an important trade. The Sloe Fair, dating from 1107, was also a popular event.

Like so many others around the country, Chichester Cathedral had suffered from centuries of decay and neglect. It had to wait until the more prosperous Victorian times for extensive restoration. Additional problems were caused by the fall of the spire in 1861, when the eroded stonework and structural weaknesses became obvious. The initial reconstruction of the spire was carried out by Sir George Gilbert Scott (1811–1878), and his work set the pattern for the continual restoration up to the present day.

One remarkable feature of Chichester Cathedral is the way in which modern works of art have been incorporated into the building in complete harmony with the medieval architecture. These include the font (1983), Graham Sutherland's painting *Noli me Tangere*, Skelton's statue of *Our Lady and the Holy Child*, the John Piper tapestry (1966) behind the high altar, the Anglo-German tapestry (1985) at the location of the Shrine of St Richard, and the modern glass of the Marc Chagall window (1978).

TOUR OF THE CATHEDRAL
Start: The west front.
Finish: The font and west door.

The **West Front (1)** is marked by its two squat towers. The northwest tower collapsed in 1635 and was not rebuilt until 1901. Further away to the northwest is the detached bell tower, the only one still remaining at any English cathedral. Dating from the first decade of the 15th century, it has three stages and is capped with an octagonal lantern; it is 120ft (36.5m) in height, matching the elevation of the two west towers. The ground floor is occupied by the cathedral giftshop.

Enter the cathedral through the much altered and renovated west door. On the right is a welcome desk; although there is no pressure to make a donation, you will probably wish to.

Step forward into the **Nave (2)**. This fine Romanesque structure clearly owes much to Winchester. It was begun in 1114, but the vaulting and much of the facing were introduced only after a serious fire in 1187. It is of unusual proportions, with the clerestory and triforium of greater combined depth than the arcade. The latter has massive multiform piers with vertical engaged shafts. The main arches of the triforium enclose smaller twin arches (as at Winchester). The clerestory, which was added a century after the rest of the nave, leads up to simple vaulting. There are double aisles on each side of the nave.

Turn back to the northwest corner of the nave to find **St Michael's Chapel (3)**, the Sailors' Chapel, dedicated in 1956 to men from Sussex who had lost their lives at sea during World War II. Note the ship's bell from HMS *Sussex*, above which is the Royal Yacht Squadron burgee flown by Sir Francis Chichester (1901–1972) when he sailed around the world in *Gypsy Moth* in 1966–7.

Leave the chapel and walk along the north aisle. Turn into the side aisle, where, on the left, is the memorial **Statue of William Huskisson (4)**. Huskisson was MP for Chichester and worked to promote the construction of the Wey and Arun Canal, but is probably best remembered as the first prominent person to be killed by a train. He was knocked down in 1830 on the day the Manchester and Liverpool Railway was opened.

Famous Sons and Daughters

Return to the north aisle and proceed eastwards. On the left is the **Arundel Tomb (5)**. The effigies are almost certainly that of Richard Fitzalan (*c*1307–1376), 13th Earl of Arundel, and his wife Eleanor. They were originally buried in the chapter house of Lewes Priory, but were brought here after the Dissolution. The lady's crossed legs and the pair's joined hands are unusual. It was once thought that the hands were linked during the Victorian restoration, but recent research has shown this feature to be original – one of the earliest examples of this concession, permitted when the husband was a knight rather than a civilian. Another unusual monument can be seen on the right of the aisle. This is the **Monument to Joan de Vere (6)**. Joan (d1293) was the daughter of Robert de Vere, Earl of Oxford. The monument is probably the first in England to show 'weepers' – figures of mourning – along the side of the tomb. John Flaxman thought it the finest medieval effigy in England.

To the right is the pulpitum or **Bell-Arundel Screen (7)**. Erected by John Arundel (in office 1459–78), it originally had two chapels within its outer arches and virtually cut off the quire from the nave. The screen was taken down in 1859, which was timely as the spire collapsed the following year and this event would undoubtedly have destroyed it. After restoration it was eventually re-erected in 1961 as a memorial to George Bell (in office 1929–58).

Walk under the screen, noting the sturdy vaulting and strong bosses, and move into the **Quire (8)**, which lies, unusually, wholly beneath the crossing. Largely 14th-century in age, the stalls, canopies and arches are original, but needed restoration after the fall of the spire. The stalls contain a fine set of misericords.

The Arts, Ancient and Modern

Return through the screen and enter the north transept. There are two features here of particular note. Set in the floor is the **Memorial to Gustav Holst (9)**. A simple plaque covers the ashes of the composer (1874–1934), who had strong connections with the city. The north wall of the transept is largely covered with 16th-century **Lambert Barnard Paintings (10)**. In the form of panelled medallions, the paintings show the heads of the bishops of Chichester from St Wilfred to Robert Sherburne. The latter, it must be surmised, probably commissioned the work, as it is his face which appears on all the bishops' heads!

Leave the transept and walk along the north quire aisle. Immediately on the left is the **Treasury (11)**. Entry is via a turnstile and there is a modest admission fee. The Treasury, which occupies the former Chapel of the Four Virgins, contains the usual collection of silverware, from both the cathedral and churches within the diocese. Of particular interest are various rings and crozier heads discovered in bishops' tombs during the repair work in the 19th century.

Cross the aisle and turn right into the presbytery. Dominating this area of the cathedral is the **John Piper Tapestry (12)**. Designed by John Piper (1903–1992) in 1966, it was woven by Pinton Frères at Felletin in France. Its vivid modern colours illustrate the theme of the Holy Trinity. The high altar in front of the tapestry is of simple modern design, using contrasting limestones, and is the work of Robert Potter.

Return to the north quire aisle. Note on the left the **Memorial to Edward Storey (13)**. Storey (in office 1478–1503) gave the city its Market Cross and provided the endowment for the Prebendal School, still attended by the cathedral's choristers. At the end of the aisle is the **Chapel of St John the Baptist (14)**. The highlight of this rather uninspiring chapel is the reredos, which takes the form of a painting (1984), the work of Patrick Procktor, that shows scenes from the life of St John the Baptist and was clearly inspired by the painting by Nicholas Poussin (1594–1665). There is little stained glass of note at Chichester (the medieval glass was presumably lost during the Reformation), so it is pleasing to see the modern glass in the window next to the Chapel of St John the Baptist. This was designed by Marc Chagall (1887–1985) and made by Charles of Marq at Rheims. It was unveiled by the Duchess of Kent in 1978.

Move across into the retrochoir, where on the right (west) is the **Anglo-German Tapestry (15)**. Designed by Ursula Benker-Schirmer in 1985, it was woven in Marktredwitz in Bavaria and at West Dean College to the north of Chichester. The largely abstract design purports to show the life of St Richard of Chichester, whose shrine was located in the area of the platform in front of the tapestry. Bishop George Bell's ashes are also interred here. The platform has a modern Purbeck Marble altar, designed by Robert Potter. The candle ornaments are the work of Geoffrey Clarke.

Turn in the opposite direction and walk into the **Lady Chapel (16)**. Originally, the chapel had only two bays, but a further three were added around 1300, with the windows in Decorated style. Note Lambert Barnard's ceiling decoration, at one time probably found throughout the cathedral. Attached to a pier on the north side of the chapel is a modern (1988) sculpture of Our Lady and the Holy Child by John Skelton.

Leave the Lady Chapel and the retroquire and move into the south quire aisle. At the extreme east end is the **Chapel of St Mary Magdelene (17)**. Behind the simple altar is another of the cathedral's modern treasures, the painting *Noli me Tangere* ('Touch me Not') by Graham Sutherland (1903–1980). It shows Christ

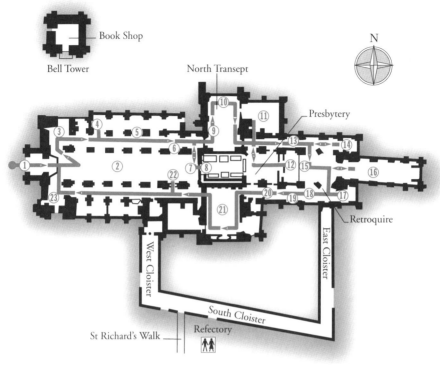

Bell Tower
Book Shop
North Transept
Presbytery
N
Retroquire
West Cloister
East Cloister
South Cloister
St Richard's Walk
Refectory

Key

1. West Front
2. Nave
3. St Michael's (Sailors') Chapel
4. Statue of William Huskisson
5. Arundel Tomb
6. Monument to Joan de Vere
7. Bell-Arundel Screen
8. Quire

9. Memorial to Gustav Holst
10. Lambert Barnard Paintings
11. Treasury
12. John Piper Tapestry
13. Memorial to Edward Storey
14. Chapel of St John the Baptist
15. Anglo-German Tapestry
16. Lady Chapel

17. Chapel of St Mary Magdlene
18. Roman Mosaic
19. 12th-Century stone carvings
20. Memorial to Robert Sherburne
21. South Transept
22. Pulpit
23. Font

appearing to Mary Magdalene after the Resurrection. The setting is Sutherland's own garden in the South of France. Further along the south quire aisle are some railings surrounding a glass panel which reveals a **Roman Mosaic (18)** from the 2nd century. It was part of the floor of a house which extended under the cathedral walls and out into the precincts and was possibly one of the major public buildings of Roman Chichester. The mosaic is made up of fragments of chalk, limestone and brick and can be illuminated by inserting a coin.

We now come to two of the most important artistic treasures in the cathedral, the **12th-Century Stone Carvings (19)** which are attached to the wall of the aisle. One shows *Christ Arriving at Bethany and Being Greeted by Mary and Martha* while the other depicts *The Raising of Lazarus*. They are thought to date from *c*1125 and may originally have formed part of a screen. These Romanesque sculptures were probably once highly coloured, and it is believed the eyes used to contain jewels.

A Reforming Bishop

Further along the aisle on the south side is the **Memorial to Robert Sherburne (20)**, bishop from 1508 until his death in 1536. This political, reforming bishop has been referred to as the 'second founder of the cathedral', and he certainly left his mark in a number of ways.

Next step into the **South Transept (21)**, where the dominating features are two more Lambert Barnard paintings, dating from the 16th century. One panel shows King Caedwalla of Wessex granting St Wilfred land on which to build a cathedral. The second depicts Henry VIII giving an assurance to the ubiquitous Sherburne that he had the right to the bishopric.

Walk into the south aisle. On the right is another of Chichester's modern additions, the **Pulpit (22)**. This was designed by Robert Potter and Geoffrey Clarke in 1966 and is made of stone-faced reinforced concrete, aluminium and leather-covered wood. Further along the aisle are two side chapels, the Chapel of St Clement and the Chapel of St George. The latter is the memorial chapel of the Royal Sussex Regiment.

Finally you come to one of the most attractive features of the cathedral, the modern **Font (23)**. It was designed by John Skelton in 1983 and is made of polyphant stone from Cornwall, with the bowl of beaten copper. On the wall behind, a miniature version acts as a sconce, and beside it is a painting by Hans Feibusch (1898–1998), *The Baptism of Christ* (1951), one of the earliest of the modern additions to the cathedral.

The tour concludes here – exit by the west door.

WALKING TOUR FROM CHICHESTER CATHEDRAL

The tour begins by exploring the cathedral precincts, including the cloisters and two ancient gateways. You then move into the historic core of the city, where there is a variety of interesting domestic architecture, particularly in the area called The Pallants. A short stretch of the city walls is walked before you return along an old Roman street to the City Cross and the cathedral. Less mobile visitors will appreciate the walk being almost entirely on the flat.

Start and finish: The west front of the cathedral.
Length: 1½ miles (2.4km).
Time: Little over an hour, but allow extra time to visit the Pallant House Gallery and the City Museum.
Refreshments: The cathedral's **refectory** (closed Sundays) is just off the south cloister, and tables spill out into the walled garden during the summer months. Near the cathedral, in South Street, is the **Medieval Crypt Restaurant**. Pubs with atmosphere are thin on the ground, but try the **White Horse** in South Street (which claims to be Chichester's oldest pub), the **Hole in the Wall Tavern** in St Martin's Street (off East Street) and the **Dolphin and Anchor** in West Street, opposite the cathedral, which also offers accommodation.

From the west front of the cathedral take the path southwards (i.e., in the opposite direction to the bell tower); the buildings of the Prebendal School are on the right.

Plate 9: *Salisbury Cathedral seen across the water meadows of the River Avon. Salisbury's spire is the highest of all the English cathedrals (see page 54), rising to a height of 404ft (123m).*

Plate 10: High Street (or North) Gate, one of several gates leading into Salisbury's Cathedral Close. High Street Gate once had a portcullis, which could be lowered if the townsfolk became rebellious (see page 57).

Plate 11: The Classical façade of the White Hart Hotel, the grandest of Salisbury's many coaching inns (see page 55). Stagecoaches left here at 10pm nightly, bound for London.

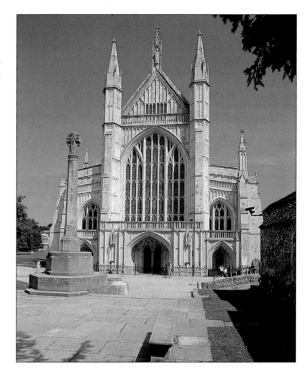

Plate 12: *The Perpendicular west front of Winchester Cathedral (see page 59). The window contains glass recovered after the vandalism of the Civil War (1642–1651).*

Plate 13: *The Great Hall at Winchester Castle (see page 66). The star exhibit is the Round Table mounted on the west wall, showing King Arthur and his knights.*

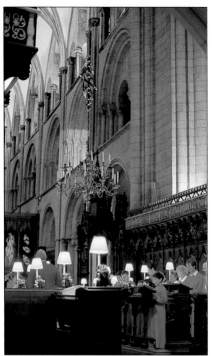

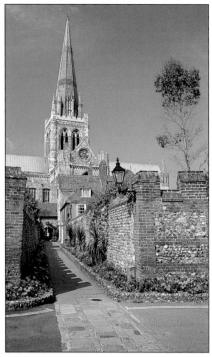

Plate 14: *The choir at Chichester Cathedral. The cathedral has architecture from many periods and some impressive modern works of art (see page 68).*

Plate 15: *Chichester Cathedral seen from the end of St Richard's Walk with its flint and brick walls (see page 73).*

Plate 16: *Vicars' Close, Chichester (see page 73). This 15th-century terrace was once occupied by the Vicars Choral (adult members of the cathedral choir). The buildings are now the homes of retired clergy.*

Swing around to the left, parallel to the south side of the cathedral; there is a good view of some of the recent restorations to the stonework.

Pass through a gateway into the **Cloisters (1)**. Built *c*1400, these were extensively restored in Victorian times. They do not form a perfect square: if they did they wouldn't fit into the shape left by the nave and the south transept. Chichester was never a monastic cathedral, so monks never strolled these cloisters in contemplation. The architecture is simple and the roof is wooden, made of Irish oak.

The west cloister leads to **St Richard's Porch (2)**, which has a double-arched entrance supported by thin Purbeck marble columns. Between the arches is a statue of St Richard dating from 1894. The south doorway beyond has some dogtooth ornamentation; this and the vaulting above are in Early English style.

Return to the south cloister and leave the area via a doorway to St Richard's Walk, which has some interesting Georgian-fronted houses. This leads to Canon Lane, with the 18th-century Deanery immediately opposite. (Look back from the end of St Richard's Walk for a superb view of the cathedral.) Walk briefly to the right, towards **Palace Gateway (3)**. This dates from the 14th century and was the gatehouse for the Bishop's Palace. Through the gateway and immediately to the right there is a view of the brick- and flint-built Bishop's Palace. Parts of the building date back to the 13th century; it is now largely used by the Prebendal School.

Return to Canon Lane and head towards the east end. Note on the left **Vicars' Close (4)**, a terrace of four 15th-century houses, once occupied by the Vicars Choral; the hall at the end of the path was once their refectory. Vicars' Close was initially a square, but the original rears of the houses to the right were converted to shops in South Street and this side blocked off with a wall. Return to Canon Lane and walk through **Canon Gate (5)**. This flint-built gatehouse was constructed in the 15th century, but had extensive renovation in 1894.

The Pallants

You are now in South Street. Turn left and walk towards the city centre. Note on the left the Medieval Crypt, now a restaurant. Most of the buildings on this side of the road are still owned by the Church Commissioners. Opposite is the White Horse Inn, which dates from 1416 and claims to be the oldest pub in the city. Cross South Street and take the narrow road – West Pallant – at the side of the White Horse.

You are now approaching the area known as **The Pallants (6)**. Four roads – North, South, East and West Pallant – form a cross. The name comes from the fact that the Archbishop of Canterbury once had a palantine, or exclusive jurisdiction here over this area. The Pallants have some delightful Georgian domestic architecture, with former wealthy merchants' house alongside those of artisans. Some of the larger buildings have now become offices and it is interesting to see how the smaller houses have been gentrified in recent years – indeed, The Pallants remains a very desirable place to live. As you walk along West Pallant, note on your left the redundant Church of All Saints, which dates back to the 13th century.

West Pallant leads to the crossroads in the centre of The Pallants, and here you find **Pallant House (7)**, claimed to be one of the finest Queen Anne houses in the England. Built in 1712 for Henry Peckham, a wealthy local wine merchant, it is now home to a good collection of porcelain, sculpture and paintings, mainly of the British

Modern School, including works by Sutherland, Moore, Piper and Nash. The rooms have been faithfully restored, each reflecting a different period in the house's history, and a peaceful walled garden in formal Georgian style can be enjoyed at the rear. The stone birds on the front gateway are dodos.

Leave The Pallants via East Pallant, turning left into Baffin's Lane. At the end of the lane, fronting East Street, is the former **Corn Exchange (8)**, with its imposing

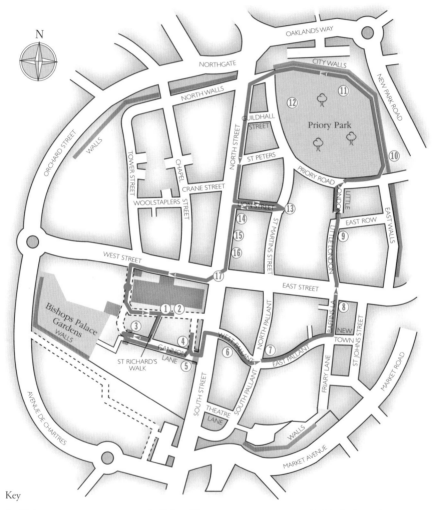

Key

1. Cloisters	7. Pallant House	13. St Mary's Hospital
2. St Richard's Porch	8. Corn Exchange	14. Council Chamber
3. Palace Gateway	9. City Museum	15. Butter Market
4. Vicars' Close	10. City Walls	16. St Olave's Church
5. Canon Gate	11. Castle Mound	17. Market Cross
6. The Pallants	12. Franciscan Friary	

The Canon Gate

Classical frontage. This has a fascinating history. Built in 1830, it was first used for the auctioning of corn and later became a popular theatre, before hosting the city's first moving-picture show in 1896. It remained a cinema until 1980, and is now, regrettably, a branch of a fast-food chain.

Cross East Street and turn into Little London. There are various fanciful suggestions – generally linked to royalty – as to how the street got its name, but none quite rings true. On the right, on the corner of East Row, is the **City Museum (9)**, housed in a former 18th-century granary; on its outer wall there is an iron hoist which was used to lift sacks of grain to the upper floors. The museum displays objects and artefacts from the Chichester area from prehistoric times to the present day.

City Defences

Continue along Little London until you reach Priory Road: Priory Park lies ahead. Turn right and walk up onto the **City Walls (10)**, first built by the Romans during the 2nd century AD. Originally made of earth, they were later faced with flint and mortar. Most of the walls survive; they can be traced for 1½ miles (2.4km) and enclose 101 acres (41 hectares) of the city. They were last used for defence in 1642, when the city was besieged by Cromwell's army during the Civil War.

Turn left and walk around the walls in an anticlockwise direction, following the edge of Priory Park. There are two main features in the park. In the northern corner is the shrub-covered **Castle Mound (11)**, once the site of a wooden Norman castle, destroyed in 1217. Nearby are the remains of the 13th-century **Franciscan Friary (12)**. All that is left of the Grey Friars is the chancel of the monastic church. This building, which stands isolated in the park, became the Guildhall and is now the Guildhall Museum. Its displays mainly concern the history of the city and Priory Park.

Leave the City Walls at what was the site of the North Gate. If you're keen to see the rest of the walls, there's a useful brochure available from the Tourist Information Centre in South Street.

Now turn left into North Street and head back towards the city centre. The pedestrianized North Street is full of interest. On the left, make a brief detour along Lion Street. This shortly leads to St Martins Square, on the far side of which is **St Mary's Hospital (13)**. The hospital dates back to 1269, later becoming an almshouse administered by the cathedral chapter, and this is still its function. At the east end of the building is a chapel where residents are obliged to attend a daily service.

Justice and Trade

Return along Lion Street to North Street. Immediately on the left is the **Council Chamber (14)**. This brick building has a Classical façade with Ionic columns and dates back to 1731, the Assembly Rooms being added at the rear some fifty years later – these were used as a courthouse until 1940. Set into the wall to the left of the main entrance is the Neptune and Minerva Stone. This slab was found nearby in 1723 and is believed to have come from a Roman temple on the site.

A few steps along from the Council Chamber is the Market House or **Butter Market (15)**, built in 1807, probably to a design by Nash, in an effort to introduce hygiene and order to market days. Thenceforth, all fresh food had to be sold under the cover of the Butter Market. It now has two storeys of specialist shops and stalls.

On the left, further towards the town centre, is the tiny **St Olave's Church (16)**, now an SPCK shop. This church has Saxon origins – indeed, is older than the cathedral. It is thought to be dedicated to King Olaf Haraldsson (995–1030), Patron Saint of Norway, who was canonized in 1164. The church may have been built by Scandinavian merchants, who traded with the city. It had some extensive Victorian restoration, but there is still lots of Saxon work to see.

The city centre is reached at the **Market Cross (17)**, the focal point of the Roman street plan. The Cross was built by Bishop Storey in 1501 as a place where the local citizens could sell their goods. Storey also founded the Prebendal School, where the cathedral choristers are still educated.

Proceed into West Street, where the cathedral – and the end of your walk – can be seen

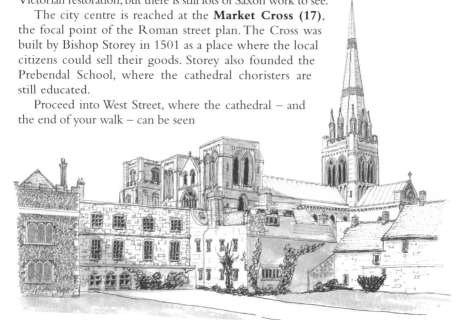

The Bishop's Palace with the Cathedral in the background

Oxford

Access: Oxford lies in the Vale of Oxford at the confluence of the Thames and the Cherwell. It is 40 miles (65km) by road from London, from which it is easily reached by the M25 and the M40. (Drivers are advised to use the 'Park and Ride' system.) The Oxford Bus Company runs frequent coach services to London's Victoria Coach Station. Trains run hourly (more frequently at busy times) from London's Paddington station. Airports within reach include Luton, Birmingham, Heathrow and Gatwick. The CityLink coach service runs regularly to both Heathrow and Gatwick, while National Express operates six services a day to Birmingham Airport.

There is evidence of Bronze Age and Iron Age settlement in the Oxford area, but its low-lying surroundings were not attractive to the Romans. At the fall of the Roman Empire, however, Roman soldiers settled in the region to become farmers. By Anglo-Saxon times the Thames had become a strategic boundary between the kingdoms of Wessex and Mercia. It is believed that around AD730 St Frideswide (d *c*735) founded the first abbey on the present site of Christ Church, and the original town clustered around the building. Frideswide was to become the Patron Saint of Oxford.

Shortly after the Norman Conquest a castle was built on the western side of the town. Early in the next century, the convent was reformed to become an Augustinian priory. The present Christ Church was begun by Prior Robert of Cricklade around 1150, and within eighty years a spire and a Lady Chapel had been completed and the chapter house rebuilt. Not until 1500, however, was the roof vaulted.

Meanwhile the town was attracting scholars from all over the country and indeed from Europe. By the 13th century much of the teaching was being carried out by friars, and students were living in halls around the town. Powerful bishop-philanthropists began to establish colleges, which initially catered only for graduates. In 1379 New College was founded and immediately accepted undergraduates, marking the start of the gradual move in influence from the academic halls to the colleges.

By 1400 Oxford had a population of 6000, making it one of the largest towns in the country. Water mills had been built along the rivers, and industries such as cloth- and leathermaking had developed, while the growing university also provided much employment. The year 1478 was marked by the first book to be printed in the town, and the first library appeared ten years later.

In 1525 Cardinal Thomas Wolsey (*c*1475–1530) founded Cardinal's College on the site of St Frideswide's Monastery, but when Wolsey fell from grace in 1529 Henry VIII took over the half-finished college and it was renamed King Henry VIII's College. The Reformation (and the consequent Dissolution of the Monasteries) was a crucial time for Oxford, but Henry decided to retain the colleges and use them to educate his supporters. The diocese of Oxford was created in 1542 and Christ Church – as King Henry VIII's College was now known – became, uniquely, both a cathedral and a college. The mid-1500s also saw the Protestant

Martyrs – Thomas Cranmer (1489–1556), Hugh Latimer (*c*1485–1555) and Nicholas Ridley (*c*1500–1555) – burnt at the stake in Oxford at what is now Broad Street. Later in the century Elizabeth I visited the city, which was expanding considerably along with the university.

During the Civil War Oxford was a Royalist centre, and Charles I used the city as his headquarters for four years. In 1646, however, Oxford was besieged by the Parliamentary army of General Thomas Fairfax (1612–1671). Charles fled in disguise and shortly afterwards the city surrendered. Thereafter Oxford continued to expand: the Botanic Gardens, the Sheldonian Theatre (designed by a young Christopher Wren) and the Ashmolean Museum date from this period. At Christ Church, Tom Quad was completed with canons' houses instead of Wolsey's proposed chapel and cloisters, while Wren's Tom Tower, with its ogee capping, also appeared.

In 1748 the Radcliffe Camera was built, and the remainder of the century saw some startling changes. In 1771 the Pavement Commission was set up, and as a result much of the medieval town was destroyed. Roads were widened and the Magdalen Bridge was constructed. The year 1790 saw the coming of the Oxford Canal; this brought coal from the Midlands and for the next half-century Oxford was a busy inland port. When the railway came in 1844 much of the canal trade disappeared, but today the canal is popular with leisure traffic. In 1879 Oxford's first two female colleges, Lady Margaret Hall and Somerville, were opened.

The Victorian period in Britain saw many cathedrals subject to restoration, which was often unfortunate. The Christ Church renovations, however, carried out by Sir George Gilbert Scott (1811–1878) in the 1870s, were largely undertaken in a sympathetic way. The neo-Norman windows at the east end belong to this period, as do the chancel stalls and the wrought-iron screens. G.F. Bodley (1827–1907) designed an ornate bell tower, but the Governing Body had second thoughts and it was never completed. The bells were rehung, rather inappropriately, under the hall stairs.

In 1913 William Morris (1877–1963) built his car factory at Cowley on the outskirts of Oxford. This was to become the major employer in the city for the rest of the century. Morris became Lord Nuffield and was an important benefactor to the university, particularly in the sciences and medicine.

Oxford suffered minimal damage during the two world wars. and also survived the proposal to build a link road across Christ Church Meadow – an outrageous scheme which was fortunately thrown out. The postwar period saw a number of additions to the Christ Church site. In 1967, the Picture Gallery was opened in the Deanery Garden. This award-winning building has an important collection of Old Masters, along with special exhibitions of contemporary art. The following year saw the opening of Blue Boar Quad, close to Blue Boar Street. Finally, in 1986, St Aldgate's Quad was built on the far side of St Aldgate's Road.

Today, Christ Church finds itself in a unique position. It is Oxford's largest and wealthiest college and also a cathedral – but one of England's smallest cathedrals in what is the country's largest diocese. Another interesting quirk is that four of its canons are also professors – all of which adds to the fascination of this building, which attracts nearly a quarter of a million visitors annually.

TOUR OF THE CATHEDRAL
Start: Meadow Buildings.
Finish: The west door.

Approach Christ Church from the city centre along St Aldgate's, but do not enter via the gateway under Tom Tower. Carry on to the end of the building and turn left at the path which leads to Christ Church Meadow. Just inside the gateway is probably the only spot to get a decent photograph of the exterior of the cathedral.

Carry on to Meadow Buildings. Halfway along the buildings is the porch where entrance is gained to the cathedral and other areas of Christ Church, and where you'll need to pay your admission fee. Follow the path round to the left and turn under an archway which leads to the **Cloisters (1)**. These were built in the 15th century along with the former refectory on the south side and the dormitory to the east. The cathedral occupies the north side, but the western side of the cloisters was destroyed by Wolsey, who planned more magnificent ones around Tom Quad.

Halfway along the east side of the cloisters (to the right) is the 13th-century

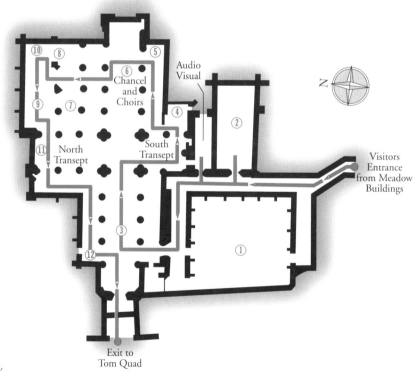

Key

1. Cloisters
2. Chapter House
3. Nave
4. Becket Window

5. St Catherine Window
6. Chancel
7. Lady Chapel
8. Shrine of St Frideswide

9. Latin Chapel
10. St Frideswide Window
11. St Michael Window
12. Jonah Window

Chapter House (2), which also functions today as a souvenir shop and the treasury. Unfortunately, the paraphernalia of the shop distracts from the essential simplicity of the Early English architecture, with its lancet windows showing detached shafts and stiff-leaved foliage in the spandrels. The chapter house has some interesting stained glass, dating from between the 15th and 17th centuries. Note also the unusual roof bosses. There is an audiovisual presentation in the room next to the chapter house.

Inside the Cathedral

Leave the chapter house and move round the north side of the cloisters to enter the southwest corner of the cathedral. On reaching the **Nave (3)** one is immediately struck by the small size of this area – but remember that Wolsey demolished the three western bays of the priory church to accommodate his Great Quadrangle. An unusual feature is that the pews in the nave face inwards, no doubt because the cathedral is also the college chapel. Note the curious double arches of the Norman arcade – probably a device for suggesting greater height, but not a successful feature. The pulpit is Jacobean. Nearby is the bust of Dean Henry Aldrich (1647–1710), the noted scholar and architect, while on a pillar close to the vice-chancellor's stall is the memorial to Bishop George Berkeley (1685–1753), after whom the Californian town is named.

Great Windows

Move along the south aisle and into the barely perceptible south transept. The east side of this area is taken up with the St Lucy Chapel, where one finds the **Becket Window (4)**. This, the oldest window in the cathedral, dates from c1320. The central panel of stained glass shows the martyrdom of Archbishop Thomas à Becket (c1118–1170), murdered in Canterbury Cathedral in 1170, although the original face of Becket is missing: it was removed after the Reformation, Becket having been posthumously declared a traitor. The removal of the face was not the act of vandalism you might at first think, because it allowed the authorities to save the window as a whole. Also in this area are a number of memorials to Cavalier supporters of Charles I in the Civil War, plus the unmarked graves of three of the king's young cousins who also died in the conflict. Note, too, the flags of the Oxfordshire and Buckinghamshire Regiment; these date from the Crimean War and World War I. In the nearby aisle is the tomb of Robert King (d1557), first Bishop of Oxford and before that last Abbot of Osney Abbey, suppressed in 1542.

Walk back into the main body of the building and turn right along the south choir aisle. At the end is the Military Chapel, which features the **St Catherine Window (5)**, designed by Edward Burne-Jones (1833–1898) in 1878. The face of the central figure, Saint Catherine of Alexandria, is based on that of Edith Liddell, whose sister Alice was the inspiration for Lewis Carroll's *Alice's Adventures in Wonderland* (1865).

You now enter the **Chancel (6)**, which includes the choir. This is the area of the cathedral which all serious students of architecture come to see. The attraction is the pendant lierne vault, which dates from the end of the 15th century, replacing the original Norman timber roof; its designer, William Orchard, did much work at the Divinity School. Each bay has a star pattern of strong lierne ribs with a series of pendant lanterns which seem to defy gravity and which were a daring design for that period of architecture. Closer inspection shows they are supported by moulded ribs which form a series of arches. The vaulting makes an elegant contrast to the simple Norman arches below. The eastern end of the chancel was rebuilt by Scott in the 1870s. The reredos behind the high altar is attributed to Bodley and includes the figures of four saints.

St Frideswide's Shrine

Move now to the north side of the cathedral, where there are two parallel chapels. The first is the 13th-century **Lady Chapel (7)**. The most significant feature here is the **Shrine of St Frideswide (8)**, built in 1289 to house the relics of the Anglo-Saxon princess who founded the original monastery on the site of Christ Church and who is now the Patron Saint of Oxford. The shrine, originally brightly painted, was destroyed at the Reformation and the saint's remains buried nearby. The shattered stonework of the shrine was recovered in the 19th century and reassembled, although the original silk canopy has been lost. Opposite the shrine is a large wooden structure which was probably a watching loft to guard the relics from visiting pilgrims. The only other watching loft existing in an English cathedral is at St Albans.

The second chapel is the **Latin Chapel (9)**, built in 1330, which gained its name from the services, traditionally said in Latin until 1861. Today the chapel is used for private prayer. On the far side of the Latin Chapel are windows with 14th-century glass, while on the south side are three tombs dating from the same period: of Lady Elizabeth Montacute, a benefactor of the original monastery; of Alexander de Sutton, a 13th-century prior of the Augustinian Monastery of St Frideswide; and of an unknown knight of the 14th century – whoever he was, he was a huge man for his day, measuring 6ft 6in (2m) tall! The feature of interest in the Latin Chapel, however, is the **St Frideswide Window (10)**, designed by Burne-Jones in 1858 and considered one of his best works. The lower windows depict the life of St Frideswide, while a roundel at the top shows a boat carrying the saint to Heaven.

Step now through the north transept, where the only item of interest is the dominating **St Michael Window (11)**, made by Clayton and Bell in the early 19th century. The glass shows St Michael (and his angels) fighting a dragon. Carry on into the north aisle, at the end of which is the altogether more interesting **Jonah Window (12)**, made by the Dutchman Abraham van Linge around 1630. The figure of Jonah, shown surveying the city of Ninevah, is made of traditional stained glass, but the remainder of the window has been produced by painting the glass with coloured ground glass mixed with oil and water – a technique later to become quite common.

Leave the cathedral by the west door, which leads out into Tom Quad.

WALKING TOUR FROM CHRIST CHURCH CATHEDRAL

The tour is in two parts. The first is a short walk around Christ Church, Oxford's most interesting and prestigious college. The longer second part is a circular walk which takes in some other well known Oxford colleges, such as Merton, Magdalen, Hertford and Trinity, along with notable city features like the Radcliffe Camera, the Bodleian Library and the Sheldonian Theatre. The tour also includes a section of Christ Church Meadow and the Botanical Gardens. Oxford is so full of fascination that half a dozen similarly intriguing walks could be made, but this tour probably contains the most interesting features of the city for those with limited time.

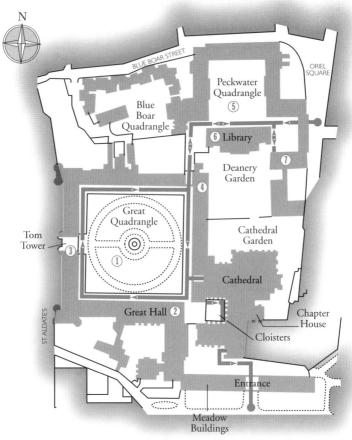

1. Great Quadrangle
2. Great Hall
3. Tom Tower

4. Deanery
5. Peckwater Quadrangle
6. Library

7. Picture Gallery

Start (shorter walk): The west front of the Cathedral.
Finish (shorter walk): The cathedral entrance.
Start (longer walk): The west front of the Cathedral.
Finish (longer walk): The Carfax Tower.
Total length: 2½ miles (4km).
Total time: 1½ hours, but allow longer for visits to museums, gardens and churches.
Refreshments: You are quite spoilt for choice at lunchtime in Oxford, with a vast range of bistros, wine bars and ancient inns. Popular student pubs include the 16th-century Turf Tavern, off Holywell Street, the King's Arms, on the corner of Holywell Street and Parks Road, the Golden Cross, in the nicely restored Golden Cross Yard and the 15th-century Chequers Inn, in the High Street.
Note: The Oxford colleges are private, working institutions. Do not wander around them without permission. Most are closed during the morning, while some will

accept visitors only if they are accompanied by the official blue-badged guides. Some colleges, such as Christ Church, charge for entry. Always check at the porter's lodge to ascertain the conditions of entry.

AROUND CHRIST CHURCH

Leave the cathedral via the West Door to the **Great Quadrangle (1)** or, as it's usually known, Tom Quad. This was the brainchild of Cardinal Thomas Wolsey, who from humble beginnings became a student at Magdalen College before rising to become Archbishop of Canterbury and Chancellor of England. He decided to found a new college in Oxford, and the project was started in 1525. Four years later, however, he fell from grace and all work ceased. It was the next century before work recommenced and the north side of the quad was completed. The Great Quadrangle is the largest in Oxford; to accommodate it Wolsey had to demolish the three westernmost bays of the cathedral nave. He had intended that the quad should be cloistered; although this plan never came to fruition, the arches can be seen set into the walls. Note the small pond in the centre of the Great Quadrangle containing the Statue of Mercury. The water in the pond was intended for use in fighting fires.

Walk clockwise around the quad. Almost immediately on the left is a doorway, with stairs leading to the **Great Hall (2)**. When climbing the stairs, note the fan vaulted ceiling, which spreads from a single elegant column. The vaulting was constructed in 1640 during the time of Dean Samuel Fell. From the landing, enter the hall, which is the biggest in Oxford. It has a superb black-and-gilded hammer-beam roof, and both the walls and the ceiling sport literally hundreds of coats-of-arms. The walls are festooned with paintings of former alumni of Christ Church, including six prime ministers and other notables such as William Penn (1644–1718), W.H. Auden (1907–1973), John Locke (1632–1704) and Charles Dodgson (1832–1898), better known as Lewis Carroll. The hall is used daily for dining by the junior and senior members of the college.

Descend the stairs and return to the Great Quadrangle. Turn left and continue around the quad in a clockwise direction. In the middle of the west side is the main entrance to the quad, capped by one of Oxford's best known landmarks, **Tom Tower (3)**. The tower dates from 1681 and was designed by Christopher Wren (1632–1723). Its bell, known as Great Tom and said to weigh seven tons, came from Osney Abbey, destroyed at the Dissolution. Great Tom is so-named not after Thomas Wolsey but after Thomas à Becket. At 21:05 each evening the bell rings 101 times, once for each member of the original college. This is done by `Oxford time', five minutes behind GMT – the city being five minutes west of Greenwich!

Continue around the north side of the quad (completed in the 17th century) until you reach the northeast corner. This is occupied by the **Deanery (4)**, which has a fine castellated parapet. The dean of the cathedral also governs the college. It was in this building that Charles I lived during much of the Civil War.

Lesser Quads

Pass through the archway and walk on into **Peckwater Quadrangle (5)**, built during the 17th-century expansion of the college on the site of the medieval Peckwater Inn. The quad's design was the work of Dean Aldrich, said to have been a disciple of Wren. One of the buildings around the quad is the **Library (6)**, completed in

1772; its style, unlike that of the rest of the quad, is Classical, with strong Corinthian columns supporting a massive cornice and balustrade. The upper floor of the library is one of the most beautiful places in the city; its shelves and columns are made of dark Norwegian oak, capped by a delightful pink-and-white stucco ceiling. But you will have to take my word for this: the library is not open to visitors.

Move along the front of the library into the small, cobbled Canterbury Quad. This was the site of Canterbury College, demolished when Wolsey redesigned the area. On the right of the quad is the **Picture Gallery (7)**. Christ Church is the only Oxford College to have an important collection of Old Master paintings: there are works here by Frans Hals (*c*1580–1666), Tintoretto (*c*1518–1594), Anthony Van Dyck (1599–1641), Michelangelo (1475–1564) and Raphael (1483–1520).

If you don't wish to take the longer walk, exit via Canterbury Quad into Orion Square, which leads northwards into the High Street. Otherwise, return to the cathedral entrance in Meadow Buildings via Peckwater Quadrangle, the Great Quadrangle and the cathedral cloisters.

BEYOND CHRIST CHURCH

Leave the cathedral entrance at Meadow Buildings and turn left along Broad Walk towards **Christ Church Meadow (8)**. Today the Meadow is largely given over to playing fields, which lead down to the River Cherwell, a popular punting venue. A recent proposal to build a relief road across the Meadow was sensibly thrown out.

After following Broad Walk for a few yards, turn left and follow the wall north-wards. Halfway along the path is a gate in the wall which gives good views towards the east end of the cathedral. Carry on to the end of the path to an iron 'kissing gate' that leads to a track between Merton and Corpus Christi colleges. Do not go through this gate, but turn right here along the path called Dead Man's Walk. The wall to your left marks the southern boundary of the grounds of **Merton College (9)**. Founded in 1264, Merton is almost certainly the oldest of the Oxford colleges in terms of both statutes and buildings, such as the medieval library. You cannot enter Merton from Christ Church Meadow. Continue along Dead Man's Walk to the cot-tages at the end of the wall. Look for the plaque in the wall marking where James Sadler (1753–1828), England's first aeronaut, made an ascent in a fire balloon on October 4 1784, landing safely near Woodeaton.

The Botanical Gardens and Magdalen College

At the cottages turn left and head towards the iron gateway. Pass through the gate and walk north along Rose Lane to its end, where it meets High Street. Turn right and enter the **Botanic Gardens (10)**, which are fronted by an attractive parterre. The oldest in the country, they were founded in 1621 by Henry Danvers as a physic garden for the School of Medicine, and renamed the Botanic Gardens in 1784. The gardens were the original home of Oxford Ragwort, a yellow flowering plant which 'escaped', spread all over the country, and is now regarded as a troublesome weed.

Leave the Botanic Gardens and turn right to **Magdalen Bridge (11)** which spans the River Cherwell. This part of the river is popular for punting in the sum-mer, and here is as good a place as any if you wish to try your hand at this tricky art. There has been a bridge here since 1004, when the original wooden structure was built. The first stone bridge appeared five centuries later, and was replaced by a drawbridge during the Civil War. The present bridge dates from 1772, when it

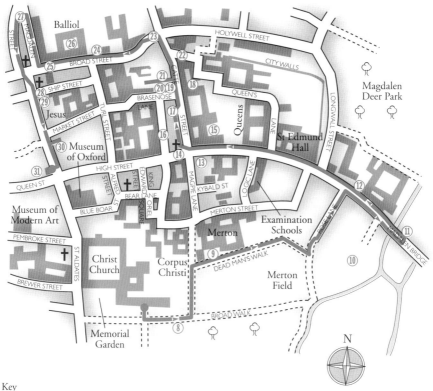

Key

8. Christ Church Meadow	16. Brasenose College	24. Trinity College
9. Merton College	17. Radcliffe Camera	25. The Oxford Story
10. Botanic Gardens	18. Hertford College	26. Balliol College
11. Magdalen Bridge	19. Bodleian Library	27. Martyrs Memorial
12. Magdalen College	20. Divinity School	28. St Michael's Church
13. University College	21. Sheldonian Theatre	29. Old Ship Inn
14. St Mary's Church	22. Bridge of Sighs	30. Covered Market
15. All Souls College	23. New Bodleian Library	31. Carfax Tower

formed part of the Pavement Commission's road-improvement schemes.

Across the road and adjacent to the bridge is **Magdalen College (12)**. Pronounced 'maudlin', the college was founded in 1485 by William Waynflete, Bishop of Winchester. Located outside the city's old walls, Magdalen College had room to spread and it has a sizeable deer park stretching along the Cherwell's water meadows. The deer were introduced in the 18th century to supply venison for the college. Note the dominating tower, which dates from 1505; choristers sing a Latin grace from the top of it each May Day morning, and it was used as a lookout point by the Royalists during the Civil War. The High Street frontage of Magdalen College features a superb range of gargoyles located just above the first floor windows. If you're allowed into the college, try to see the two delightful quadrangles and the chapel, which dates back to 1480.

University College and the University Church of St Mary the Virgin

Continue west along the High Street towards the town centre. The architecture here is magnificent – it led Nikolaus Pevsner to describe this as 'one of the world's greatest streets'. To the left is **University College (13)**, another to stake a claim to be the oldest college in Oxford. None of the original 13th-century buildings remain, however, as much of the college was rebuilt in the 17th century. There are two fine quadrangles to see, the Front Quad and the Radcliffe Quad, both almost identical in design, and also some statues of note: Queen Anne and Queen Mary adorn the Gate Towers, while the Front Quad has a statue of the unpopular James II (one of only two in the country). Elsewhere, a small dome covers the monument to the poet Percy Bysshe Shelley (1792–1822), expelled from University College for writing what were considered revolutionary pamphlets.

Cross the High Street opposite St Mary's Church and go through the narrow entrance to Catte Street. Turn immediately left before reaching the Radcliffe Camera and enter the **University Church of St Mary the Virgin (14)**. This church is full of interest and should not be missed. Pass through the shop to the nave, which is 15th-century Perpendicular in style. The Oxford Martyrs – Latimer, Ridley and Cranmer – were tried here for heresy before being burnt at the stake in Broad Street; the pillar opposite the pulpit was partly cut away so a wooden platform could be installed for Cranmer's trial. John Wesley (1703–1791) preached many a sermon from the pulpit before leaving to found the Methodist Church. John Henry Newman (1801–1890) was vicar here 1828–43 before converting to Catholicism and eventually becoming a cardinal. Another significant preacher was John Keble (1792–1866), whose sermon in 1833 launched the Oxford Movement. Certainly the galleries on the east and west walls help to form an auditorium worthy of the preaching of such men.

The oldest part of the church is the Adam de Brone Chapel, dating from 1328. De Brone was Rector of St Mary's and founder of what was later to become Oriel College. Note his tomb, made of Purbeck Marble and recently restored by Oriel.

Two other parts of St Mary's should not be missed. The Coffee Shop is in fact the old convocation house, built in 1320, in which for two centuries university meetings and ceremonies were held. And finally, do climb the 127 steps of the tower. The view from its parapet of the city's 'dreaming spires' is undoubtedly the best available.

Scholars and the Stage

Step out from St Mary's into Radcliffe Square. To the right is **All Souls College (15)**, the only Oxford college with no students – only graduate research Fellows. It was founded in 1473 by Henry Chichele, Archbishop of Canterbury. The main attractions are the North Quad, designed by Nicholas Hawksmoor (1661–1736), the Codrington Library, built with the proceeds of the sugar trade, and the chapel, which has a screen designed by Wren. Wren was also responsible for the attractive sundial in the quad. On the other side of Radcliffe Square is **Brasenose College (16)**. The name comes from the 'brazen nose' door knocker once attached to the main gate. At one stage it was stolen, and on recovery it was resited in the main hall. The quad dates from 1516 and features another interesting sundial.

Dominating the square is the circular **Radcliffe Camera (17)**. This Classical building surmounted by a dome was the idea of Hawksmoor and designed by James

Gibbs (1545–1754). It was completed in 1749 and named after Dr James Radcliffe (1689–1716), physician to William III. Radcliffe left £40,000 in his will for the construction of a library, and the building originally housed scientific books; it is now a reading room of the larger Bodleian Library. The Radcliffe Camera (the word means 'vaulted chamber') is not open to the public.

Pass to the right of Radcliffe Camera along Catte Street. On your right is **Hertford College (18)**, which had the distinction of being closed down in 1805 for lack of students; it was refounded in 1874. Opposite Hertford is a small square, to the south of which is the **Bodleian Library (19)**. A small opening leads into the Old Schools Quadrangle, which is built in Jacobean-Gothic style. Note the gate tower, known as the Tower of the Five Orders, which was supposedly designed to introduce students to the five orders of Classical architecture: Doric, Tuscan, Ionic, Corinthian and Composite. The library was founded by Thomas Bodley (1545–1613), who donated the initial 2000 books and made a deal with the Stationers' Company in 1610 that they would send the library a copy of every book published. It is still purely a reading library: no books can be borrowed.

Also in the complex of buildings here is the **Divinity School (20)**, entered through the doors behind the Earl of Pembroke's statue. Work began on this building in 1426 and took sixty years to complete, but the result is the finest interior in Oxford. The main attraction is the pendant lierne vaulted ceiling, with sculptured figures and 455 carved bosses. It is no surprise to learn that the architect was William Orchard, responsible for the similar ceiling in the chancel of Christ Church Cathedral.

Housed above the Divinity School is Duke Humphrey's Library, which contains a collection of manuscripts donated by Humphrey, Duke of Gloucester, in 1440. Note the sturdy beamed ceiling.

Nearby is the **Sheldonian Theatre (21)**. Described as a 'roofed-over Roman theatre', the Sheldonian is used for concerts, lectures and degree ceremonies. It was one of the first buildings designed by a youthful Christopher Wren, then still a professor of astronomy in Oxford. One of its main attractions is the flat painted ceiling. You can climb into the cupola for excellent views over the city.

Trinity and Balliol Colleges

Return to Catte Street and the junction with New College Lane, which is straddled by the **Bridge of Sighs (22)**, linking the two parts of Hertford College. The bridge was clearly inspired by the Venetian original. Continue to the end of Catte Street, where you find the junction with Broad Street, Holywell Street and Parks Road. Note on the corner the King's Arms, a popular student pub. Turn left here and proceed along Broad Street. On the right is the **New Bodleian Library (23)**, which was opened in 1930 to take the increased amount of books being published. It is connected to the old library and the Radcliffe Camera by a system of underground passages.

The next group of buildings on the right (north) side of Broad Street form **Trinity College (24)**. The original college buildings here were set up by a group of monks from Durham in 1286 but were closed down in the Reformation. The college was refounded as Trinity College by Thomas Pope (c1507–1559) in 1555.

Trinity has a Baroque chapel with limewood carvings attributed to Grinling Gibbons (1648–1721), plus some extensive gardens.

Broad Street now widens out. This was the site of the Horse Fair in the Middle Ages and the place where the Oxford Martyrs – bishops Latimer, Ridley and Cranmer – were burnt at the stake in 1555, the spot being marked by a cross. The south side of Broad Street is distinguished by a row of attractive coloured-wash buildings, among which is **The Oxford Story (25)**, a museum which describes the history of the university. Visitors go first to a 'common room', thence being whisked through the ages on a motorized desk with a headset commentary.

On the other side of Broad Street is **Balliol College (26)**, yet another claimant to the title of Oxford's oldest college. It was set up in 1263 by John de Balliol or Baliol (d1269), reputedly as a penance for insulting the Bishop of Durham. Most of its present buildings are Victorian, however, including its uninspiring little chapel. It is well known for producing politicians; alumni have included Harold Macmillan (1894–1986), Edward Heath (b1916) and Lord Jenkins of Hillhead (b1920).

You now reach the city centre and the main shopping area. To the right, St Giles splits into two around the Church of St Mary Magdalen. Take the right-hand arm. After about fifty yards you find on the left the **Martyrs' Memorial (27)**, erected in 1841 in memory of the Oxford Martyrs.

Return to the road junction along the left-hand arm and continue across into Cornmarket Street. Shortly you'll see to your left the **Church of St Michael-at-the-Northgate (28)**. Its late-Saxon tower – the oldest stone building in the city – was used as a lookout point. The tower was connected to the old North Gate – removed by the Pavement Commission in the late 18th century – by the Bocardo Prison, where the three bishops were held before their martyrdom.

The church itself has a number of interesting features. The window above the altar has some stained-glass medallions dating from 1290, almost certainly the oldest examples of stained glass in Oxford. The font is late-14th-century, and it is claimed that William Shakespeare (1564–1616) stood by it when acting as godfather to a Cornmarket innkeeper's child. Note also the 15th-century pulpit, from which Wesley preached a sermon in 1726. Entry to the church is free, but there is a charge to climb the tower, from where there a good views of the city's roofscapes.

You are now at Ship Street where, on the corner, is the former **Ship Inn (29)**, a picturesque half-timbered Tudor building with jettied walls. It was recently restored by Jesus College and is now partially occupied by Laura Ashley. Further along on the left, Market Street leads to the **Covered Market (30)**, yet another feature established by the Pavement Commission. It is full of atmosphere, with butchers, delicatessens and other food outlets alongside florists, boutiques and other specialist shops.

You finally arrive at the end of Cornmarket Street, at the crossroads known as the Carfax, overlooked by the **Carfax Tower (31)**. This is all that remains of the Church of St Martin's, demolished in 1896 as part of the Pavement Commission's road-widening plans. On the east side of the tower is a splendid clock, with quarterboys striking the two bells at fifteen-minute intervals. There are excellent views of the city from the top of the tower.

The walk ends at this point, some three hundred yards from Christ Church, where it began.

Gloucester

Access: Road links are good. The city is less than 5 miles (8km) from the M5, leading to the Midlands and the Southwest, while the M4, which connects with London, is a 30-minute drive to the south. National Express coach services link with many parts of the country, and seats may be booked through the Tourist Information Office. Rail links are also excellent: trains from Paddington take under 2hr, and there are also direct services to Bristol, Bath, South Wales and the Midlands. The nearest international airport, at Bristol, deals mainly with charter flights.

Although there is evidence of Iron Age occupation in the area, Gloucester's significant history begins with the Romans. Around AD48, the Romans built a fortress, Gleven, at Kingsholm to guard what was then the lowest crossing point of the River Severn. Twenty years later a new fortress was built on what is now the modern city centre. The main Roman legions withdrew from Britain around AD400, to be replaced by the Saxons, who took Gloucester in 577. The next three centuries were a time of decline for the city, despite the founding of St Peter's Abbey on the present cathedral's site. Gloucester saw better times in the 10th century, due to the patronage of Aethelflaeda or Ethelflaed (d.c917), daughter of King Alfred. In 1058 the Benedictines again rebuilt St Peter's Abbey.

William the Conqueror built the first castle at Gloucester in 1068. Fifty years later his son, Henry I, built a second castle on the site of the modern prison. In 1072 Serlo, the first Norman abbot, was appointed to the rather moribund abbey. A man of great energy and foresight, he began to build a new abbey church in 1089, the foundation stone being laid by Robert Bishop of Hereford. By 1100 the whole of the east end was completed and the church was dedicated. Serlo's successor built the nave and the cloisters, and the Norman abbey church was complete by 1126.

There was some minor rebuilding in Early English and Decorated style, and then a major reconstruction in the 14th century. The finance for this project came from a rather macabre source. In 1327, the unfortunate King Edward II was murdered in Berkeley Castle. He was buried in the north choir aisle of Gloucester's Abbey Church. His son, Edward III, provided funds to transform the area around the tomb. These funds were augmented by the contributions of the pilgrims who flocked to the site. The result was one of the finest Perpendicular sections of any English cathedral and – largely due to the influx of pilgrims – the city of Gloucester became the 15th wealthiest town in the country.

Work began on the south transept in 1331, followed by the complete remodelling of the choir and presbytery. Although the Norman aisles and galleries were retained, the Perpendicular panelling gives a cage-like effect. Above, clerestory windows and a lierne vault were added. The east end was graced with a superb window, probably the largest in Medieval Europe. Attention turned in 1360 to the north transept and then in the latter part of the 14th century to the cloister, with its magnificent fan vaulting. The following century saw the addition of the superb

Perpendicular tower. The rebuilding work on the cathedral was completed with the Lady Chapel, again in the Perpendicular style.

Meanwhile, the city of Gloucester had been granted a town council by Richard III and the county of Gloucestershire had been established. The city had also developed as a religious centre, with the foundation of Carmelite, Franciscan and Dominican friaries, although these were soon to be suppressed. During the Reformation, in 1539, St Peter's Abbey was dissolved by Henry VIII. Three years later the Abbey Church became a cathedral in its own right. Although some of the monastic buildings were destroyed, along with a number of statues and other furnishings, the cathedral came through the Reformation in reasonable condition.

Gloucester saw a considerable amount of action during the Civil War. The city was a Parliamentarian stronghold and in 1643 Charles I and 30,000 men besieged it for over a month. They eventually ended the siege when a Parliamentary force marched in from London. After the Restoration, Charles II took his revenge by knocking down the defensive walls and reducing the boundaries of the city.

The 18th century was largely a period of stagnation for the cathedral – although the city was thriving, thanks to its agriculture-based industries. This century saw the birth in Gloucester of three famous men – George Whitefield (1714–1770), the charismatic evangelist; Robert Raikes (1735–1811), the prison reformer and pioneer of Sunday Schools; and John Stafford Smith (1750–1836), who did the arrangement of a traditional English tune that Francis Scott Key (1779–1843) put words to for the US national song, *The Star-Spangled Banner*.

The 19th century saw the opening of the Gloucester and Berkeley Canal, which enabled small ships to avoid the sand banks of the Severn and stimulated an important transhipment trade in the port. Life improved in the city with the introduction of public baths, electric lighting and horse-drawn trams. This was also a time for major restoration at the cathedral, the work being largely carried out by F.S. Waller (1842–1923) and Sir George Gilbert Scott (1811–1878). The choir and presbytery were paved; the choir sub-stalls and Bishop's Throne were introduced; and a new high altar reredos designed. A considerable amount of Victorian glass appeared, mainly by Charles Eamer Kempe (1837–1907) and Christopher Whall.

Gloucester continued to develop in the 20th century, and by the 1990s had over 100,000 inhabitants. By the middle of the century, the city's docks were in terminal decline and many surrounding buildings were derelict. In the 1980s an imaginative plan was devised to revive the area. The city council started the ball rolling by moving its administration to the docks and the remaining warehouses soon converted to museums, galleries and restaurants. Gloucester Docks is now a major tourist attraction.

TOUR OF THE CATHEDRAL

Start: The south porch.
Finish: The cloisters.

Enter the cathedral via the south porch, with its recently restored stonework and ancient wooden door. Proceed past the bookshop to the east end of the nave, where there is the alabaster **Statue of Edward Jenner (1)**, the Gloucestershire man who discovered the technique of vaccination against smallpox. Jenner (1749–1823) figured on one of the Royal Mail's special stamps in the lead-up to the Millennium.

Now have a look at the **Nave (2)**. The first impression most visitors have on entering Gloucester Cathedral is of the simplicity and severity of the massive Norman columns – something of a surprise, given that the exterior of the building is almost entirely Perpendicular in style. Above the cylindrical columns are simple arches with chevron and dogtooth decoration. At the middle level is a tiny double-arched triforium. The proportions cannot be considered aesthetically pleasing. The original wooden Norman roof was replaced in 1242 by stone vaulting which springs from the base of the triforium.

Turn to face the west end. The window, in Perpendicular style, was constructed in the early 15th century, but the glass is Victorian. It shows biblical events including the birth of Jesus, at the centre of the window, and Moses at the Red Sea.

The Great and the Good

Walk to the south nave aisle, where you see the first of over four hundred memorial tablets and plaques to the great and good of Gloucester. The majority are of little interest, but a few will be picked out on the tour. Halfway along the aisle is the **Raikes Memorial (3)** – a testament not to the founder of the Sunday Schools but to his younger brother, the

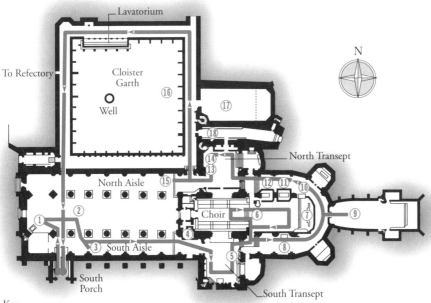

Key

1. Statue of Edward Jenner
2. Nave
3. Raikes Memorial
4. Seabroke Chantry Chapel
5. Mason's Bracket
6. Quire
7. East Window
8. Effigy of Robert, Duke of Normandy
9. Lady Chapel
10. Effigy of Osric
11. Tomb of Edward II
12. Effigy of William Parker
13. Bower Monument
14. Gloucester Cathedral Exhibition
15. Machen Memorial
16. Cloisters
17. Chapter House
18. Treasury

Reverend Richard Raikes (c1743–1823). The memorial was designed by Thomas Rickman, who is credited with devising the terms 'Early English', 'Decorated' and 'Perpendicular' to describe the different styles of Gothic architecture. Nearby a Victorian stained-glass window shows the coronation of the boy king Henry III, crowned here in 1216 at age nine – the only English king since the Norman Conquest not to be crowned at Westminster Abbey.

Continue to the end of the aisle. On the left is the delightful little **Seabroke Chantry Chapel (4)**. Thomas Seabroke was Abbot of St Peters 1450–57. In addition to his alabaster effigy, there is an interesting hanging pyx which would have held communion bread and wine.

Move into the south transept, where there are two chapels – the Chapel of St John the Baptist, located behind the choir stalls, and, on the east side of the transept, St Andrew's Chapel, now used by scouts and guides. There are two items of interest in the transept itself: the huge buttress crossing the Perpendicular tracery on the east side and designed to support the old Norman tower; and the **Mason's Bracket (5)** on the west wall. Made of stone, this L-shaped monument is thought to have been made by the master mason in memory of an apprentice who fell to his death from the cathedral roof. Nearby is the entrance to the crypt, which is not usually open to visitors.

The Mason's Bracket in the south transept

The Quire and Lady Chapel

Leave the south transept and walk eastwards, turning left into the **Quire (6)**. You now see a complete change from what has been on view before. Here we have archetypal Perpendicular architecture, the earliest in any English cathedral. The work started in the 1330s after the abbot of the time acquired the remains of the murdered King Edward II. Encouraged by his son, Edward III, and helped by the money from pilgrims who flocked to the dead king's shrine, the abbot completely remodelled the east end of the building to provide what was effectively a royal chapel within a medieval monastic church. Look first at the choir itself, which retains some of the monastic stalls, some with excellent misericords. At the west end you can admire the finely carved and decorated organ case, dating from 1665.

Turn now to the east to fully appreciate the Perpendicular architecture. It is clear that a cage-like structure masks the Norman work, which can still be seen in the aisles. The proportions here are pleasing, with a large tribune gallery topped with a massive clerestory allowing light to flood in. The imposing **East Window (7)** is almost certainly the largest cathedral window in England – it's as big as a vertical tennis court! Dating from *c*1350, it includes most of its original glass. Close inspection shows that it is not in fact flat but has two slanting 'wings', like those of a gigantic triptych. The window is said to commemorate those who fought with Edward III at the Battle of Crécy (1346). The floor of the presbytery was retiled in Victorian times, but near the high altar the steps contain a wide range of 14th-century tiles. Finally, look up at the superb lierne vaulting, showing a network of struts, three of which run parallel along the highest area. There are numerous gilded bosses, mostly foliated, but over the high altar you can see a series of angelic musicians. Few people leave this part of the cathedral without experiencing a feeling of uplift at its beauty.

Step back into the south choir aisle, now in effect the south ambulatory. Immediately on your right is a large semicircular cope chest, which dates from the 1500s. Opposite is one of the oldest memorials in the cathedral, the **Effigy of Robert, Duke of Normandy (8)**. Made of wood, it dates from *c*1260. Robert (*c*1054–1134), Duke of Normandy, the eldest son of William the Conqueror, had hoped to succeed him but was imprisoned at Cardiff Castle by his brother, Henry, so that his younger brother, William Rufus (c1056–1100), became king. Robert died at Cardiff in 1134 and is probably buried in the chapter house.

Pass the south ambulatory chapel on the right and head into the **Lady Chapel (9)**. Built 1457–99, this occupies the site of the apsidal chapel of the earlier Norman church. Built once more in Perpendicular style, it was the last major work during the time of the abbey. There is also some fine lierne vaulting to be seen, echoing that in the quire. The Lady Chapel is unusual in that it has two chantry chapels (with singing galleries above), like mini-transepts. Behind the altar is a stone reredos, which must have been an impressive sight its time, although most of the statuary has been destroyed and the three main niches are now filled with modern tapestries.

Turn back towards the west to see the gallery above the entrance vestibule. Beneath the gallery is an ancient lead font mounted on a modern concrete plinth. The font dates from *c*1140 and came from a church in the Wye Valley. There are two monuments of note. On the north wall is the effigy to Elizabeth Williams, who died in 1622, while on the opposite wall is that of her sister Margery. Both died in childbirth, always a danger in those days. They were the daughters of Miles Smith, Bishop of Gloucester 1612–24, who played an important part in the translation of the King James Bible.

Memories of Famous Men

Leave the Lady Chapel and walk along the north ambulatory, passing on the right the War Memorial Chapel of St Edmund and St Edward. On the left are three of the most important monuments in the cathedral. First is the **Effigy of Osric (10)**. Osric, Prince of Mercia, founded St Peter's Abbey in 681. On his death he was buried in the abbey church, but his remains have been moved several times. His effigy, which holds a model of the abbey, has occupied this position since 1530. On the wall next to the effigy is a glass case containing the Carne Cross, carved by Lt.-Col. James Power Carne VC (1906–1986), commander of the `Glorious Gloucesters', while he was a prisoner during the Korean War.

You next reach the **Tomb of Edward II (11)**. The alabaster tomb, with its soaring pinnacles, was ordered by Edward III in memory of his father, murdered in Berkeley Castle in 1327. Edward II, despite the picture of him we might gain from

Marlowe's play, was at the time thought to have been a good king, and the tomb soon attracted pilgrims in large numbers. Note the recesses cut into the adjacent pillars to allow pilgrims to walk around the tomb.

The third memorial of this trio is the **Effigy of William Parker (12)**, the last Abbot of St Peter's. The chantry was built during his lifetime, but the stone chest does not in fact contain his remains – their actual whereabouts is a mystery.

Step past St Paul's Chapel (on the right) and into the north transept. Look on the west wall for the **Bower Monument (13)**. This unusual wooden monument shows John and Ann Bower along with their seven daughters and nine sons (boys on the left, girls on the right). Above are shields with the children's names. Some names are repeated or have a shield that is painted black, suggesting that many of the children died while young. John Bower (d1615) was an apothecary. There is an ironic inscription on the canopy: 'Vayne Vanytie, all is Vayne.'

A door in the corner of the north transept leads up narrow stairs to the **Gloucester Cathedral Exhibition (14)**. This stretches around the tribune gallery and includes the 'whispering gallery', a stone passageway which runs behind the east window. The exhibition traces the history of the cathedral from the building of the monastery by Osric in Saxon times up to the present day. There is a small charge for this exhibition, which is highly recommended, particularly for the views it gives of the east window and looking down into the choir.

Returning to ground level, turn briefly into the north nave aisle where, on the right, is another monument from the same historical period as the Bower Memorial: the **Machen Memorial (15)**. It shows the figures of Thomas and Christian Machen kneeling before their prayer books. Below are the 'weepers' of their thirteen children – seven boys on the left and six girls on the right. Some of the figures are half-sized, and it is assumed these represent children who died in infancy. Machen (d1615) was an ex-mayor of Gloucester. The Machen and Bower memorials have many similarities, and the two men may have known each other well.

Cloisters and Chapter House

Go back towards the north transept and walk out into the **Cloisters (16)**, built 1351–1412. The cloisters formed a square walkway which connected the various monastic buildings – such as chapter house, dormitory, refectory and infirmary – so that the monks could reach them under cover. They also provided an opportunity for study and contemplation – look for the recesses (carrels) where the monks could work. The north cloister has a well preserved lavatorium, a long stone trough where the monks could wash. The water came from a well that you can still see in the cloister garth. Opposite the lavatorium is another recess, an open cupboard for storing towels. The Gloucester cloisters are noted for their splendid fan vaulting, the first to appear in any English cathedral and later widely copied.

Just off the east cloister is the **Chapter House (17)**, where the monks met daily to discuss business and read from the rule of St Benedict. It is highly probable that the chapter house was the site where William the Conqueror's Christmas Council ordered the Domesday Survey. Alongside the chapter house is an alleyway (slype) which the monks used as a locutorium, a place where they could relax their rule of silence. This area is now the cathedral's **Treasury (18)**.

The tour concludes at the cloisters. Leave by the southwest or southeast doors or the refectory in the west cloister.

WALKING TOUR FROM GLOUCESTER CATHEDRAL

The walk first circumnavigates the cathedral and views some of the old buildings and gates dating back to the days of the abbey. It then follows part of the Via Sacra, the old Roman walls, before arriving at Gloucester Docks. Although commercial water traffic has more or less ceased, the leisure industry has taken over the docks, making them a major tourist attraction. The return route to the cathedral passes by the remains of two of the city's ancient friaries.

Start and finish: The south porch of the cathedral.
Length: 2 miles (3.3km).
Time: Under 1hr, but you will probably wish to visit at least some of the many churches and museums along the route.
Refreshments: The excellent cathedral refectory is to the west of the cloisters. Plenty of city-centre pubs offer bar meals, but some are pretty rough inside: choose with care! The Fountain Inn in Westgate, first licensed in 1216, can certainly be relied upon. The New Inn in Northgate has a galleried courtyard; it was built around 1450 to accommodate pilgrims visiting the grave of Edward II. Other old inns include The Fleece and Dick Whittington's, both in Westgate. The New County Hotel in Southgate Street, more up-market, also provides accommodation.

Standing at the south porch of the cathedral you are on the cathedral close, known as **College Green (1)** because, after the Dissolution in 1541, the cathedral came under the jurisdiction of a college of clergy. Walk past the west front of the cathedral and the War Memorial and over Lower College Green to **St Mary's Gate (2)**. The arch dates from the 13th century and was the main entrance to the abbey. It is said that the room over the arch was a viewing place when Bishop John Hooper (1495–1555) was burnt at the stake in 1555. A fine range of houses to the south of the gate includes the monastic almonry and granary.

Turn right and pass under the 14th-century inner gate of the monastery to reach **Miller's Green (3)**, the monastery's inner courtyard. If you're interested in domestic architecture you'll have a field day here. Buildings include a schoolmaster's house, an old mill, the organist's house and the deanery. The most important, however, is the **Parliament Room (4)**, a half-timbered house resting on a 13th-century stone undercroft. This was almost certainly the monastery guest hall, and derives its later name from the fact that Richard II summoned parliament here in 1378.

Leave Miller's Green via the alleyway past Little Cloister House, which has an interesting timber supported window. Ahead are the remains of the abbey **Infirmary (5)**. After the Dissolution, this building quickly became derelict; the arches and the west wall are all that is left today. Nearby were the monastery's herb garden and vineyard. You have from here a good opportunity to view the external features of the east end of the cathedral and appreciate the fine Perpendicular architecture, particularly that of the tower, built in the time of Abbot Seabroke. Take the path around the east end and back to the south porch.

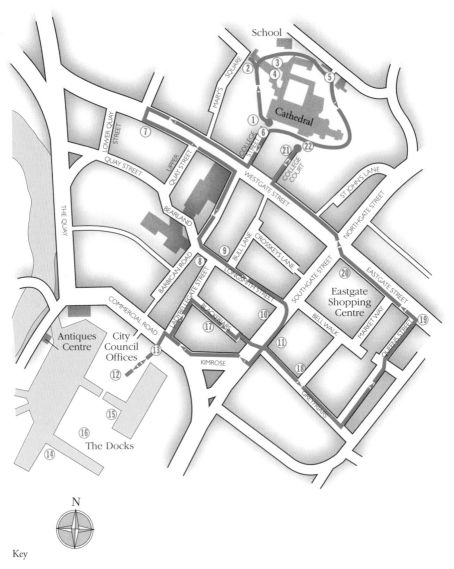

School

Cathedral

N

Key

1. College Green
2. St Mary's Gate
3. Miller's Green
4. Parliament Room
5. Infirmary
6. King Edward's Gate
7. Folk Museum
8. Transport Museum

9. Ladybellegate House
10. Golden Cross Inn
11. Church of St Mary de Crypt
12. Gloucester Docks
13. Soldiers of Gloucester Museum
14. National Waterways Museum
15. Museum of Advertising and Packaging

16. Mariners' Church
17. Blackfriars Friary
18. Greyfriars Friary
19. East Gate Viewing Chamber
20. St Michaels Tower
21. House of the Tailor of Gloucester
22. St Michael's Gate

St Mary's Gate

Harsh Discipline

From here leave the Cathedral Close by **King Edward's Gate (6)**, the place where King Edward's body was received. Little of the gateway remains today except part of the west tower, upon which the arms of Osric, the founder of the abbey, may be seen. The wrought-iron gates were added in 1989.

Move into the short College Street and turn right into Westgate Street. A few yards along on the left you find the monolithic Shire Hall, built in 1815. Almost opposite is the redundant Church of St Nicholas, with its curiously shaped leaning spire. On the other side of the road is the **Folk Museum (7)**, located in a range of half-timbered and Jacobean houses. It is thought that the main house was the place where Bishop John Hooper spent his last night in 1555 before being burnt at the stake. The buildings housed a pin factory in the 18th and 19th centuries. Today there are displays showing local crafts and industries plus mock-ups of a dairy, an iron-monger's shop and wheelwright's and carpenter's workshops. The top floor features a Victorian schoolroom, where visiting schoolchildren are obliged to dress up in period clothes and experience the harsh discipline of those times!

Leave the museum and return along Westgate Street towards the city centre. On passing the Shire Hall, turn immediately right into Berkeley Street. This is part of the Via Sacra, which follows the route of the old city walls. Turn left on reaching Longsmith Street. Opposite is the small **Transport Museum (8)**, which is housed in the old fire station and will not be a high priority for those with limited time.

On the north side of Longsmith Street is **Ladybellgate House (9)**, a superb Georgian townhouse dating from 1705. The Raikes family lived here for a number of years. The building is now the offices of a firm of solicitors.

Continue along Longsmith Street until you reach Southgate Street, and turn right. Immediately to your right is another Raikes house: the **Golden Cross Inn (10)**, a half-timbered 16th-century building with a double-jettied wall. There are more connections with Robert Raikes across the road at the **Church of St Mary de Crypt (11)**, where the Sunday School stalwart is buried. This is one of Gloucester's oldest churches, with Norman origins, having been founded about 1100, although all the windows are Perpendicular in style. There are a number of medieval wall paintings and some interesting brasses. George Whitfield, the rousing 18th-century preacher, gave his first sermon here. Regrettably, the church is often closed to visitors.

Gloucester Docks

Towards the end of Southgate Street, fork right via Kimrose Way into Commercial Road. At the pedestrian crossing, walk over to the building labelled 'Custom House'. An alleyway to the left of the building leads down to **Gloucester Docks (12)**. The River Severn, with its sandbanks and rocks, was never an easy river to navigate, and in 1793 an Act of Parliament gave permission for the construction of a canal to link Gloucester with Berkeley. In 1812 it was decided to end the canal at Sharpness, and shortly afterwards the dock basins at Gloucester were opened. A local rail company terminated its railroad at the docks, enabling the transhipment of goods, and by 1820 the canal was linked with the national network, thereby connecting Gloucester with London and the Midlands. The docks dealt initially with products such as corn and timber and prosperity seemed assured. Unfortunately, the growth of the railways and the development of ports downstream, such as Avonmouth, led to a gradual decline. By the 1970s the docks were almost derelict. To arrest the decline, the City Council decided to move its administration to the docks, acquiring several warehouses. Soon a number of leisure and retail outlets moved in. Some of the warehouses, which are named after the companies who originally owned them, have been converted into imaginative museums. Within a few years the Docks had become one of Britain's most popular tourist destinations and has been used as a setting for countless films.

The Custom House, when viewed from the Docks, is seen to be the **Soldiers of Gloucester Museum (13)**. Displays follow in the footsteps of the Gloucester regiments in their campaigns over the past three centuries, with lifelike models of World War I trenches, guns, medals and other souvenirs. The **National Waterways Museum (14)**, based in Llanthony Warehouse, is also not to be missed. This presents a vibrant display of the history of our canals and waterways, with models and audiovisual displays, and provides an insight into the life of those who worked on the canals. There are a number of historic boats in the neighbouring docks. The museum runs boat trips using the *Queen Boadicea II*, a small ship which was present at the Dunkirk evacuations.

The Albert Warehouse is the home of the Robert Opie Collection at the **Museum of Advertising and Packaging (15)**. Claimed to be the only museum of its type in the world, this displays products and packaging from the Victorian era to the present day. And don't miss the delightful little Victorian **Mariners' Church (16)**, built for the sailors and dock workers, but also popular with townsfolk. There are also an antiques centre and numerous pubs and eating places, plus some specialist shops. Little wonder that some coach parties spend the whole day here!

Returning to the Cathedral

Leave Gloucester Docks by the same route as you entered – the alleyway at the side of the Soldiers of Gloucester Museum. This brings you back to Commercial Road. Go over the pedestrian crossing and walk up Ladybellgate Street. Turn right into Blackfriars. On the right is the **Blackfriars Friary (17)**, said to be the most complete of its type in the country. It was founded in 1239 and at its height accommodated 30–40 friars. After the Dissolution in 1539 the site was bought by a wealthy local clothier, Thomas Bell, who converted the cloisters into his workshop and the church into his mansion. Blackfriars is not normally open to the public.

Continue to the end of Blackfriars, which leads to Southgate Street. Cross over the road and take the path at the side of St Mary de Crypt Church. Pass the Music and Drama Library on the left and keep going until you reach a gap in the stone wall that leads into the ruins of **Greyfriars Friary (18)**. This Franciscan friary church was founded *c*1231 by Thomas Berkeley, but only parts of the nave and north aisle remain and nothing of the other friary buildings. After the Dissolution in the 16th century the church was converted into tenements and workshops.

Continue to the end of Greyfriars and reach the stone-built public library. Turn left along Constitution Walk at the back of the library to go through part of the modern Eastgate Shopping Centre to Eastgate Street. Immediately on your right you'll see the concrete and glass cover of the **East Gate Viewing Chamber (19)**, entry to which is from Queen's Walk. There are good views from here of the medieval walls and the city's East Gate. The original Roman gate was made of wood, part of a fortress built in AD68, but it changed greatly over the years. The view shows one of two towers that date from *c*1230 and a B-shaped gateway. There was evidently a moat, crossed by a drawbridge, and a horsepool, built *c*1550 to wash horses and swell timber in carts, plus a toilet dated *c*1700. The tower served at various times as a prison, a school and a house.

Turn left and walk along Eastgate Street to the central crossroads (The Cross), which is dominated by **St Michael's Tower (20)**, where you can see the arms of Richard III, who granted the city its charter in 1483. The arms were unveiled by the Duke of Gloucester in 1983 to commemorate five centuries of city status. The tower is all that remains of the medieval St Michael's Church.

Cross over into Westgate Street and, after a short distance, turn right along the narrow College Court. On the left is the **House of the Tailor of Gloucester (21)**. Beatrix Potter (1866–1943) used this small building as the model for the tailor's house in one of her best-loved books, *The Tailor of Gloucester* (1903). Since 1979 it has been a giftshop and museum owned by Frederick Warne, her publishers. Potter fans will be in their element here. Younger visitors will be fascinated by the moving tableau of mice at work on the mayor's coat!

At the end of College Court is the minute **St Michael's Gate (22)**, probably the route taken by pilgrims visiting the tomb of Edward II. Pass through the gateway and back into the Cathedral Close, where the walk ends.

Hereford

Access: Hereford can easily be reached by road: the nearest motorways are the M50 to the southeast and the M6 to the east. It is 135 miles (220km) from London, a journey which can be achieved in 3hr. National Express coaches run from London. Hereford can also be reached from Paddington by rail. The nearest international airport is at Birmingham, some 58 miles (93km) to the east.

Hereford is located on the north bank of the River Wye at a traditional early fording point. Its role in defending Saxon territory against the Celts meant that armies often occupied the town; the name 'Hereford' means 'army ford'. Its strategic importance in Saxon times meant a number of Saxon kings came to the town, and some had their coins minted here. This was also the time when the first Hereford Castle was built, although the Normans later built a larger structure on the site. The Saxons also built the first cathedral at Hereford, probably of wood, in AD676. A later stone cathedral was destroyed by Welsh invaders in 1055. When Offa, King of Mercia, had Ethelbert, King of the East Angles, killed, Ethelbert was buried at Hereford, and his remains have always attracted pilgrims to the cathedral.

Following the Conquest, the first Norman bishops began rebuilding the cathedral, starting in 1080 under Bishop de Losinga (in office 1079–95) and his successor Raynhelm (in office 1095–1107). The oldest parts of the cathedral are accordingly in the Norman style. The cathedral went through bad times during the reign of the unfortunate King Stephen in the 12th century, but things picked up during the early 13th century, when the Lady Chapel and the crypt beneath it were completed in Early English style. The north transept was built later in the century by Bishop Aquablanca (in office 1240–1268) and reflects the work which was going on at Westminster Abbey at that time. The 13th century was also important for the relic known as the Mappa Mundi, the cathedral's greatest treasure. This pictorial map of the world dates from 1290 and was probably brought to the cathedral to support the canonization of Bishop Thomas Cantalupe (in office 1275–82). By the end of this century, however, the city of Hereford was losing its importance as a military centre following the conquest of Wales by Edward I.

During the 15th century there were a number of additions to the cathedral in Perpendicular style, including the cloisters, the great west window and some chantry chapels. Hereford Cathedral suffered badly during the Reformation, with a series of reforming bishops who made sure that the building was despoiled of many of its treasures. Further problems came with the Civil War, when both the bishop and the citizens supported the Royalist cause. Despite being taken and retaken, the city suffered little damage until it was besieged in 1645 by Lord Leven and a Scottish army, great damage then being done. The Scots were eventually driven away by the army of Charles I, but later the city was taken again, apparently due to the treachery of its governor, one Colonel Birch. This time the cathedral was ransacked: brasses were destroyed, windows were smashed and the library was pillaged. The courageous dean of the time is said to have preached to the soldiers, condemning their sacrilege. Although they levelled their muskets at him, he was, remarkably, not killed.

By the end of the 18th century the cathedral was in an appalling condition and the architect James Wyatt (1746-1813) was called in to undertake restoration. Although he was highly regarded, he was an unfortunate choice, as several other cathedrals found to their cost. He built a new west front, shortened the nave, removed the Norman triforium and clerestory and used plaster unsparingly. The Victorians continued the restoration, directed mainly by N.J. Cottingham (1823–1854), who provided the reredos behind the high altar, the choir floor and pew ends and the replica Norman arch. Sir George Gilbert Scott (1811–1878) designed an inappropriate metal screen between the crossing and the choir; this has recently been removed for 'restoration', but thankfully will not return. The Victorians also provided a considerable amount of stained glass of mixed quality. Overall it would be fair to say that the changes made here by the Victorians are not as objectionable as in many other cathedrals. Today, the cathedral has a friendly, welcoming ambience and attracts over 200,000 visitors annually, many attracted by the Mappa Mundi and the remarkable Chained Library.

The city, meanwhile, has maintained much of its market-town atmosphere. It has avoided the heavy industrial development which many places attracted during Victorian times. Its industries, such as cidermaking, are light, being mainly connected to farming. It has also developed as a tourist centre, being a gateway to the Welsh mountains and the Wye Valley. The Three Choirs Festival is based at Hereford every third year.

TOUR OF THE CATHEDRAL

Start: The north porch.
Finish: Chapter House Yard.
Hereford does not have a ceremonial entrance on its west front, which was redesigned in the early 20th century. Enter the cathedral via the **North Porch (1)**, which is sometimes known as the Booth Porch, after Bishop Charles Booth (d1535), and dates from 1519. Once a chantry chapel, approached by a spiral staircase, this occupied the space above the porch. Note the porch's superb modern iron gates.

Proceed into the cathedral and turn immediately left to find the **Memorial to Bishop Booth (2)**, set into the north aisle wall. The ornately painted and gilded tomb is protected by heavy iron railings. Booth was the last medieval bishop of Hereford, dying in 1535, immediately before the Reformation.

Step from here into the centre of the **Nave (3)**. The massive piers and arches are Norman and were built around 1100. The arches are decorated with chevron designs, each one being subtly different. The triforium and clerestory levels date from Wyatt's work at the end of the 18th century, and you may feel that the two styles do not sit comfortably together. Walk across to the southwest corner of the nave, where there are a number of items of interest. Between the piers is the alabaster **Effigy of Sir Richard Pembridge (4)**. Pembridge fought at Poitiers (1356) and was one of the first Knights of the Garter – note the garter on his left leg. His right leg is a Victorian replacement for an earlier wooden one, itself a substitute. Nearby is the late-Norman **Font (5)**, the sides of which have carvings of the apostles, their faces erased during the Reformation. The circular, mosaic-topped base is Victorian.

In the corner of the aisle is normally kept a **Mobile Organ (6)**, which can be

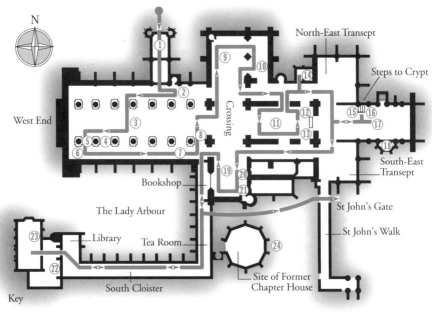

Key

1. North Porch
2. Memorial to Bishop Booth
3. Nave
4. Effigy of Sir Richard
   Pembridge
5. Font
6. Mobile Organ
7. North Aisle
8. Corona

9. North Transept
10. Shrine of St Thomas
    Cantalupe
11. Choir
12. King Stephen's Chair
13. Ethelbert's Statue
14. Stanbury Chantry Chapel
15. Crypt
16. Facsimile of Mappa Mundi

17. Lady Chapel
18. Audley Chantry
19. South Transept
20. John Piper Tapestries
21. Denton Tomb
22. Mappa Mundi
23. Chained Library
24. Chapter House Yard

trundled around the cathedral on its wheeled platform; its main use is during the Three Choirs Festival. There are two other organs in the cathedral: the main 'Father' Willis organ in the choir and one in the Lady Chapel's chantry.

Proceed east along the **North Aisle (7)**. There are two stone effigies set into the wall of Thomas de Pembridge, treasurer of the cathedral in the mid-14th century, and Stephen de Ledbury, dean of the cathedral at about the same time. This brings you to the beautifully carved Jacobean pulpit (the base and steps are modern).

Cross in front of the pulpit. Dominating the crossing to the right is the **Corona (8)**, a modern wrought-iron crown which hangs above the nave altar. The chevron design matches the decoration on the nave's Norman arches. Proceed to the north aisle and on into the **North Transept (9)**. This was built by Bishop Peter Aquablanca *c*1250 and is of an unusual Geometrical Decorated design, with almost pointed, triangular arches, reminiscent of work at Westminster Abbey; this replaced the original Norman design, which can still be seen in the south transept. The transept also has a number of monuments to bishops, the most interesting of which is the alabaster bust of Bishop Field, who came to Hereford after being bishop successively of Llandaff and St David's and who died in office in 1636. In the corner of the north transept is the **Shrine of St Thomas Cantalupe (10)**, which dates from 1287. The lower part of the shrine, which is made of Purbeck Marble, shows 15 Knights Templar; the bishop was a Provincial Grand Master of this order. He was also the last Englishmen to be canonized before the Reformation. His shrine attracted many pilgrims and was the source of much revenue for the cathedral. Walk into the north choir aisle, where on the right you see a showcase depicting the last journey of St Thomas. Opposite is the tomb of Bishop Aquablanca.

Two Thrones

Continue along the aisle and turn into the **Choir (11)**, which is full of interest. The main arches and the triforium are Norman, but the clerestory and vaulting are Early English, dating from c1250. The choir stalls and canopies are richly carved in the Decorated style and have a good collection of misericords. The Bishop's Throne dates from the same period. The other 'chair' of interest is **King Stephen's Chair (12)**, on which Stephen is supposed to have sat during his visit to the cathedral in 1142. If this were true – and it is doubtful – then it would be one of the oldest pieces of furniture in the country. Elizabeth II has used the chair on two recent visits.

Statue of St Ethelbert

Elsewhere in the choir, the high altar reredos, the flooring and the mock Norman arch were the work of N.J. Cottingham during the Victorian restorations. The wooden woodpecker plaque on the organ casing reflects the fact that the restoration of the organ was sponsored by Bulmers, the local cidermaker, whose emblem is a woodpecker. Before you leave the choir area, inspect the Victorian tiled floor in front of the high altar. One of the tiles shows the rather gory death of St Ethelbert, the cathedral's patron, murdered in 794 on the orders of King Offa of Mercia. **Ethelbert's Statue (13)**, minus hands and facial features, can be found nearby, against the wall to the right of the high altar.

Return to the north choir aisle, where on the north side is one of the most delightful parts of the cathedral – the **Stanbury Chantry Chapel (14)**. John Stanbury (in office 1453–74) was originally a Carmelite friar before becoming confessor to Henry VI. He was thereafter the first Provost of Eton, then Bishop of Hereford. His chantry chapel, built in the 1470s, is in an ornate Perpendicular style, with intricate wall carving and some superb fan vaulting. It is rare to get so close to such fine vaulting, so enjoy the detail. The 20th-century glass (paid for by Eton College) shows scenes from Stanbury's life. Note that the impression of Hereford Cathedral shows the tower capped by the wooden spire removed in 1790. The chapel also has a finely carved wooden triptych above the altar. (During Lent all the cathedral's triptychs are folded up.)

You are now approaching the east end of the cathedral, which once had an apsidal end. This was replaced by two shallow transepts, an ambulatory (sometimes referred to as the retrochoir) and the Lady Chapel. The whole area is in Transitional or Early English style. To the left of the entrance to the Lady Chapel are stairs leading down to the **Crypt (15)**; said to be the only example of a cathedral crypt built later than the 11th century, this is today used for private prayer. Apparently it was at one time called `Golgotha', as it was used as a charnel house. There are few features of interest in the crypt, but don't miss the tomb at the west end, which in place of effigies on the top has the incumbents' figures etched on the lid.

Tombs and Effigies

Climb the steps back to the Lady Chapel, where there is a **Facsimile of the Mappa Mundi (16)**. It's worth spending some time looking at this, as it is considerably easier to decipher than the original. Head next into the **Lady Chapel (17)**. This and the crypt below were built in Early English style around 1225, but suffered considerable alteration in Victorian times, and all the stained glass dates from this era. The Lady Chapel once contained the Shrine of St Thomas and until the 19th century was the home of the Chained Library. On the north wall is an intricately painted and gilded tomb, believed to be that of Peter de Grandisson. Nearby, kept behind glass because of its fragility, is a Victorian tapestry altar frontal designed by Sir George Gilbert Scott and made in Belgium.

On the south side of the Lady Chapel is the two-storey **Audley Chantry (18)**. Erected by Bishop Edmund Audley (in office 1492–1502), it contains the cathedral's third organ. It is separated from the Lady Chapel by a fine decorated screen bearing the painted figures of numerous saints. Audley was successively Bishop of Rochester, Hereford and Salisbury, and it was while he was at Hereford that he had the chantry built. He later had another one constructed at Salisbury, where he is buried.

Leave the east end and turn into the south choir aisle, where there are identical effigies of four medieval bishops. Their probable names are shown on the wall, but it is not accurately known which effigy is of which bishop.

You next reach the **South Transept (19)**, which has a variety of architectural styles. The north wall is pure Norman, with five tiers of rounded arches of varying size. In the three largest arches in the second tier are the **John Piper Tapestries (20)**. These show three trees from the Bible: the Tree of Knowledge of Good and Evil (note Adam and Eve), the Tree of the Cross and the Tree of Life. In the southeast corner of the transept is the **Denton Tomb (21)**, dating from 1566, which shows the effigies of Sir Alexander Denton, his wife Elizabeth and their infant child. Both the south and west walls of the transept have large Perpendicular windows, and the vaulting also dates from this period. The west wall of the transept has two interesting items – a Norman fireplace (the only other known example is at Durham) and a triptych from Hereford's twin town of Nuremberg.

The Mappa Mundi and the Chained Library

Leave the south transept, turn left and go through the cathedral shop and the tearoom, both located in the east cloister. Turn into the south cloister, at the end of which is the New Library Building. An entrance fee (with concessions) is required here to see the Mappa Mundi and the Chained Library Exhibition. The New Library Building was completed in 1996 and was given the Building of the Year Award in 1997.

The **Mappa Mundi (22)** dates from the end of the 13th century and is believed to be the work of Richard of Haldingham, a canon at the cathedral. It is a map of

Plate 17: *Christ Church Cathedral, Oxford, seen from Broad Walk (see page 77). Christ Church is unique in that it is both a college chapel and one of England's smallest cathedrals.*

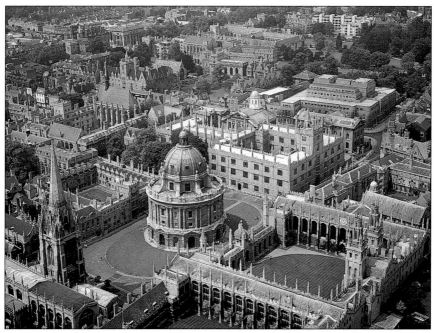

Plate 18: *Aerial view of the 'dreaming spires' of Oxford. In the centre of the picture is the Radcliffe Camera (see page 36), while surrounding colleges include Brasenose, All Souls and Hertford.*

Plate 19: Gloucester
Docks have become one of
the country's most popular
tourist destinations (see
page 98). The redundant
docks and warehouses
have been converted into
museums, restaurants and
retail outlets.

Plate 20: Gloucester
Cathedral. Some of the best
Perpendicular architecture in
England can be seen at
Gloucester, along with some
exquisite fan vaulting (see
page 94).

Plate 21: *Hereford's pink sandstone cathedral dominates the view across the River Wye, with its ancient stone bridge. The cathedral contains the priceless 13th-century Mappa Mundi (see page 100).*

Plate 22: *The Old House Museum in Hereford's Market Place (see page 108). A fine half-timbered building, the museum dates from 1621 and was once a butcher's shop.*

Plate 23: *Worcester Cathedral, seen from College Green. There has been a diocese based at Worcester since the 7th century (see page 109), but the present cathedral was begun in 1084.*

Plate 24: *Worcester's largely pedestrianized city centre has some fine domestic architecture including this half-timbered building which is now the Museum of Local Life (see page 117).*

the world as conceived in the Middle Ages, with the Mediterranean Sea and Jerusalem at the centre and England and Wales near the lower left-hand edge. The imagery is fascinating: the Garden of Eden is complete with Adam, Eve and an apple tree; Babylon is marked by the Tower of Babel; and Lot's wife stands by the shore of the Dead Sea. There is much more to see, including a whole range of strange animals with a dodgy distribution – for example, a monkey inhabits Norway!

The **Chained Library (23)** is a rich collection of medieval manuscripts from both England and abroad. There are nearly 1500 books with chains attached in what is probably the largest such collection in the world. The practice of chaining came about because during the Middle Ages and even in the Renaissance books were rare and their readers not necessarily honest. The exhibition, which uses models and computer technology, is an essential part of a visit to Hereford Cathedral.

Return through the cloisters to the tearoom, and move outside into **Chapter House Yard (24)**. The chapter house, which was a fine 14th-century building, was unfortunately pulled down *c*1715, and all that remain are the stone foundations, including the bases of the buttresses – excellent seating when people overflow from the tearoom on warm summer days.

Leave the yard through St John's Gate. On the right is St John's Walk, a covered way with carved roof beams that led to the College of the Vicars Choral. Here the tour ends.

WALKING TOUR FROM HEREFORD CATHEDRAL

The tour begins in the Cathedral Close and proceeds down to the Wye Bridge and a riverside walk. You cross the river to see the site of Hereford Castle before going on into the heart of the city, with its superb domestic architecture, ancient parish churches and pedestrianized shopping areas. There is an optional extension of the walk to the Cider Museum to get a flavour, as it were, of the area's main industry.

Start and finish: The north porch of the cathedral.
Length: 2 miles (3.2km), plus a 1 mile (1.6km) for the diversion to the Cider Museum.
Time: A little over 1hr, but add time if you want to visits the museums.
Refreshments: The small cathedral tearoom only serves light snacks. There are plenty of ancient inns *en route*, many with coaching origins. However, although interesting from the exterior, some can be rough inside. At the top of the range is the Green Dragon Hotel in Broad Street, whence coaches once left for London. Other possibilities are the Orange Tree Inn in King Street and the Grapes Tavern in Capuchin Lane. There is a unique 'community' restaurant in the nave of All Saints' Church.

The tour begins in the **Cathedral Close (1)**, a grassy area with mature trees which is well used by visitors and the citizens of Hereford. It was open land in medieval days, when it was the site of St Ethelbert's Fair, and it was the city's only graveyard until 1791. It is said that at one time pigs roamed here at will, occasionally digging up bodies, so the cathedral authorities had to enclose the site. Here you have a good opportunity to look at the external features of the cathedral. Dominating the exterior is the magnificent tower, which has much in common with those of the neighbouring cathedrals of Gloucester and Worcester. The tower dates from *c*1300 and is Decorated in style, with a profusion of ball flower decoration. You don't have to look closely to see that much of the pink sandstone of the cathedral's exterior is in bad condition, and the cathedral's stone masons are kept very busy. You can watch them working in their small yard between the north and northeast transepts.

Leave the close from the west side and walk into Broad Street. Ahead is the **City Art Gallery, Museum and Library (2)**. This multi-purpose building was constructed in 1874 and extended early in the 20th century. It has a good archaeological section and changing exhibitions of art and sculpture. Opposite the museum notice the Roman Catholic **Church of St Francis Xavier (3)**. This ochre-coloured church has a Classical frontage and was one of the first post-Reformation Catholic churches to be built in the country.

By the River

Walk south towards the Tourist Information Office and turn right along King Street to its junction with Bridge Street. At this point, in the middle of the road, once stood St Nicholas' Church, but in the early years of the 19th century it was removed stone by stone to a new home in Victoria Street. Walk down Bridge Street towards the River Wye and **Wye Bridge (4)**. In Roman times there was a ford just to the east, and later a wooden bridge. The present stone bridge, with its elegant arches and pedestrian refuge places, dates from the late 15th century.

At the far side of the bridge, take the steps down past the Bridge Inn to **Bishop's Meadow (5)**. This recreational area, once owned by the cathedral authorities, was eventually given to the city. A shady riverside walk gives views across the Wye towards the cathedral, with the Bishop's Palace to the left and the College of Vicars Choral to the right. Some of the dead trees along the walk have been imaginatively carved by local artists. Cross over the river via **Victoria Footbridge (6)**; this suspension bridge, replacing a ferry, was built to celebrate Queen Victoria's Diamond Jubilee in 1897.

From Castle Green to the Old House

After crossing the bridge, climb the steps up to the left to reach **Castle Green (7)**. This open space was once the castle bailey. In the centre of the green is a local version of Nelson's Column – Nelson was a frequent visitor to Hereford.

Walk round the edge of the green, passing some public toilets on the left. On the right is Castle Pool, all that remains of the castle moat. The first castle on this site was Saxon, dating from 1052. It was later strengthened by the Normans. Behind the pool is the back of St Ethelbert's Almshouses (see below).

Turn back to the left along Castle Hill. On the left is a grassy area, Redcliffe Gardens. This was the site of the castle keep, demolished in the 17th century. At the southern end of the gardens is Castle Cliffe, once the castle's watergate. At the end of Castle Hill is a water fountain set into the wall. This is the site of **St Ethelbert's Well (8)**, once renowned for its healing waters. Above the fountain there is a much eroded stone head, believed to have once been in the cathedral.

Turn right into Quay Street; the Cathedral School occupies most of the buildings to both right and left. At the end of Quay Street, turn right into Castle Street. On the right you can see the front of St Ethelbert's Almshouses. The present buildings date from 1805, but there were almshouses here bearing this name centuries earlier.

Now swing left into St Ethelbert Street, where there are some impressive houses, mainly in Georgian style and many with wrought-iron balconies. Turn left again into the broad St Owen Street. Halfway along on the left is the **Town Hall (9)**. This

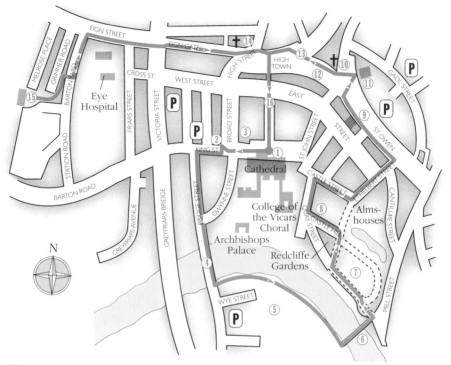

Key

1. Cathedral Close
2. City Art Gallery, Museum and
   Library
3. Church of St Francis Xavier
4. Wye Bridge
5. Bishop's Meadow
6. Victoria Footbridge
7. Castle Green
8. St Ethelbert's Well
9. Town Hall
10. St Peter's Church
11. Shire Hall
12. The Old House
13. Market Place
14. All Saints' Church
15. Cider Museum
16. Church Street

imposing building, completed in 1904 in Edwardian Baroque style, contains the council chamber, the mayor's parlour and many of the city's civic treasures and regalia.

You now reach St Peter's Square, named after the 11th-century **St Peter's Church (10)**, the oldest church in the city. Built in the traditional pink sandstone, the church has a prominent spire, but the overall effect is spoiled at the front by a sheltered walkway that looks like a glass conservatory. Opposite is the **Shire Hall (11)**, once the centre of the county's administration but less important since the merger of Herefordshire with Worcestershire. Built in Classical style, it was designed by Sir Robert Smirke (1781–1867), also responsible for the British Museum in London. Outside the Shire Hall is a statue of Sir George Cornewall Lewis, MP for the city in the mid-19th century.

Walking to the left of St Peter's Church, you now approach the heart of the city, known as Hightown. Immediately ahead is the **Old House (12)**. This half-timbered, three-storied building with jettied walls dates from 1621 and has a profusion of latticed windows and carved gables. Over the main door is the coat-of-arms of the

Butchers' Guild. The Old House is the last remaining building in a terraced row of butchers' shops (shambles) which once stood here – this is why the jettied walls are found on only three sides. The building has had a variety of uses in its long history, being by turns a fish shop, a saddlery, a hardware store and a bank before being handed over to the city authorities, who have converted it into a highly atmospheric museum. Apart from the furniture and other artefacts, which go back to the 16th century, there is an informative display about the effect of the Civil War on Hereford.

Commerce and Spirit

You have now reached the bustling **Market Place (13)**. There has been a market here since Norman times. The large timber-framed Guildhall was demolished in 1862 because of its ruinous condition, but you can still see its position marked out by a line of coloured bricks set into the pavement.

Go to the end of the Market Place, cross the High Street and walk along the pedestrianized Eign Gate. Immediately on your right is **All Saints' Church (14)**. There has been a church here since *c*1200, the present building dating from 1330. The top third of its dominating, slightly crooked, spire was rebuilt in 1994, but the whole is still slightly out of kilter. Step inside for a real surprise: the whole of the west end of the nave and its gallery have been converted into a highly popular restaurant. The rest of this parish church is full of interest. There is a fine hammer-beam roof, a pulpit dating back to 1621 and a Queen Anne reredos in the Chapel of St Anthony. Don't miss the font, which is claimed to be as old as the church itself. The actor David Garrick (1717–1779) was baptised here.

The Cider Museum

From All Saints' Church there is an optional excursion to the Cider Museum. Walk to the end of Eign Gate and take the pedestrian subway under Victoria Street to emerge in Eign Street. Pass the Eye Hospital on the left. At the traffic lights, turn left along Barton Road. Almost immediately cross Barton Road by the pedestrian crossing into Grimmer Road. The **Cider Museum (15)** is signposted just a few yards away. The museum has a reconstructed farm ciderhouse with some of the presses and other equipment from past centuries, plus the traditional 'tack' of the travelling cidermaker. The cellars can be visited, as can the distillery, which makes fortified products such as cider champagne, cider liqueurs and cider brandy. You can taste the cider, and a giftshop sells cider and other items.

Return by the same route to All Saints' Church to resume the main tour. Leave the Market Square on the south side by a narrow alley known as Capuchin Lane. This crosses East Street, widens, and becomes known as **Church Street (16)**. On the corner is the Grapes Tavern; here, in the 18th century, the 'London Letter' was read to the eager citizens. Church Street is full of specialist shops and restored half-timbered buildings. A number of plaques on the walls above the shops show historical items of interest. One indicates the house where Roger Kemble (1721–1802) was born: he was the father of a theatrical family that included Sarah Siddons (1755–1831). As you near the cathedral, another plaque points out a house containing a medieval hall, the former home of the cathedral organist Dr Sinclair, an associate of Elgar. Finally, don't miss Capuchin Yard, a small alleyway devoted mainly to craft workshops.

Church Street leads back to the Cathedral Close and the end of the tour.

Worcester

Access: Worcester is located close to the M5 and therefore has good road links via the motorway system to all parts of the country. The city is 113 miles (181km) from London, 27 miles (43km) from Birmingham and 111 miles (178km) from Manchester; leave the M5 at junction 7. Parking in Worcester is not usually a problem: the nearest carparks to the cathedral are in Copenhagen Street and King Street. National Express coaches stop on the outskirts of Worcester, with scheduled local bus services to the city centre. There are regular trains from London Paddington to Shrub Hill Station Worcester, the journey taking 2½ hours. Trains from Birmingham arrive at Foregate Street Station. The nearest airport is at Birmingham. Coaches from London Heathrow Airport run twice daily.

Worcester was an important Roman town, protected by an earth embankment. It appears that towards the end of the Roman occupation Christianity had made an impact – certainly two graves recently discovered beneath the undercroft of College Hall suggest a Christian burial. In Anglo-Saxon times a diocese of Worcester was created, sometime towards the end of the 7th century. The first bishop was called Bosel and his simple cathedral was dedicated to St Peter. In 971 Bishop Oswald founded a Benedictine monastery on the site. He built a new church to replace the old one and dedicated it to St Mary. Oswald died in 992 and was later canonized. His shrine became a place of pilgrimage.

The year 1062 saw the appointment of Wulfstan as prior and bishop. Four years later came the Norman Conquest, but the able Wulfstan proved acceptable to King William and kept his positions. He decided to build a new cathedral in the Romanesque style, and a start was made with the crypt in 1084; this remains the largest Norman crypt in England. Above the crypt the east end of the cathedral was completed within five years. The design was typified by alternating bands of white limestone and green sandstone – a pattern which can be seen today in the chapter house. Wulfstan was likewise canonized after his death, and this meant pilgrims had a second shrine to visit. In 1216, King John was buried in the cathedral, as stipulated in his will, attracting to his tomb yet further visitors. The pilgrims' offerings were an important revenue in the continual restoration of the Norman cathedral.

Changes came with the appointment in the 1220s of Bishop William de Blois. He built a Lady Chapel at the east end in Early English style. The effect was obviously pleasing, because de Blois and his successors, bishops Cantelupe and Gifford, continued the process in the rest of the cathedral, gradually replacing Wulfstan's Romanesque with Gothic work as far as the crossing. In 1317 Bishop Thomas de Cobham started on the nave. There was evidently a gap in the work, probably coinciding with the Black Death, with the result that the nave was completed in Decorated and Perpendicular styles. All that remained was the construction of the tower, the revaulting of the nave and the building of the north porch. By the end of the 14th century the cathedral was to all events and purposes the building we see today.

The monastery, meanwhile, was also thriving. Monastic buildings included the infirmary, refectory, dormitory and, of course, the cloisters. When Prince Arthur (1486–1502), the brother of Henry VIII, died in 1502 at Ludlow Castle, he was buried in the cathedral, and an imposing chantry, just to the right of the high altar, was constructed to house his tomb. This represented what was to be the pinnacle of the monastery's influence: changes were soon to come.

At the Reformation Henry VIII dissolved the monastery (1540). The cathedral was refounded and the prior, Henry Holbeach, became the first dean. Regrettably, the shrines of Oswald and Wulfstan were destroyed and the whereabouts of the saints' bodies remains unknown. Considerable damage was also done to statues and other fittings and stained glass.

As with many cathedral cities, Worcester saw plenty of action during the Civil War, which both started and ended here. There was a skirmish between Cavaliers and Roundheads at Powick Bridge in 1642, while the Battle of Worcester in 1651 was the decisive action of the campaign, resulting in the rout of the Royalist army and the flight of the future Charles II to France. Cromwell's troops were billeted in the nave of the cathedral for some time, inflicting predictable damage.

The 17th century saw the cathedral in a sad state of repair and, although there was some restoration work done in the 18th century, it was piecemeal and of poor quality. It was left to the Victorians to save the fabric of the cathedral. The soft pink sandstone of which most of it is constructed was severely eroded in places and much needed to be replaced. Work at Worcester started in 1854, with Sir George Gilbert Scott (1811–1878) playing an important role. Much Victorian glass appeared, along with the west door, the Bishop's Throne, the nave pulpit, the high altar reredos and the vault paintings. One of Scott's better moves was to remove the organ (and its screen) from the west end of the choir and replace it with a light screen, thus allowing uninterrupted views along the length of the cathedral. Whether it was wise to relocate the organ screen in the south transept is debatable. Perhaps it is charitable to say that, despite the controversial nature of the work, Worcester Cathedral provides an excellent opportunity to study the full range of Victorian sculpture, glass and artwork.

The city of Worcester also developed during Victorian times, with the railways gradually replacing the canal as the main means of moving both freight and passengers. The Industrial Revolution did not bring the ugly development found in many cities in the Midlands and the North. Worcester developed light industries based around agriculture plus specialist glove and pottery making. Fortunately the two world wars inflicted little damage on either the city or its cathedral. The second half of the 20th century saw the coming of the motorways, allowing tourists, the modern pilgrims, even easier access to the city and its cathedral. Some 300,000 visitors come annually to Worcester Cathedral, their contributions helping the ongoing fight to maintain the fabric of this magnificent building. The 1990s were a cause of some celebration for Worcester, as 1992 was the Millennium of St Oswald and 1995 was the 900th anniversary of St Wulfstan.

TOUR OF THE CATHEDRAL

Start: The north porch.
Finish: The east cloister and College Green.

Enter via the north porch and move towards the west end. On the right is a simple
Wall Plaque to Edward Elgar (1). Above is the Elgar Window, based on the poem
The Dream of Gerontius (1865) by Cardinal John Henry Newman (1801–1890). Sir
Edward Elgar (1857–1934), a local man, was organist at the local Roman Catholic
church but had many links with the cathedral.

It is often suggested that, to appreciate the architectural features of Worcester's **Nave
(2)**, the visitor should stand near the second pier on the south side. All the features west
of here are in the Transitional Norman style, while to the east the architecture is
Perpendicular and Decorated. The proportions of the various levels are pleasing. The
triforium is of particular interest. Each bay has a pair of arches, with sculptures filling
the tympanum. The shafts are of Purbeck Marble. Just behind is a subsidiary arcade with
smaller and lower arches, a pattern which continues in the east end of the cathedral.
The glass in the west window is Victorian and shows the story of the Creation.

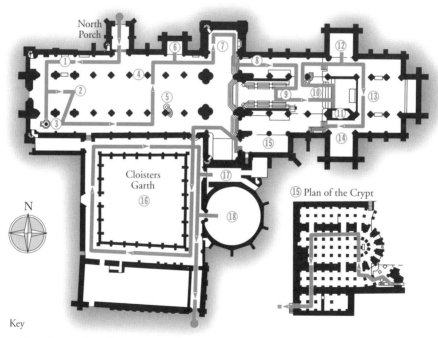

Key

1. Elgar Plaque and Window
2. Nave
3. Font
4. Beauchamp Tomb
5. Pulpit
6. Jesus Chapel
7. North Transept
8. Oriel Window
9. Quire
10. Tomb of King John
11. Chantry of Prince Arthur
12. St George's Chapel
13. Lady Chapel
14. Dean's Chapel
15. Crypt
16. Cloisters
17. Slype
18. Chapter House

Walk across to the southwest corner of the nave, where, in the aisle, is the **Font (3)**. This is remarkable for its extraordinary wooden and gilded cover which soars away to the roof and has doors at its lower end giving access to the font itself. Only the Victorians could have designed something as extraordinary as this!

Move along the nave eastwards and cross over to a gap in the pews to the north side, where you find one of the more interesting of the many memorials in the cathedral. This is the **Beauchamp Tomb (4)**, bearing effigies of Sir John Beauchamp and his wife. Beauchamp was a favourite of Richard II, but fell foul of the Merciless Parliament in 1388 and was executed. The heads of him and his wife rest on black swans. Over to the right is Scott's ornate marble **Pulpit (5)**; this would no doubt be admirable for a Methodist chapel, but in a Gothic cathedral it stands out like a sore thumb. Move to the left for a quick look into the 14th-century **Jesus Chapel (6)**, reserved for private prayer and once the baptistry. The ornately carved oak reredos that dominates the chapel dates from 1899.

Walk round into the **North Transept (7)**, which is festooned with monuments to the great and good of the city. The most distinctive is the white marble monument to John Hough, Bishop of Worcester 1717–43. He was a Fellow of Magdalen College, Oxford and was elected President by the Fellows in 1687, but then dismissed by James II's Commissioner, who required a Roman Catholic president. The Magdalen scene is depicted on the memorial.

Leave the transept and walk along the north quire aisle. On the left is a small **Oriel Window (8)**, which was part of the sacrist's house built on the outside of the cathedral wall. The window enabled the sacrist to watch over the pilgrims visiting the shrines in the sanctuary.

The Quire and Altar

Turn right into the **Quire (9)**. This area of the cathedral dates from the early 13th century and is in Early English style. Note the pointed arches, the slender Purbeck Marble pillars, the bold carving on the capitals and the sculptures in the spandrels of the triforium. Some of these carvings were restored in Victorian times, but the majority are 13th-century. Turn to the choir stalls. The back rows on each side date from the 14th century and have a superb collection of 37 carved misericords. Move into the sanctuary, dominated by the over-ornate Victorian marble reredos showing Christ in Majesty seated between the four evangelists. Far more pleasing is the modern altar-front collage tapestry showing the cathedral and nearby buildings reflected in the River Severn. Look up at the vaulting. The painting was designed by Sir George Gilbert Scott based on 13th-century originals. If you've been to Salisbury and Winchester cathedrals you'll see the similarities.

Immediately in front of the altar is the **Tomb of King John (10)**. A friend of Wulfstan, John left a codicil to his will expressing his wish to be buried at Worcester. The marble top of the tomb is the lid of the original coffin, while the base dates from the 15th century. This is claimed to be the earliest extant royal effigy in the country.

To the right of the sanctuary is the magnificent stone **Chantry of Prince Arthur (11)**. Arthur, the elder brother of Henry VIII, had just married Catherine of Aragon when he died, aged 15, at Ludlow Castle. (Catherine went on to marry Henry.) His body was brought with great pomp to Worcester, where a long series of funeral services was held involving three bishops, eight abbots and the Prior of Worcester. The chantry, which contains Arthur's tomb, has some superb vaulting and imagery. It is believed to have been built by masons from Westminster Abbey, where they were working on a chapel for Henry VII. A good view of the chantry can also be had from the south choir aisle.

Chapels

Return to the north aisle. On the left stands **St George's Chapel (12)**, the chapel of the Royal Worcestershire Regiment. It has a number of military memorials, including one to the World War I chaplain G.A. Studdert Kennedy (1883–1929), better known as `Woodbine Willie'. Note the exterior stone screen, which dates from the 15th century and which occupied a place behind the high altar until the Victorian renovations. Opposite the chapel is a stretch of wall with some faintly discernible medieval paintings. Covered with limewash during the Puritan regime, these were exposed during the Victorian renovations and left in pre-restoration condition to show the previous state of the cathedral. There are two tombs beneath the wall paintings; although the incumbents cannot be identified, the ball flower decoration on the arch of the eastern tomb is *c*1320.

We have now reached the east end of the cathedral, dominated by the **Lady Chapel (13)**. Apart from the stained glass and the roof decoration, the chapel is much as it was when built by Bishop de Blois in the early 13th century. It is typically Early English in style with pointed lancet windows and free use of Purbeck Marble shafts; the carved scenes in the spandrels are an important feature. The two tombs at the sides of its entrance are those of bishops de Blois (in office 1218–36) and Cantelupe (in office 1237–66), who were responsible for the reconstruction of the east end of the cathedral.

Leave the Lady Chapel and walk back along the south side of the cathedral. To the right is the **Dean's Chapel (14)** or southeast transept, where there are a number of examples of the original 13th-century sculpture in the spandrels. The tomb in the centre of the chapel is that of Sir Griffith Ryce, standard-bearer to Prince Arthur. Note the similarities between the tombs of Ryce, King John and Prince Arthur. Also in the southeast transept, in a glass recess in the west wall, is a triptych of Our Lady and the Holy Child, made of Derbyshire alabaster in the late 15th century and thought to be by Sir W. St John Hope. From this position it is possible to view the exterior of Arthur's Chantry, decorated with a number of heraldic devices and the pomegranate, symbol of the city of Granada, Catherine of Aragon's home. The tombs beneath the chantry, believed to be those of Bishop Gifford (in office 1267–1301) and Lady Gifford, were already in position when the chantry was constructed over them.

Crypt and Cloisters

Take the steps down into the **Crypt (15)**. The oldest part of the cathedral, built by Wulfstan 1084–9, this is the largest Norman crypt in England – and was once even larger, before the eastern end was filled in to support the new choir above. The crypt

Ruins of the monastery Guesten House

is a good example of the strong but simple Romanesque architecture. It is believed the columns were re-used from an earlier building. The crypt is regularly used for exhibitions; at the time of writing there were displays on Oswald, Wulfstan and the Worcester Pilgrim.

Leave the crypt by the exit stairs to the south transept. This area is almost entirely filled with the organ case, once at the west end of the choir but placed here by Scott during the Victorian restoration, reportedly against his better judgement. From the transept turn into the **Cloisters (16)**, built during the 14th and 15th centuries and once at the core of the monastic community. All four cloister walks have items of interest. The west walk has a lavatorium (washing place) for the monks; the doors leading to their dormitory have now been filled in with stone. In the east walk is a row of five bells of various sizes, all that remain of the original peal of eight bells; the oldest dates back to 1374. The space behind the bells once contained cupboards for the monks' books as they worked at desks in the spaces by the windows. The cloisters have a fine range of bosses in the vaulting. Finally, note the attractive cloister garth or garden, which contains the types of herb which the monks would have grown; there are also a few gravestones, but these would not have been there in monastic times – monks were usually buried on the west side of their church, but at Worcester many of the graves were removed so the Lady Chapel could be built. The bones were transferred to a specially built charnel house, probably near the north porch.

From the east cloister look into the **Slype (17)**. This narrow passage led from the cloisters to the cemetery and was the place where the monks were allowed to converse. Note the walls, into which small arches and pillars are set; they probably came from the earlier Saxon cathedral. The slype is now the cathedral tearoom.

Also on the side of the east cloister is the **Chapter House (18)**, where the monastic community held its daily meetings. This was built in the early 12th century with alternating bands of green sandstone and white limestone set against interlocking arches (it is possible that much of the early Norman cathedral was in this style). The upper part of the building, including the windows, dates from the late 14th century and is in Perpendicular style. The vaulting is supported by a slender pillar. This chapter house is claimed to be the earliest of any English cathedral. A curiosity is that, although the building is circular inside, the exterior is decagonal because of the wall-strengthening in the 14th century.

Leave the cathedral by the east cloister and the passage which runs past the end of the monks' refectory (now the King's School Hall). This leads you to College Green, on the south side of the cathedral, and the end of the tour.

WALKING TOUR FROM WORCESTER CATHEDRAL

The tour begins and ends in the monastic surroundings of the cathedral. The Royal Worcester Porcelain Factory gives a glimpse of one of the city's most important industries before you move on to look at Worcester's role in the Civil War. The tour then proceeds into the largely pedestrianized city centre, with its wealth of well preserved historic buildings. Waterways are represented by the River Severn and the Worcester and Birmingham Canal.

Start: The south side of the cathedral, at the cloister entrance.
Finish: The north porch of the cathedral.
Length: 1½ miles (2.6km).
Time: Just over 1hr, but you will probably want to visit one or more of the museums.
Refreshments: The cathedral tea room is small and offers only a limited range of snacks, but plenty of historic pubs in the city centre offer good lunchtime food, including the King Charles II Restaurant in New Street, the Salmon's Leap opposite the Royal Worcester works, Ye Olde Talbot Hotel and the Cardinal's Hat (*c*1482), both in Friar Street, and the Old Pheasant and the Swan With Two Necks, both in New Street. An unusual eatery is RSVP in the redundant St Nicholas Church, which has been converted into a trendy café-bar.

College Green (1) is Worcester's version of a cathedral close; it gained its name at the time of the Dissolution, when the administration of the cathedral was taken over by a college of the dean and canons. Some of the buildings are used by the King's School. Leave the green by the archway under **Edgar Tower (2)**; this pink sandstone structure was built in the 13th century on the orders of King John and was the main entrance to the monastery. Passing through the arch, pause to look at the huge wooden gates, which it is believed are the originals.

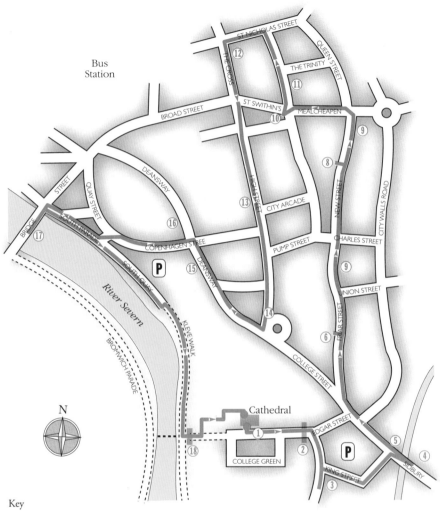

Key

1. College Green
2. Edgar Tower
3. Royal Worcester Pocelain Works
4. The Commandery
5. Worcester and Birmingham Canal
6. Museum of Local Life
7. The Greyfriars
8. Reindeer Court Shopping Centre
9. King Charles Restaurant
10. St Swithan's Church
11. Queen Elizabeth's House
12. Church of St Nicholas
13. Guildhall
14. Statue of Sir Edward Elgar
15. St Alban's Church
16. St Andrew's Spire
17. Worcester Bridge
18. Watergate

From Edgar Tower, turn right past the King's School Tuck Shop and proceed down Severn Street. On the left, just past the junction with King Street, is the **Royal Worcester Porcelain Company (3)**. The firm was founded in 1751 by Dr John Wall and gained its first Royal Warrant in 1789 from George III. Today the company's china and porcelain are world famous, and there is much here to see.

Royal Connections

Head back towards the cathedral, turning right almost immediately along King Street, which skirts around the carpark to the road called Sidbury. Cross Sidbury with care and head for the half-timbered building known as the **Commandery (4)**. This dates largely from the 15th century and was founded as the Hospital of St Wulfstan. After the Reformation it was in the hands of the Wylde family. In more recent years it served as a college for the blind and then a printing works, before being purchased by the City Council in 1977. It now houses a museum, the Civil War Centre. The entrance is deceptively small, the museum in fact being a rambling complex of buildings with oak-panelled rooms where audio-visuals are used to tell the tale of the Civil War. The Commandery was the Royalist headquarters at the Battle of Worcester in 1651, and just outside the building was the Sidbury Gate, which was stormed by the Parliamentarian forces. The Royalists were overwhelmed and Charles II subsequently had to flee for his life to France. The Commandery has a giftshop and a popular canal-side restaurant.

Alongside the Commandery is Sidbury Bridge, which crosses the **Worcester and Birmingham Canal (5)**. One of the locks is just below the bridge. The canal was built in the 18th century and was busy with freight until the railways came onto the scene. It is 30 miles (50km) long and has five tunnels and 58 locks, which are narrow and only one gate wide.

Continue towards the city centre, forking right into Friar Street. This pedestrianized street has a wealth of ancient buildings, many half-timbered. A good example can be seen immediately on the left – the **Museum of Local Life (6)**. The building dates from the 16th century and has a post and pan and a fine jettied wall. The museum reflects the social life and history of Worcester, particularly over the last two centuries. Further along Friar Street, on the right, is another half-timbered building, **The Greyfriars (7)**, now owned by the National Trust. Built in 1480 with early-17th- and late-18th-century additions, it was rescued from demolition during World War II and has been carefully restored.

Friar Street progresses into New Street. On the left is the imaginative **Reindeer Court Shopping Centre (8)**, which has many small specialist shops and restaurants. The main entrance is through an old 16th-century coaching inn, The Reindeer, originally called The Rayned Deer. Continue along New Street until on the right you see the **King Charles II Restaurant (9)**. This and the florist's shop around the corner date from 1577 and comprise the building in which King Charles II stayed before evading Cromwell's soldiers.

You have now reached the Cornmarket, a small square which once contained the city's stocks. Turn left into Mealcheapen Street, where at the end is the plain wall of **St Swithun's Church (10)**. Now redundant, this 18th-century church is looked after by the Churches Conservation Trust. It is normally closed, but if you would like to look inside you can ask for keys at the Tourist Information Centre in the Guildhall.

Now turn right into Trinity Street. On the right is a simple half-timbered building with a large balcony, **Queen Elizabeth's House (11)**; from here Queen

Elizabeth I is reputed to have addressed the citizens of Worcester when she visited the city in 1575. At the end of Trinity Street, turn left into St Nicholas Street and then left again into The Cross. This was the point where the four main roads of the city met, a prime position – as shown by the imposing bank frontages. Also prominent here is the redundant **Church of St Nicholas (12)**, dating from the 18th century but built on the site of an earlier church. Today it has been converted into an imaginative café-bar, RSVP: the stained-glass windows and pulpit have been retained among the tables, while the font forms a flower-covered centrepiece. This place is proving a popular watering hole.

A Many-Faceted City
Wander down the pedestrianized High Street. On the right is the impressive frontage of the Queen Anne-style **Guildhall (13)**. Dating from 1724, with major renovations in 1870, this was the site of the City Assizes for over two centuries. You are free to look around and perhaps take tea in the first-floor Assembly Room. Note the exterior, showing the city's coat-of-arms, with the motto 'City Faithful in War and Peace' – you'll recall that Worcester supported the Royalists during the Civil War. The statues of Charles I and Charles II can be seen on either side of the main door. The Guildhall is also the site of the helpful Tourist Information Centre.

Continue to the end of the High Street, marked by the **Statue of Sir Edward Elgar (14)**. Facing the cathedral, the statue was unveiled by Prince Charles in 1981. Elgar spent much of his childhood in the family music shop, marked by a blue plaque on the wall just a few yards from the statue. Regarded as one of the great English composers, Elgar was also an organist, violinist and teacher. Although a Roman Catholic, he had many connections with the cathedral and was closely associated with the Three Choirs Festival. His birthplace, at Lower Broadheath, some three miles (5km) from the centre of Worcester, is open to the public.

Turn right into Deansway and walk down to the junction with Copenhagen Street. Look across the road to the modern college, sandwiched between two churches. On the left is the minute **St Alban's Church (15)**, built of pink sandstone and dating from the 12th century. It has joined the ranks of Worcester's many redundant churches and today is a day-care centre for the homeless. On the right is the 246ft (75m) **St Andrew's Spire (16)**, all that remains of the church of the same name, which was demolished in 1940. Known during the prime of the Worcester glove industry as 'The Glover's Needle', the spire is surrounded by attractive gardens.

Cross Deansway by the pedestrian crossing and walk down Copenhagen Street to the River Severn. Turn right along South Parade to **Worcester Bridge (17)**. There has been a bridge here since 1313. The present structure was built in 1781 and widened in the 1930s. Worcestershire County Cricket Ground lies just beyond the bridge, and the racecourse is a few hundred yards upstream. From here you get magnificent views of the cathedral.

Return along South Parade to the riverside thoroughfare called Kleve Walk, after one of Worcester's twinned towns. Follow Kleve Walk for about two hundred yards until you reach the **Watergate (18)**, which was the westerly entrance to the monastery and the traditional landing-point for the ferry across the River Severn; the ferrymen lived in the house above the gate. Note the wall on the right, which has a series of plaques showing the height the river has reached at various times. The Severn carries away most of the rain that falls on the highlands of Central Wales and is thus prone to flooding – flood waters have even stopped play at the cricket ground!

Pass through the Watergate. The path straight ahead up the hill takes you directly back to College Green, but for a more interesting route to the cathedral turn left and head through the gardens towards some ruins. These turn out to be the reredorter, the drainage conduit from the monks' toilets in the old dormitory (dorter). Climb the steps past the west window of the cathedral, with its rose window, and proceed along the north side of the building to the North Door, where the tour ends.

Courtyard of the Commandery Museum

Coventry

Access: The M6 motorway runs just to the north of the city, giving easy connections to the M5, the M42, the M69, the M1 and the M54. Coach services use these routes for speedy links with many parts of the country. Coventry is also on one of the busiest railway lines in England. The nearest international airports are at Birmingham, ten miles (16km) to the west, and East Midlands, at Castle Donnington, 45 miles (60km) to the northeast. There is also a canal basin close to the city centre, although the waterway is now almost entirely confined to leisure traffic. Coventry has a park-and-ride system. There are plenty of carparks between the inner ring road and the city centre, and visitors to the cathedral will not find parking a problem.

There is no archaeological evidence of Roman occupation in the area which is now central Coventry. It is known that Saint Osburga founded a nunnery here some time in the 7th century; this was destroyed in 1016, when Mercia was in revolt against King Canute (c995–1035). In 1043 Edward the Confessor granted a charter to Earl Leofric (d1057) and his wife Godiva (c1040–1080) to set up a Benedictine monastery at Coventry – this is the Godiva whom legend says rode naked through the streets in an attempt to save the citizens from unfair taxation. The priory flourished and, as was often the case in those days, a settlement grew around it. After the Conquest the Norman earls of Chester played an important part in encouraging the growth of the town. They built a motte and bailey castle in the late 11th century, later demolishing it to accommodate a new street plan. The monks, meanwhile, having built their priory and church, constructed two parish churches for the townsfolk: Holy Trinity Church was completed in 1113 and St Michael's Parish Church in 1145. The three church spires were to be the town's most notable landmarks for centuries. At the end of the 11th century, the priory church was designated a cathedral and the diocese of Coventry and Lichfield set up.

Over the next three centuries Coventry's prosperity was based on the textile industry, particularly wool-making, with leather- and glassmaking also important. By the mid-14th century it was the fourth largest town in England (after London, Bristol and York), and the rich merchants constructed some magnificent houses, a few of which remain today, plus the superb St Mary's Guildhall (1342). It was during this period that St Michael's Parish Church was rebuilt in Perpendicular style.

This prosperity did not last. The wool trade was already declining when Henry VIII dissolved the priory in 1538. The monastic buildings went into private hands before gradually falling into decay as the stonework was removed for other building projects. The see of Coventry and Lichfield was transferred at this time to Lichfield.

After the lean years, Coventry's second period of economic growth came with the Industrial Revolution. Progress was led by the watch- and clockmaking industry, which employed over 2000 people and set the town on the way to becoming a notable centre of engineering. The manufacture of cycles was followed by that of motorbikes and then, as the 20th century evolved, the making of cars. An important landmark was 1918, when the diocese of Coventry was founded, with St Michael's Parish Church becoming the city's second cathedral.

The two World Wars saw Coventry's factories making planes, vehicles and munitions, work which attracted people from far and wide and doubled the city's population. Coventry's factories, however, were a prime target for German bombers during World War II, and St Michael's Cathedral was to suffer too. On the night of November 14 1941, Luftwaffe bombs destroyed much of Coventry's city centre; 568 lives were lost and there were hundreds of injuries. The cathedral suffered several direct hits and the wooden roof soon fell. The local fire brigade could not cope, and the cathedral officials were reduced to saving what valuable artefacts they could. Remarkably, the tower and spire remained unscathed among the ruins, along with the nave walls, crypt and south porch.

The following day it was agreed that the cathedral would be rebuilt. Sir Giles Gilbert Scott submitted designs, but it was soon realized that it would be too expensive to renovate the existing building. A competition was held to design a new cathedral, and 219 plans were submitted. The winner, although his nontraditional design was not universally popular, was Basil Spence (1907–1976), then a little-known architect, Work began on the new cathedral in 1955 and the foundation stone was laid by Queen Elizabeth II a year later.

In May 1962, in the presence of the Queen, the new Coventry Cathedral was consecrated. A Visitor Centre was opened in 1984; here high-technology audiovisual material tells the story of Coventry, concentrating on the theme of reconciliation. The cathedral celebrated its Silver Jubilee in 1987.

TOUR OF THE CATHEDRALS
Start (old cathedral): St Michael's Porch.
Finish (old cathedral): The north door.
Start (new cathedral): Priory Street by St Michael's Steps.
Finish (new cathedral): Exit door in southwest corner.

Before touring the two buildings, it is crucial to understand the rationale behind Spence's design for the new cathedral. His approach was always to consider the ruins of the old cathedral and the new cathedral as a single entity, with St Michael's Porch providing the physical link: the old building would signify crucifixion and sacrifice, the new cathedral resurrection. The common theme throughout is reconciliation.

The Old Cathedral
Though razed in 1940, the old cathedral, remains consecrated ground and, indeed, services still take place in the crypt chapels and at the Altar of Reconciliation. The ruins form a shell of pink sandstone walls with Perpendicular windows that lack, of course, their glass. The nave pillars are mere stumps, interspersed with seats. The tower, with its tall spire, has remarkably remained intact.

Enter the ruins from the north door via St Michael's Porch and what are known as the Queen's Steps. Turn right and note the plaque on the wall telling something of the history of the building. One fascinating point here is that the iron struts introduced to strengthen the tie beams of the wooden roof twisted in the heat of the fire

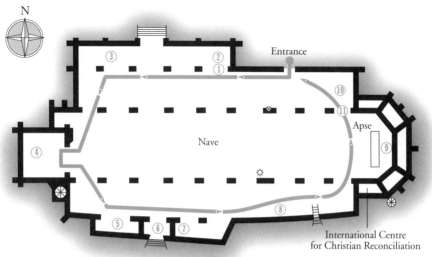

Key

1. Statue of Reconciliation
2. Girdlers' Chapel
3. Smiths' Chapel
4. Tower
5. Dyers' Chapel

6. Bishop Haigh's Memorial
   Chapel
7. Cappers' Room
8. Ecce Homo
9. Altar of Reconciliation

10. Drapers' Chapel
11. Effigy of Bishop Yeatman-Biggs

caused by the incendiary bombs and were responsible for bringing down much of the upper masonry. Further on the right is the **Statue of Reconciliation (1)** by Josefina de Vasconcellos, showing two kneeling figures. It was made by the artist when she was 90 and given to the cathedral by Richard Branson in 1995 to mark the 50th anniversary of the end of World War II.

You then come to the first of numerous guild chapels around the nave aisles; they show the strength of the woollen craft industries in the city in the 1300s and 1400s. The chapels were primarily chantries where masses were sung for deceased members, but were used also as meeting places for the conduct of the guilds' affairs. They had private entrances and were not open to the public. The guilds paid for chantry priests; in 1522 there were six of these. By the end of the 16th century, however, the guild chapels and all their possessions had passed to the city authorities. The chapels are marked by 'hallowing places' depicted on engraved plaques. Immediately behind the Statue of Reconciliation is the **Girdlers' Chapel (2)**, and this is followed shortly afterwards by the remains of the **Smiths' Chapel (3)**.

Step across to the **Tower (4)**, built between 1373 and 1394. The spire, added in 1433, is at 294ft (90m) the third highest in England (after Salisbury and Norwich). Built on unstable ground, the tower was in bad shape by the time it was comprehensively restored in 1895, using red sandstone from the Runcorn quarries. The spire, one of three to grace the central Coventry skyline over the centuries, would have been immediately recognizable by the four flying arches at the junction of spire and tower. Also distinctive are the statues of the Botoner family, generous 14th-century benefactors. The tower's twelve bells were rehung in 1987 to celebrate the cathedral's Silver Jubilee, and were rung for the first time when Coventry City won the FA Cup Final. It is possible to climb the tower for marvellous views over the city, but be warned: there are 180 steps, and they're steep.

Now proceed along the south side of the ruins. First you find the **Dyers' Chapel (5)**, which still contains one rather decrepit monument. Next is the enclosed **Bishop Haigh's Memorial Chapel (6)**, claimed to be one of the oldest parts of the building and named after the bishop at the time of the destruction; it is known also as the Chapel of Resurrection. Above Bishop Haigh's Chapel is the **Cappers' Room (7)**, the only above-ground guild chapel to have survived. It is still used for meetings.

Further along the south side is the *Ecce Homo* **(8)**, a statue carved by Sir Jacob Epstein (1880–1959) in 1934–5 from a block of Subiaco marble. It was presented to the cathedral by Lady Epstein in 1969. The *Ecce Homo* represents Christ on trial before Pilate, with his hands bound and the crown of thorns on his head.

You now approach the sanctuary and the east end of the ruins. In the southeast corner is the place where the old organ used to be, and just past here is the International Centre for Christian Reconciliation. The east end is in the form of an apse, with fine Perpendicular windows. In its centre is the **Altar of Reconciliation (9)**, topped by the Charred Cross. When the cathedral burned in 1940, two of the roof beams fell in the form of a cross. An altar was hastily built from broken masonry and the charred cross placed upon it. The carved words 'Father Forgive' form an important part of the Coventry Litany of Reconciliation, a prayer based on the Seven Deadly Sins.

Turn back now to the south side to the last guild chapel, the **Drapers' Chapel (10)**. The feature here is the bronze **Effigy of Bishop Yeatman–Biggs (11)**; he was bishop when the See of Coventry was revived in 1918. The swastika on his mitre reminds us that this was a symbol of good luck long before the Nazis adopted it.

Leave the ruins through the north door. You can either go straight on to the new cathedral or go round the ruins anticlockwise via Cuckoo Lane and Bayley Lane to Priory Street, and start the second part of the walk from there.

THE NEW CATHEDRAL

Bear in mind that the new building is aligned north–south, instead of the traditional east–west, so the normal directional terms used in other cathedrals do not apply. All the features described have a symbolism and meaning, and the theme of reconciliation is continued from the old building.

From Priory Street, with the university to your east, approach the main entrance by climbing St Michael's Steps. This is a good position to appreciate the exterior of the building, which is predominantly constructed of pink Hollington Sandstone with, in places, a contrast provided by blue-green Lakeland Stone. On the right of the steps is the huge bronze **Sculpture of St Michael and the Devil (12)**, the last of Epstein's religious works. The sculpture suggests that good will always triumph over spiritual guilt and evil.

Climb the steps to St Michael's Porch. Pause to look at the south end of the cathedral, which is in reality a **Glass Screen (13)**, the work of John Hutton (b1906). In many of the panels the glass has been incised with figures of angels, apostles, saints, prophets and patriarchs. As well as providing a link between the old and new cathedrals, the screen allows a view through to the nave, showing that the building is open to the world rather than cut off from the wider community.

Step into the building, noting the cherubs on the door handles – more of Epstein's work. At the information desk to the right the friendly staff will suggest a donation for the upkeep of the cathedral. Turn back to face the glass screen, which may well give a different impression when seen from the interior of the building, particularly if the sunlight is streaming in from the south.

Depictions of Christ

Move across to the circular **Chapel of Unity (14)** in the southwest corner. On the right of the entrance is a collage showing in pictorial form the diocese of Coventry, while opposite is a sculpture by Helen Huntingdon-Jennings of the head of the crucified Christ, made from the metal of a crashed car. Entering the chapel, you are immediately struck by the mosaic floor, which shows the continents and the symbols of the four gospels; designed by Einar Forseth, it was a gift from the people of Sweden. There is a simple central glass altar, below which a dove can be seen in the mosaic. Above the altar is a tall cross, painted black to reflect the fact that the 'church' is still not united. The narrow windows were designed by Margaret Traherne and given by German Christians.

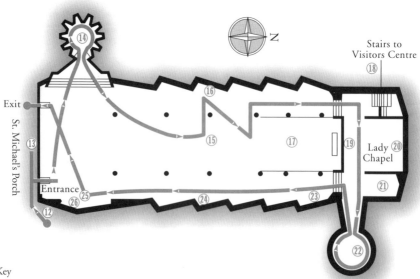

Key

12. Sculpture of St Michael and the Devil
13. Glass Screen
14. Chapel of Unity
15. Nave
16. Tablets of the Word

17. Chancel
18. Visitors Centre
19. High Altar
20. Sutherland's Tapestry of Christ
21. Chapel of Christ in Gethsemane

22. Chapel of Christ the Servant
23. The Plumb Line and the City
24. Nave Windows
25. Font
26. Baptistry Window

Walk back into the **Nave (15)**. This is a good spot to take a long-distance view of the Sutherland tapestry, which will be examined more closely later. As you look north, the zigzag roughcast walls and the slim concrete pillars give an impression of height, but in fact the walls are a mere 70ft (22m) high. The south-facing lower parts of the walls are distinguished by eight **Tablets of the Word (16)**. They contain New Testament texts and were inscribed by Ralph Beyer in uneven lettering to emphasize that they are the work of man, rather than machine, and that man is still dependent on the primitive truths of the church.

Move along the nave to the **Chancel (17)**. The stalls for the canons and choir have a canopy of spikes, resembling thorns or birds in flight, which tower up above the Provost's stall and the bishop's *cathedra*. Note, too, the modern organ console. In front of the stalls are the pulpit and lectern, designed by Basil Spence. Both the eagle on the lectern and the crucifix on the pulpit are the work of Dame Elisabeth Frink (1930-1994).

Walk to the left (north) side of the chancel to find a wooden Norwegian organ, a gift to the Coventry Song School. Ahead, steps lead down to the **Visitor Centre (18)** in the

Geoffrey Clarke's High Altar Cross

undercroft. The complex also includes the Song School, lecture hall, broadcasting studio, restaurant and shop. The Visitor Centre opened in 1984 and uses high technology in its audiovisual presentation to tell the story of Coventry Cathedral.

From the top of the Visitor Centre steps, turn right behind the **High Altar (19)**. A simple concrete affair, the altar is flanked by six tall pottery candles, while surmounting it is Geoffrey Clarke's abstract cross. Made of gilded silver, it contains in its centre the original cross of nails from the old cathedral.

Turn now in the opposite direction, towards the Lady Chapel, to view **Sutherland's Tapestry of Christ (20)**. This is a neck-craning exercise, because the tapestry, which replaces the traditional east window, measures 74ft (23m) by 38ft (12m). Designed by Graham Sutherland (1903–1980), it was made in France by Pinton Frères and paid for by an anonymous resident of Coventry. The tapestry shows a huge seated figure of Christ wearing a carpenter's apron. Note the normal sized human being between his feet. On either side are the four traditional symbols of the evangelists, Matthew, Mark, Luke and John, while to his right the Devil is shown being thrown down into Hell. At the base is the crucifixion scene. Sutherland's original plans and paintings of the tapestry can be seen in the undercroft and in the Herbert Art Gallery (see page 131). The tapestry dominates the cathedral and is undoubtedly its most precious asset.

Places of Strength

Move past the Lady Chapel to the delightful little **Chapel of Christ in Gethsemane (21)**. When Jesus went to the Garden of Gethsemane to pray on the night before his crucifixion he was visited by an angel, who brought him strength. Here in Coventry this chapel is today used for private prayer and meditation. The gold-and-grey mural behind the simple altar shows an angel holding the cup of suffering. The metal screen enclosing the chapel represents the crown of thorns and was made by the Royal Engineers.

Walk up the sloping corridor into the **Chapel of Christ the Servant (22)** or, as it is often known, the Chapel of Industry. This circular chapel, designed by Basil Spence, has clear glass windows through which you can see many of the buildings of central Coventry; the idea is that the cathedral is part of the wider city community and that worship and life in general are closely entwined. In the centre of the chapel is a stone base bearing the words 'I AM AMONG YOU AS ONE THAT SERVES', and above this is an oak altar table inlaid with boxwood. Both were the work of apprentices at the city's technology college. Rising above the altar is a white aluminium cross enveloped by a crown of thorns made by Geoffrey Clarke.

Return now to the nave. Immediately on the left is a sculpture entitled *The Plumb Line and the City* **(23)**, made in 1971 by Clarke FitzGerald from Cincinatti. Composed of a collage of metal items, the 'city' contains factories, churches, schools, office blocks, cars, etc. The symbolism of the plumb line, based on *Amos* 7:8, poses the question: are the inhabitants of the city upright or not?

From this point you can view the **Nave Windows (24)**, not visible when you were walking in the opposite direction. There are five windows on each side of the nave. Their modern stained glass – by Lawrence Lee, Keith New and Geoffrey Clarke – depicts human life through the stages of Birth, Youth, Maturity, Old Age and Resurrection. The windows are 70ft (22m) high. Their angled south-facing position ensures maximum light and they look quite stunning on days when the sun is streaming through.

Walk finally to the southeast corner of the cathedral. Backed by the baptistry window, the **Font (25)** is a rough three-ton boulder from the Valley of Barakat, near Bethlehem. A scallop-shaped basin has been hollowed out on the top. The whole thing is mounted on a black marble base. Behind the font is the massive, curved **Baptistry Window (26)**, designed by John Piper (1903–1992) and made by Patrick Reyntiens. The window, 81ft (24.6m) high and 51ft (15.5m) across and stretching from floor to ceiling, contains 195 panels of brilliantly coloured glass, mainly deep blue and red on the outside and merging to a sunburst of white and yellow in the centre. The symbolism is of baptism. This is regarded by experts as possibly the greatest stained-glass window in the country.

Leave the cathedral by the exit door in the southwest corner.

WALKING TOUR FROM THE CATHEDRALS

Unfortunately, much of the historic core of Coventry was destroyed in the Blitz, but enough remains to offer an interesting walk. This short circular tour includes historic features such as the remains of the priory, some fine Elizabethan houses, a medieval guildhall and some remnants of the city walls, with gates at each end, plus one of the most interesting parish churches in the country. There are two museums to see – the Herbert Art Gallery and Museum and the superb Museum of British Road Transport. The tour ends at the Tourist Information Office, under which is the city's only medieval vaulted cellar open to the public.

Start: St Michael's Porch, between the old and new cathedrals.
Finish: The Tourist Information Centre in Priory Street.
Length: 1½ miles (2km).
Time: Under 1hr, but allow considerably more time if visiting the Transport Museum, the Herbert Gallery and Holy Trinity Church.
Refreshments: Benedict's Coffee Shop in the cathedral's Visitor Centre is worth a visit. Of the numerous pubs in the city centre along the walking route, few can be recommended for lunch apart from the old half-timbered Golden Cross on the corner of Hay Lane and, opposite, the modern Newt and Cucumber.

Leave St Michael's Porch, which links the two cathedrals, and head northwest past the circular exterior of the Chapel of Unity to the end of **Priory Row (1)**, where there is a range of domestic buildings from various architectural periods. No 11, the Provost's House (or Gorton House), is an early-18th-century town house with a brick frontage and pillars in the Ionic style. It was severely damaged during World War II but has been faithfully restored. Nos 9–10, today part of the Coventry International Studies Centre, are early-

16th century houses, Priory Row

127

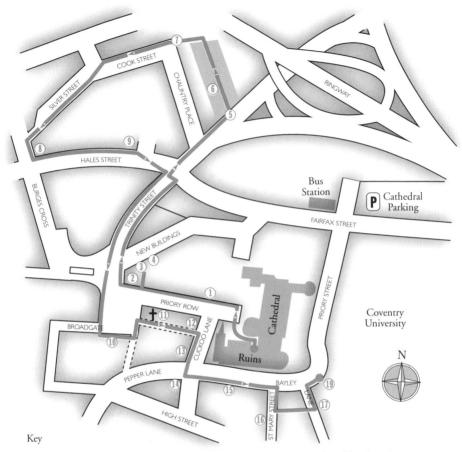

Key

1. Priory Row
2. 3-5 Priory Row
3. Blue Coat School
4. New Buildings
5. Swanswell Gate
6. Lady Herbert's Garden
7. Cook Street Gate
8. Hospital of St John the Baptist
9. Museum of British Road Transport
10. Statue of Lady Godiva
11. Holy Trinity Church
12. Coventry Cross
13. County Hall
14. Golden Cross Inn
15. St Mary's Hall
16. Council House
17. Herbert Art Gallery and Museum
18. Drapers' Hall
19. Tourist Information Office

19th-century town houses; their cellars are possibly part of the priory foundations and are some 30ft (9m) below the present street level. No 7, now the office of the Friends of Coventry Cathedral, was built around 1800; John Gulson, a mayor of the town and a public benefactor, lived here between 1835 and 1904.

Walk to the end of Priory Row. Just before the half-timbered house, an alleyway leads to the right. Beneath the railings, there is an excellent view of the foundations of what is believed to be west front of the Benedictine Priory Church built by Leofric and Godiva, and this Saxon couple are thought to be buried nearby. Excavations have shown that the east end of the church was near the present-day cathedral Visitor Centre, so the building would have been larger than either Holy Trinity, St Michael's or the modern cathedral. The priory was demolished during the Reformation, although the central tower remained. On the other side of Priory Row you can view the exterior of Holy Trinity Church, the red sandstone of the tower contrasting with the cream limestone of the nave.

You now reach **3–5 Priory Row (2)**, a collection of half-timbered buildings dating from the late 16th or early 17th century. They form one of only three surviving double-jettied buildings in the city. The alleyway to the right, parallel with the foundations, leads to the **Blue Coat School (3)**, opened as a charity school in 1714 and rebuilt on the same site in 1856–7 in the style of a French château. It was during these 19th-century renovations that the foundations of the priory were discovered. The Blue Coat School closed in 1940.

Quiet Places

Return to Priory Row. Turn right and right again into Trinity Street. Shortly on the right are the **New Buildings (4)**, a four-storey industrial site dating from 1849–50 and originally a steam-powered ribbonmaking factory. When this industry declined, John Gulson bought the building, which thereafter had a number of uses, including being used as a `Ragged School' for poor children.

Cross Trinity Street at the traffic lights and head towards the Art Deco Hippodrome with its peeling paintwork. Cross Hales Street and, shortly along on the left, come to the only surviving stretch of the city's medieval walls, largely demolished in the 1660s on the orders of Charles II. At the southern end of the wall is the pink sandstone **Swanswell Gate (5)**, believed to date from the mid-15th century and probably the main gate into St Mary's Priory – it led in the other direction to the priory's fishpools. In the early years of the 20th century the gate was used as a residence, but in 1931 it was given to the city by Sir Alfred Herbert, a wealthy local industrialist, and carefully restored the following year.

Turn under the arch of the gate and enter **Lady Herbert's Garden (6)**. This was created in the 1930s as a memorial to Lady Herbert, Sir Alfred's second wife. With a pond and some exotic shrubs, it makes a peaceful change from the hustle and bustle of the city centre. Follow the right-hand path parallel to the old city wall until, at the top of the gardens, you reach **Cook Street Gate (7)**, a second survivor of the original twelve town gates. Believed to have been completed around 1385, it was largely derelict during the 19th century. It was given to the city in 1913 by Colonel W.F. Wyley, a local mayor and alderman, and restored after the end of World War I. A scheduled ancient monument, it still has road traffic running under it.

Pass through the gateway and walk down Cook Street and via Silver Street to Bishop Street. Turn left here and, on the corner of Hales Street, you find the **Hospital of St John the Baptist (8)**. This was founded in 1340, and its buildings once extended across what is now Hales Street. All that remains today is the 14th-century church that replaced the hospital's original chapel. The hospital was dissolved, along with monasteries, in the mid-16th century. In 1557 the building was converted into a `Free Grammar School', which remained here until Victorian times, when it moved to Warwick Road; it is now known somewhat ironically as the Henry VIII School.

Road Transport

Continue along Hales Street until you see, on the left on the corner of St Agnes Lane, the **Museum of British Road Transport (9)**. Don't be put off by the rather unprepossessing exterior: this is a wonderland of cycles, motorbikes, cars and commercial vehicles, from 'penny farthings' to Thrust, the holder of the world land-speed record. The amazing thing is that the vast majority of the exhibits were built in the Coventry area, a fact that brings home to you the former importance of the city's engineering and metalworking trades. There are also mock-ups of Victorian shops and a rather alarming 'experience' of what it was like to be in the Coventry Blitz.

Leave the museum and turn right, back up Trinity Street, into the modern town centre, rebuilt after the wartime destruction. Carry on into Broadgate, where you will see the huge canopy covering the **Statue of Lady Godiva (10)**. Legend has it that Lady Godiva rode naked through the streets of Coventry in protest at the taxes her husband Leofric had imposed on the townspeople. Most averted their eyes but, of course, not Peeping Tom. The bronze statue, the work of Sir William Reid Dick (1879–1961), was unveiled in 1949.

Church and Tavern

Leave the modern Broadgate and go back to **Holy Trinity Church (11)**. This is one of the most interesting parish churches in the country. A church stood on this site as early as 1113, built by the Benedictine monks for their tenants, but this was destroyed by fire in 1250. The oldest part of the present building is the 13th-century north porch. There is a priest's room above the door, which was probably the main exit to the priory. In the Middle Ages the church had fifteen chapels; few of these remain, although the Tanners' Chapel on the north side has a medieval piscina. The south side of the nave has some stone seats (for the weakest to go to the wall). Holy Trinity has some interesting stained glass, both old and modern; there is some particularly good modern glass in the Great West Window by Hugh Easton. Other items of interest include the pulpit, dating from *c*1470 (the foliage beneath contains carved heads of, possibly, Henry VI and Queen Margaret of Anjou), the eagle lectern and the font (both 15th-century).

Exit from Holy Trinity and go along the alleyway called Trinity Churchyard to the right of the building. At the end is the **Coventry Cross (12)**. The present cross is a replica of the original, erected in 1541 in Broadgate but demolished in the 18th century. With four tiers and surrounded by a flight of four steps, the new cross was unveiled in 1976.

Turn right at the cross and go along the short Cuckoo Lane. Immediately on the right is the old **County Hall (13)**, a solid stone building in Classical style built in the 18th century and probably the city's only public building of this period to survive. Its rear was once the town gaol. The last public execution in Coventry took place in the street outside County Hall in 1849.

Next on the right is the **Golden Cross Inn (14)**, a 15th-century half-timbered building with double-jettied walls. It was comprehensively restored in the 19th century. Inside it there is a dragon beam in the ground-floor ceiling. Turn left past the modern Newt and Cucumber pub into Bayley Lane, believed to have been named after the motte and bailey of the Earl of Chester's castle, pulled down in the mid-

12th century; the lane probably ran along the side of the castle's ditch. On the left are the walls of the ruined second cathedral, while on the right are a series of ancient buildings: first is a half-timbered house with jettied walls on brick foundations, probably dating from *c*1500. Note the elaborate carving on the beams.

Civic Buildings

You now come to **St Mary's Guildhall (15)**, on your right, justifiably claimed to be one of the finest medieval guildhalls in the country. It was built *c*1340 and probably included parts of a 12th-century castle in the south wall. Built for the Trinity guild, it in due course became the first seat of local government in the town. At first-floor level is the stunning Great Hall, which has a late-14th-century wooden roof. Below is a large vaulted undercroft. Set in the walls is a tower in which, it is claimed, Mary Queen of Scots was once imprisoned.

Now turn right along the narrow St Mary's Street. On the right is the **Council House (16)**, with its main frontage on the High Street. It was built 1913–17 and few would consider it an architectural gem; its main point of interest is the clock tower on the corner, featuring a number of statues including portrayals of Leofric and Godiva.

Halfway along St Mary's Street, turn left through some small gardens that contain an outdoor exhibition showing the history of the Bayley Lane area from the 11th century to the present. This part of the city was the centre of the wool industry, and many of the wealthy merchants, particularly drapers, had their homes here. Coventry cloth was famous for both its quality and its colour – a blue dye which never faded (hence the term 'true blue'). Later, when the woollen industry declined, so did the Bayley Street area. Much of it was destroyed during World War II.

Cross the road to the **Herbert Art Gallery and Museum (17)**. Named after Sir Alfred Herbert, the museum opened in 1959. Many of its exhibits relate to the Coventry area and include the drawings for Sutherland's cathedral tapestry. The gallery has works by L.S. Lowry (1887–1976) and Henry Moore (1898–1986).

Opposite the museum is the **Drapers' Hall (18)**, the headquarters for centuries of the Drapers' Guild. The present building, probably the third on the site, can hardly be called distinguished. It was built in 1832 and has a Greek Revival stone frontage, whose symmetry has been ruined by later alterations. The arms of the Drapers' Company can be seen over the upper corners. The rest of the exterior of the hall is of dull Midlands brick.

On the same side of the road as the museum is a Peace Garden, opened in 1990 on the 50th anniversary of the Blitz which destroyed the cathedral. The main feature is a Peace Stone, which has lines pointing to Coventry's twin towns (there are 28 of them!).

Nearby is our last port of call, the **Tourist Information Office (19)**, located in a modern building (opened 1990) erected over a 14th-century vaulted cellar, which is open to the public and can be reached down a flight of steps. The cellar measures 22ft (6.7m) long and 11½ft (3.5m) wide, in two nearly square bays. The ceiling has simple groyne ribs in the local red sandstone. In one of the bays is a display case showing some of the artefacts found during excavations, including cowhorns, clay pipes, ceramics and tiles.

Return to street level, where, opposite the cathedral, the tour concludes.

Lichfield

Access: The A38 and A5 trunk roads link the city to the Midlands motorway network, including the M42, M40, M6 and M1. Lichfield is fortunate in having two railway stations: trains from London Euston call at Lichfield Trent Valley, while trains from Birmingham run to both this station and Lichfield City. The nearest airports are Birmingham International and East Midlands, both within a 45min drive.

Archaeological evidence suggests there were settlements in the area in prehistoric and Celtic times. Later, during the Roman occupation of Britain, two roads crossed some two miles (3km) southwest of the present city: Ryknild Street (the present A38) and Watling Street (the present A5). At this point the Romans built a posting station, known as Letocetum ('Wall Village'), which became a military base. The site has been excavated to reveal the remains of a fort, baths, granary and an inn.

The story of Lichfield Cathedral begins with St Chad (d672). He was a pupil of St Aidan at Lindisfarne before being appointed Bishop of Mercia in 669. He immediately moved the see from Repton to Lichfield, where there was already a small church called St Mary's. Chad was not to last long in the post, however: he died three years later, being initially buried near St Mary's Church. Pilgrims flocked to his grave after miracles were reported. A new cathedral of St Peter was built to house his shrine, while pilgrims also visited St Chad's Well, about half a mile to the east.

The Saxon church was quickly replaced after the Conquest by a new cathedral in Norman style. Begun in 1085, the building was further expanded in the 12th century under the leadership of Bishop de Clinton, who was to die during the Second Crusade in 1148. The Norman cathedral must have been unsatisfactory, because in 1195, work began to replace by a new building in Gothic style; nothing remains of the Norman cathedral except a few foundations discovered during excavations in the area of the present-day choir, but, almost certainly, St Chad's Shrine would have been placed behind the high altar. The transepts (in Early English style) of its replacement and St Chad's Head Chapel were completed by 1240 and the chapter house nine years later. Then came the nave, in Geometric Decorated Gothic, and by 1327 the west front was finished. The Lady Chapel followed between 1330 and 1340, so that by the end of the 14th century the cathedral was more or less complete. This was to be the Golden Age of Lichfield Cathedral, and the town itself became an important ecclesiastic centre. The cathedral and its close had been surrounded by sturdy sandstone walls in Bishop de Clinton's time, but this was not to work in the cathedral's favour in the centuries to come.

Always a secular establishment never attached to a monastery, Lichfield survived the Reformation relatively well. However, it did not escape unscathed, as Henry VIII's commissioners destroyed the Shrine of St Chad and removed the relics along with other treasures. Many statues were smashed, although structurally the fabric survived.

During the Civil War Lichfield suffered more than any other English cathedral. The sandstone walls and sturdy gates made the close an ideal fortress, and it was soon occupied by Royalist forces. However, in March 1643 the Roundheads, despite the death of their leader Lord Brooke (1611–1643), took the close. It was recovered by the Royalists one month later, Prince Rupert (1619–1682) firing cannons from the mound to the north of the cathedral. In 1643, it was taken back by the Roundheads, whose soldiers wreaked havoc in the cathedral, smashing statues, looting tombs and defacing monuments. There was very little stained glass left intact and the central spire had already been felled by cannonballs.

After things had quietened down with the Restoration, Bishop Hackett (d1669) set about rebuilding the spire and patching up the rest of the damage. For two centuries, nevertheless, Lichfield Cathedral was a pale shadow of its former greatness. In 1788 James Wyatt (1746–1813) began alterations: admittedly he saved the nave from falling down by removing much of the heavy vaulting and replacing it with lighter plaster, but many of his renovations and changes can in retrospect be considered nothing but disastrous. His most appalling alteration was to block up the arches of the choir aisles to create what has been described as a 'church within a church'.

The city of Lichfield, meanwhile, had become a thriving place. Its citizens of the time included the writer and lexicographer Samuel Johnson (1709–1784), the actor David Garrick (1717–1779) and the inventor Erasmus Darwin (1731–1802).

By the 19th century the Industrial Revolution was well under way. Despite coal deposits in the nearby South Staffordshire coalfield, Lichfield did not become a place of heavy industry like many of its neighbours – rather, it maintained its position as a prosperous market town and ecclesiastic centre. The middle part of the century saw the start of Sir George Gilbert Scott's restorations to the cathedral. Many Victorian renovations to English cathedrals are regarded as little more than vandalism, but Scott's work at Lichfield was done sympathetically and went a long way towards returning the cathedral to its medieval splendour. He redeemed Wyatt's insensitive work in the choir, which he provided with a colourful Minton tiled floor and an attractive metal screen linking it to the nave; he also restored the statues on the west front and St Chad's Head Chapel in the south aisle. Although the Victorian glass is not particularly distinguished, the early years of the century saw the introduction to the Lady Chapel of superb 16th-century stained glass from the suppressed convent of Herckenrode in Belgium. In the Close, the episcopal palace at last had a bishop in residence. George Selwyn (in office 1867–78) extended the building, and it is now the choir school.

Lichfield and its cathedral were largely unscathed during the two world wars, and today the cathedral has resumed its medieval role as a meeting place and venue for the local community. Foremost is the annual July International Festival of music, drama and entertainment. The building is in good shape thanks to a rolling maintenance programme.

TOUR OF THE CATHEDRAL
Start: The Cathedral Close.
Finish: The west end.

The **West Front (1)** is best viewed from halfway across the Cathedral Close. From here you can see the three spires (the main central spire and the two western ones), collectively known as the Ladies of the Vale. The stonework on the west front is the same as on the rest of the building – pink sandstone to which a residue of industrial pollution gives a curious mottled effect.

You will be immediately struck by the large number of statues on the west front: there are over a hundred, all but three being Victorian replacements. Central, high above the main door, is Jesus; this figure replaced that of Charles II, now found by the south transept door. The other statues, found in five rows, represent Saxon and Norman kings, early bishops, apostles and missionaries. The middle row includes a statue of Queen Victoria sculpted by her daughter Princess Louise. Artistically the statues have little merit – Alec Clifton Taylor observed in connection with the identical fussy little curls on each statue that they might pass as 'an advertisement for a local hairdresser'.

The architecture is more interesting. The two spires merge via heavily crocketed ornamentation into the towers, which in turn lose their identity within the five ranks of statues. The central window at the third level is in Geometrical Decorated style, a pattern repeated around the ground-level doors. A curious feature is the way the horizontal layers 'wrap around' the side of the west front; this in fact helps relieve the general flatness of this part of the building.

Enter the cathedral through the southwest door. Proceed into the **Nave (2)**. This is short, with only seven bays, and low – a mere 57ft (17.4m) from floor to vault – but the proportions are very satisfying. The arcade takes up 50 per cent of the height, with the rest being equally divided between the triforium and the clerestory. The vaulting, mainly in wood and plaster, is of the tierceron type. The style throughout the nave is Geometric Decorated. Of particular interest are the thin triple-attached shafts that sweep right up from floor to vault, taking the eye to the unique triforium windows. These are in the form of curved triangles containing three circles filled with a trefoil. They look equally effective on the outside of the building. The trefoil pattern is repeated in the spandrels of the arcade. Note, too, the well carved oak-leaved capitals on the arcade's main pillars (which lean inwards rather alarmingly). Looking back to the west end, you can see the modern gallery, built by the Friends of Lichfield Cathedral.

Move over to the **North Aisle (3)**. Here there is blind arcading and, below that, stone seating where, in the days when the congregation stood in the nave, 'the weakest went to the wall'. Here also we see the first of many monuments in the cathedral – in this case brass wall plaques in memory of those who fell while serving in the South Staffordshire Regiment.

Walk ahead to the **Crossing (4)**, beneath the central tower. Dominating this area is the unusual choir screen: made of metal, it is painted and gilded. It was designed by Francis Skidmore (1816–1896) and erected during Sir George Gilbert Scott's renovations. The screen is complemented by the pulpit, made of similar materials.

Cross to the **North Transept (5)**, which is regrettably often used as a storage space. Of various undistinguished monuments here the most important is in the northwest corner: the remains of the 15th-century stone monument to Dean Haywood, which was smashed during the Civil War. Also in the transept is the 19th-century marble font, carved with biblical scenes. On the north side of the transept is the St Stephen's Chapel, which has a number of memorial tablets to former organists.

The Lichfield Gospels

Proceed now into the north choir aisle and turn left into a **Vestibule (6)** which leads to the chapter house. The vestibule has finely carved double arcading, below which is a medieval pedilavium, where feet were washed. Note, too, the vaulting, with stone infilling and impressive bosses. At the far end of the vestibule is a modern memorial bust of Bishop Edward Woods (1877–1953) by Jacob Epstein (1880–1959).

The **Chapter House (7)** dates from 1249 and is an elongated octagon vaulted from a central pier. The architecture is Early English. Note the stained glass in Kempe's window showing the life of St Chad. The main interest here, however, is the display on the Lichfield Gospels. Probably dating from around 730, they spent some time in Wales, but have been at Lichfield since the 10th century. Remarkably, they survived the desecrations of the Civil War, when they were protected by the Duchess of Somerset. The illuminated Gospels are written in Latin; there were once all four gospels, but only *Matthew, Mark* and part of *Luke* remain. Outstanding is the marvellous `carpet page', whose design is based on the cross. The style is similar to that of the Lindisfarne Gospels and the Book of Kells at Trinity College, Dublin. The pages of the Gospels are made of vellum. The scribe's name is not known, but he was almost certainly a monk who devoted his life to the project.

The cathedral library, above the chapter house, is not normally open to the public.

The Retrochoir and Lady Chapel

Return via the vestibule to the main body of the cathedral and proceed along the north choir aisle. At the far end are memorials to the 19th-century bishops Lonsdale and Ryder. Turn right here into the **Retrochoir (8)**, where there is a tablet in the floor marking the place where St Chad's Shrine once stood. The shrine was provided by Bishop Langton in the 14th century at a cost of £2000, but was destroyed

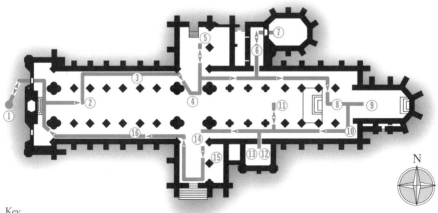

Key

1. West Front
2. Nave
3. North Aisle
4. Crossing
5. North Transept
6. Vestibule

7. Chapter House
8. Retrochoir
9. Lady Chapel
10. The Sleeping Children
11. Choir and Presbytery
12. Consistory Court

13. St Chad's Head Chapel
14. South Transept
15. St Michael's Chapel
16. South Aisle

during the Reformation. Behind the tablet is the effigy of Bishop George Selwyn (in office 1867–78), who became the first bishop of New Zealand. Tiles around the tomb depict his work in that country.

Step into the **Lady Chapel (9)**, arguably the most impressive part of the cathedral. It follows the same height as the choir, but without, of course, the aisles. With its tall, narrow windows and angled east end, it has a distinctly continental feel about it. Set between the windows are statues of angels, each beneath a crocketed canopy; these are Victorian replacements, the originals having been destroyed during the Reformation. Blind arcading runs beneath the windows. Behind the altar is a gilded reredos, carved in Oberammergau. The main delight of the Lady Chapel, however, is undoubtedly the 16th-century stained glass brought from the suppressed convent of Herckenrode in Flanders by Sir Brooke Boothby (1744–1824) in 1803.

The Sleeping Children

From the Lady Chapel, move into the south choir aisle. Immediately on the left is the cathedral's most notable monument, **The Sleeping Children (10)**, an alabaster carving by Sir Francis Chantrey (1781–1841), who was also responsible for the Bishop Ryder Monument in the north choir aisle. Dating from 1817, the sculpture shows two young sisters, Ellen-Jane and Marianne, a cathedral prebendary's daughters who died in childhood. Nearby is a medieval piscina with traces of a mural, thought to date from around 1400. The south choir aisle is notable also for its collection of tombs and monuments of former bishops. Look for, successively, Bishop Hackett (d1669), who restored the cathedral after the ravages of the Civil War, Bishop de Langton (d1321), who built the Lady Chapel, and Bishop Patteshall (d1245), plus a number of lesser-known deans and archdeacons.

Halfway along the north choir aisle, turn right into the **Choir and Presbytery (11)**. To the right, the high altar is made of local stone, with the reredos of alabaster. The sedilia was put together in the 19th century using medieval stone. The choir was also revamped by Scott in the 19th century, reversing Wyatt's earlier meddling. Note the superb Minton tiled floor, with its roundels showing scenes from the life of St Chad. Behind the choir stalls are a series of shields. Finally, on the south side, is the richly carved Bishop's Throne.

Consistory Court and St Chad's Head Chapel

Return to the north choir aisle. Immediately on the left is the old **Consistory Court (12)**, now the cathedral treasury, containing robes, vestments and silverware. There is, unusually, some stunning modern silverware dating from the early 1990s, the Lang Lichfield Silver Collection, named after Dean Lang (in office 1980–83). Also on display are reproductions of the pendants which pilgrims would buy after visiting St Chad's Shrine or the Holy Well. A door in the wall leads to the Duckpit, which was the original, and more secure, treasury. On the west side of the room are some wooden seats, believed to be the original chairs in which the bishop sat during court hearings.

Now take the stairs up into the 13th-century **St Chad's Head Chapel (13)**. The head of St Chad, covered in gold leaf, was shown to pilgrims passing through the gallery outside the chapel. The gallery, incidentally, gives fine views of the Minton tiled floor in the presbytery. The chapel itself has robust sandstone vaulting.

Descend the stairs and return to the aisle. Move into the **South Transept (14)**, where there is a return to the Early English style of architecture – this is the oldest part of the cathedral. Look at the nearest pillar of the crossing, where there is a rummer, an early-18th-century bottle used to measure out the daily 2½-pint (1.4l) ration of ale for the adult members of the choir (or Vicars Choral).

On the east side of the transept is **St Michael's Chapel (15)**, which contains the colours of the South Staffordshire Regiment along with a Book of Remembrance. The chapel also has memorials to local notables Samuel Johnson and David Garrick. The windows of the chapel display a few fragments of medieval glass which survived the destruction of the Civil War.

Leave the south transept and walk down the **South Aisle (16)**. Of interest here is the second window on the left, which tells the story of David and Goliath, reminding us that, in times when most of the congregation could not read, the stained glass was relied upon to tell the Bible stories. Further along the aisle are some unusual wall monuments which have traces of medieval paintwork.

The tour concludes at the west end of the cathedral.

WALKING TOUR FROM LICHFIELD CATHEDRAL

The walk begins in the Cathedral Close, where a number of fine buildings may be seen and there is also the opportunity to inspect the external features of the cathedral. The walk continues into the city centre, following the grid pattern of roads established by Bishop de Clinton in the 12th century. You are treated to a wide range of domestic architecture, and the walk has many literary associations. The three museums *en route* are well worth a visit, as are some of the city's old coaching inns.

Start and finish: The west front of the cathedral.
Length: 1 mile (1.6km). The walk is almost entirely on flat land.
Time: 45 minutes, but allow extra time for the museums.
Refreshments: Bird Street has three famous old coaching inns – The Swan, The George and The King's Head – which have plenty of atmosphere and serve excellent lunches. Nearer the cathedral, the Angel Croft Hotel provides good bar meals. There are a number of bistros and coffee shops in the pedestrianized part of the city.

The **Cathedral Close (1)** was originally laid out by Bishop de Clinton (in office 1129–48) in the 12th century, when it was surrounded by a ditch; a sturdy stone wall followed. These defences led to the close being used as a fortress during the Civil War, when it was subjected to three sieges. As a result many of the medieval buildings were destroyed and in due course Parliament ordered the wall to be pulled down so that the cathedral could never again be a Royalist stronghold. Most of the present buildings were constructed in the 17th and 18th centuries, but behind their façades there are often medieval cores.

A Circumnavigation of the Cathedral

Immediately to the left of the west front, on the south side of the close at no 21, is the modest **Bishop's House (2)**, which has been the residence of the Bishop of

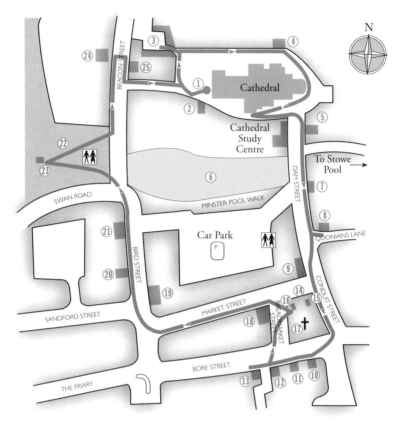

Key

1. Cathedral Close
2. Bishop's House
3. Vicars' Close
4. Old Bishop's Palace
5. St Mary's House
6. Minster Pool
7. Brooke House
8. Quonians Lane
9. Corn Exchange and
   Market Hall

10. Five Gables
11. Guildhall
12. Donegal House
13. Tudor Cafe
14. Market Place
15. Statue of Boswell
16. Statue of Johnson
17. St Mary's Church
18. Samuel Johnson
    Birthplace Museum

19. The George
20. The King's Head
21. The Swan
22. Museum Gardens
23. Statue of John Smith
24. Angel Croft Hotel
25. Erasmus Darwin Museum

Lichfield only since 1954. The house was rebuilt in the 1790s, but its interior has some medieval remains, probably of a canon's house.

Head now to the northwest corner of the close, past an old pump, part of a water supply system which dates back to the 12th century – probably one of the first examples of a piped water supply in England. Walk down a narrow alleyway into **Vicars' Close (3)**, a grassy square surrounded by recently restored half-timbered buildings. This was the northern of two courtyards built to provide accommodation for the Vicars Choral, the adult members of the cathedral choir. Returning to the close, note the terrace of houses at the west end. These buildings were once part of the southern courtyard of Vicars' Close and originally their frontages faced inwards to the close, but by the end of the 18th century they had reversed their orientation to face the cathedral.

Walk along the north side of the close, where there is a range of 17th- and 18th-century buildings, including the school house and the deanery. One half-timbered building, apparently used as a garage, shows the remains of a cruck framework. At the far end is the **Old Bishop's Palace (4)**, built in 1687 to replace an earlier medieval building. Surprisingly, few bishops chose to live in the close, and this palace was often rented out; one of its famous tenants was Anna Seward (1742–1809), the poet. Bishop Selwyn, in the 1860s, was the first bishop to live in the palace, and the east and west wings were added during his occupancy. Selwyn's widow lived in Selwyn House at the east end of the close, from where there is a view over Stowe Pool.

The walk along the north side of the close gives you an opportunity to view some of the external features of the cathedral, including the flying buttresses which support the tilting pillars of the nave, the trefoiled windows of the clerestory, the beautifully carved north transept doorway and the 'continental' look of the Lady Chapel – note the double line of statues between the chapel's windows.

Walk further round to the south side of the cathedral, where on the corner of the south transept is a much-eroded statue of Charles II. This once occupied a key position on the west front, but was removed during the 19th-century restorations. After the ravages of the Civil War, Charles gave money and timber to help repair the cathedral. Note, too, the carving on the south transept door, with its seven bishops.

Domestic Architecture

Leave the Cathedral Close by the southeast corner. On the right is the Visitors' Study Centre and on the left is **St Mary's House (5)**, once the vicarage for St Mary's

Half-timbered buildings in Vicars' Cross

Church in the city centre and now the diocesan office. St Mary's House embraces part of the old stone walls of the close, including a corner turret. The path at the side of the house gives views of some of the blocked arrowslits. Archaeological research has shown this was the site of a huge stone gatehouse destroyed in the 18th century.

Head now along the pedestrianized Dam Street, named after the embankment which blocked the stream to form **Minster Pool (6)**, now a pleasant lake containing a selection of wildfowl. Minster Pool was originally one of three lakes, but the upper pool has been drained and is now Museum Gardens. The lower and larger lake, to the east, is Stowe Pool.

Continue towards the city centre along Dam Street, where there is a variety of domestic architecture to be seen. Note on the left the Georgian **Brooke House (7)**, where a plaque notes that Lord Brooke (1611–1664), a leader of the Parliamentary forces in the Civil War, received his fatal wound on this spot. The shot was fired from the battlements of the steeple by the deaf Royalist John Dyott. Further along Dam Street, make a short diversion into **Quonians Lane (8)**, where immediately on the left is a half-timbered house of the type which would have housed an artisan in medieval times. There is some interesting stone carving on the wall.

Pass the Market Place (see below) to the right as Dam Street merges into Conduit Street. Above the shop fronts to the right you see the **Corn Exchange and Market Hall (9)**, built in 1849. The arcaded ground-floor area once contained a poultry market and a buttery; the arcades were filled in with shops in the 1970s. Ahead is the impressive frontage of Boots the Chemists: although it appears to be of some antiquity, it actually dates from the early years of the 20th century.

Turn right into Bore Street to find many of the more interesting and historic houses in the city. First on the left is **Five Gables (10)**, a half-timbered building probably dating from the late 16th century. It displays some intricate carving and herringbone pattern work. Next on the left is the **Guildhall (11)**, largely in Gothic style, constructed 1846–8 by the Trustees of Lichfield Conduit Lands, although parts of it go back to the early 15th century. It was not the first guildhall in the city, however; there is believed to have been one by 1387, in the time of Richard II. Guilds have always been powerful in Lichfield, particularly the religious Guild of St Mary, founded by Bishop Langton in 1295, which ruled the city for two centuries until it was dissolved in 1548.

Now you come to **Donegal House (12)**, a Georgian town house built for the Robinson family in 1730. A plaque outside the building states that it was given to the manor, aldermen and citizens of the city by Mrs M.A. Swinfen-Broun of Swinton Hall, Lichfield, in 1928. The ground floor is presently occupied by the helpful Tourist Information Centre. It is worth walking up the stairs to the first floor to view the Sketchbook Exhibition, where a number of the panelled rooms have been used to depict such topics as 'The Life of a Georgian Lady' and the work of various tradesmen such as millers, carpenters and scribes. The rooms have informative illustrative plaques, while waxwork models dressed in the clothing of the time add a lifelike touch.

To the right of Donegal House is the **Tudor Café (13)**, a 16th-century half-timbered building with jettied walls. The timberwork is in a variety of styles – post and pan, square, herringbone and, in the gables, patterned. The large amount of expensive wood in the building suggests the original owner was one of the more affluent members of Lichfield society. At the side of the Tudor Café is Tudor Row, a narrow alleyway leading to some small specialist shops.

Johnson and Boswell

Cross Bore Street and head along the short Breadmarket Street into the **Market Place (14)**. A market has been held here since 1153, when King Stephen granted Bishop Durdent, also Lord of the Manor of Lichfield, the right to hold a Sunday market. Since then this area has always been the centre of city life, whether for trade, socializing, public meetings or watching people being burnt at the stake (look at the plaques on the side of St Mary's Church for further gory details).

There are two statues of note in the Market Place. On the east side is the **Statue of Boswell (15)**. James Boswell was an associate of Samuel Johnson during the latter's London days, and they remained firm friends. Boswell's masterpiece was *The Life of Samuel Johnson* (1791), described by Macauley as 'the greatest biography in the English language'. Johnson often brought Boswell to Lichfield to experience country life at its best. At the opposite end of the Market Place is the **Statue of Johnson (16)**, which fittingly looks across the road to his birthplace and museum.

Do not leave the Market Place without visiting **St Mary's Church (17)**. There has been a church on this site since the 9th century and the present building is the fourth to be constructed here. Sadly, this parish church is now redundant and has been converted into a sort of civic centre and tourist attraction. The small Dyott Chapel has been retained as a place of worship, and elsewhere on the ground floor is an Old Peoples' Day Centre and an attractive coffee shop. The whole of the nave has been given a mezzanine level and this houses the Heritage Centre, which boasts audiovisual displays, dioramas and models describing the history and development of Lichfield. A metal spiral staircase leads up to a viewing platform on the tower, where you can enjoy superb vistas over the city's rooftops and away to the spires of the cathedral.

Cross Breadmarket Street to the **Samuel Johnson Birthplace Museum (18)**. Johnson was born in this building in 1709, the son of a bookseller. He was educated at a local Dame School before going on to Lichfield Grammar School, followed by a short spell at Pembroke College, Oxford, before lack of funds forced him to leave. For a brief period he ran a school just outside Lichfield, where one of his pupils was David Garrick. Johnson later moved to London, where he was to make his reputation. He wrote the first dictionary of the English language plus other works of literature and was the central figure in a group of the leading writers and scholars of his day. He made many return visits to Lichfield before his death in London in 1784. His birthplace is now a museum. In the basement is a mock-up of the 18th-century kitchen with the precocious nine-year-old Johnson reading the ghost scene from Shakespeare's *Hamlet*. Other rooms are devoted to 'Johnson and his Century' and 'London Life'.

Coaching Inns

Leave the Johnson Museum and turn left along Market Street, where there is a fascinating mixture of ancient and modern shop fronts, inns, bistros, and occasional

Georgian and Tudor buildings. At the end of Market Street turn right into Bird Street. This Georgian road is notable for its former coaching inns. The heyday of the coaching inn was from the end of the 18th century to about 1840, when the railways took over the trade. In 1831 it is recorded that 31 coaches a day passed through Lichfield to such destinations as Birmingham, Liverpool and London, plus three Royal Mail routes to Chester, Liverpool and Sheffield. The first of these coaching inns you come across, on the right hand side of Bird Street, is the **The George (19)**. It retains its Regency ballroom, with ships' timbers in the ceiling. The Irish dramatist George Farquahar (1678–1707) was billeted at the George in 1704, and it was here that he wrote *The Recruiting Officer* and *The Beaux' Stratagem*. Opposite the George is the **The King's Head (20)**, which is full of military history and memorabilia. A plaque on the wall outside records that in 1705 Colonel Luke Lillington raised a Regiment of Foot here – this was later to become the South Staffordshire Regiment. Further along, on the left, is the **The Swan (21)**, the oldest surviving inn in the city, probably dating to the 15th century. Famous visitors have included Johnson, Boswell and Elias Ashmole (1617–1692), the scholar who founded the Ashmolean Museum in Oxford. Another, perhaps less welcome, visitor is the resident ghost – an apparently friendly White Lady. The Swan and the George were not only coaching but political rivals, with the Tory headquarters at the Swan and Whigs drinking at the George. Presumably neutrals went to the King's Head!

Continue along Bird Street until you see Minster Pool on the right. Underneath the road are the foundations of a medieval bridge. Turn into **Museum Gardens (22)** on the other side of the road. Here there are two statues of note, one of King Edward VII, erected in 1908, and the other, on the far side of the gardens, the **Statue of John Edward Smith, Captain of the** *Titanic* **(23)**. The statue was unveiled in 1914 and attracted little interest until the 1990s, when James Cameron's film *Titanic* was released. Now the statue attracts hordes of camera-wielding visitors, much to the wry amusement of locals. Smith, who went down with his ship, was actually born in Hanley and has no connection at all with Lichfield, so after the success of the film Hanley suggested the statue should go there ... an offer the Lichfield authorities politely refused! The statue was the work of Kathleen, Lady Scott, whose first husband was Robert Falcon Scott (1868–1912) – Scott of the Antarctic.

Leave the Museum Gardens and turn left along Beacon Street (known until Georgian times as Bacon Street and famous for its brothels). On the left is the **Angel Croft Hotel (24)**, a Georgian building whose 18th-century railings have survived various war efforts. Opposite is the **Erasmus Darwin Centre (25)**, which opened in April 1999. Erasmus Darwin (1731–1802), the grandfather of Charles Darwin (1809–1882), was a remarkable man in his own right. A well liked local doctor, he was also a philosopher, inventor, poet and botanist. He was a friend of the potter Josiah Wedgwood (1730–1795) and introduced the inventors Matthew Boulton (1728–1809) and James Watt (1736–1819) to each other, possibly in this house, which was his home between 1758 and 1781.

Walk along the side of the Darwin Museum, past the remains of the old West Gate and back into the Cathedral Close, where the tour concludes.

Chester

Access: Chester is well placed to take advantage of both the north–south and cross-Pennine motorways, while the A55 expressway leads to North Wales and Holyhead (for ferries from Ireland). London is 188 miles (302km) and Birmingham 85 miles (136km) away. National Express provides coach links with many other towns and cities. There are good rail links with the rest of the country: trains from London Euston take 2½ hours. The nearest international airport is at Manchester, a 45min motorway drive to the northeast.

Chester's history begins with the Romans, who in AD79 built a fortress on a low sandstone plateau within a meander of the River Dee and constructed the original city walls. They named the fortress Deva (after the river), and its main purpose was to act as a military base for operations against the Welsh. The site of the fortress was superb – the river was on three sides and it could be forded and later bridged – and, since the Dee was deeper in those days, sea-going ships could easily reach the site. The fortress became one of three main Roman garrisons in Britain and is thought to have housed up to 6000 troops, being particularly associated with Agricola's 20th Valeria Vatrix Legion. Deva had the typical rectangular shape of a Roman fort, and the Roman street plan is still largely in place today. The Via Principalis (now Eastgate and Watergate streets) ran east–west and the Via Decumana (now Northgate Street) and the Via Praetoria (now Bridge Street) north–south.

By AD383 the Romans had withdrawn from the area, but the site was probably never completely deserted. Some 500 years later the Saxons, under Aethelflaeda or Ethelflaed (d.917), a daughter of King Alfred, refortified Deva and extended the walls to counter the Welsh and the Vikings. Cestre, as it was now known, became a busy port. Aethelflaeda, meanwhile, had dedicated a church to St Werburgh. An Irish–Norse community had also established itself and was involved in the tanning of hides in the riverside area. Chester was sufficiently important to have its own mint and in AD937 received a visit from King Edgar (the first King of All England), who was rowed along the river by eight Celtic kings as a sign of their allegiance.

After the Conquest, William built a castle at Chester as part of his campaign to control the north of the country. He installed his nephew, Hugh Lupus, the Wolf, as Earl of Chester; this title remains today and is automatically given to the eldest son of the monarch. After subduing the local inhabitants, Hugh converted the Saxon minster into a Benedictine abbey with the help of Anselm, the Abbot of Bec in Normandy. Over the next 150 years the monks pulled down the Saxon building and replaced it with a Norman-style church; there are a few remains today of this Norman building in the north transept of the current cathedral. Later, the monks were dissatisfied with the heavy Norman architecture and began to replace it piece by piece with a lighter, more elegant, Gothic-style building. They had just completed this church when Henry VIII dissolved the monastery in 1540. A year later Henry declared the abbey church a cathedral and created the diocese of Chester. The last abbot became the first dean.

By this time the Dee had silted up and Chester was finding it difficult to maintain its prosperity as a port. It had further problems during the Civil War. The city supported the Royalist cause and the citizens were under siege by the Parliamentarians for over a year before being starved into submission. By the end of the century, however, Chester was once more thriving: it became an important regional centre and its industries supplied many of the goods required for the North American colonies.

In the early 18th century, with the turnpike system coming into being, Chester became an important coaching centre. With this came the growth of inns – some 150 are known to have been licensed at this time. Elegant Georgian houses were built, such as those in Abbey Square, while the old medieval gateways were replaced by modern arches. The riverside area, known as The Groves, became a well used promenade for local people. Across the Dee, the silted-up Roman harbour was now used as a popular racecourse. Chester was also becoming a prestigious resort for the gentry. In addition, the city linked up with the national canal network, the Chester Canal joining with the Shropshire Union System. For the cathedral, however, these were hard times, with the fabric and exterior stonework in bad condition.

The Victorian era was significant for both city and cathedral. Chester continued to prosper and, mercifully, did not attract the heavy industry of many of its northern neighbours. Medieval Revival was the name of the game and many of Chester's black-and-white half-timbered buildings are not in fact Elizabethan but Victorian. The city fathers made sure that The Rows – the lines of shops at both ground and first-floor level – were preserved and extended. The city walls, too, were maintained; today Chester is the only English town with a complete circuit of medieval walls. The railway came to Chester in 1840, with links to Crewe and Birkenhead. A new road led from the General Railway Station to the newly built Grosvenor Bridge, making the first change to the medieval road pattern; this was the largest stone single-span bridge in the world. Another innovation was the new suspension bridge from The Groves to the west bank of the Dee, opened by the youthful Princess Victoria. Towards the end of the century the Eastgate Clock was erected to celebrate the same Victoria's Diamond Jubilee.

It was the Victorians who saved the cathedral from ruin. The restoration, as for many other English cathedrals, was in the hands of Sir George Gilbert Scott (1811–1878), and as usual his schemes were controversial. His renovations were mainly to the floors and ceilings, but much of the stained glass dates from his time, along with the mosaics on the wall of the north nave aisle.

Today, the cathedral looks in good condition, although the exterior stonework needs constant attention. Fortunately, the thousands of tourists who visit Chester annually regard the cathedral as an essential port of call and contribute generously.

TOUR OF THE CATHEDRAL
Start and finish: The northwest porch.

Enter the cathedral through the door at the northern corner of the west front. Proceed past a small area called the Abbot's Passage, built in the 12th century to provide a route for the abbot to step into the cathedral; today it contains a continuous video presentation describing the history of the cathedral.

Plate 25: *The font and baptistry window at the new Coventry Cathedral, completed 1962. The unusual font is shaped from a three-ton boulder brought from Bethlehem (see page 126).*

Plate 26: The old Coventry Cathedral, which was destroyed by enemy bombs during World War II. The tower and spire miraculously remained unscathed (see page 121).

Plate 27: Vicars' Close, a small square of half-timbered buildings in Lichfield's Cathedral Close (see page 139). The houses were built to provide accommodation for the adult members of the cathedral choir.

Plate 28: The west front of Lichfield Cathedral, showing the three spires known collectively as the Ladies of the Vale (see page 133).

Plate 29: The Eastgate Clock on the city walls at Chester (see page 153). This is the only English city which has its city walls fully intact.

Plate 30: The nave at Chester Cathedral was built between 1360 and 1490 (see page 145). Only six bays in length, it is one of the smallest naves in any English cathedral.

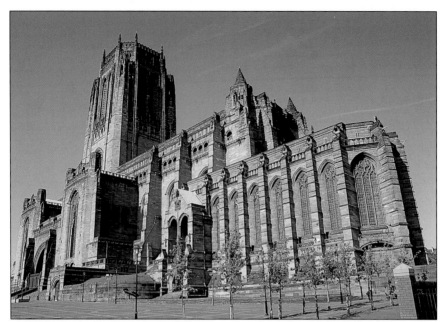

Plate 31: *The massive structure of Liverpool's Anglican Cathedral, with its immense central tower (see page 155). Designed by Giles Gilbert Scott, the style can be termed Edwardian Gothic.*

Plate 32: *The front of Liverpool's Roman Catholic Cathedral. It was built in the post-war years to a radical design by Sir Frederick Gibberd (see page 161).*

Walk into the **Undercroft (1)**, which has some sturdy vaulting and was the cellar of the monastery. After being a workshop for many years, it was converted into a permanent exhibition centre in 1992.

Pass briefly into the southwest corner of the cloisters before entering the **Nave (2)**. This is small – only six bays long – and was built between 1360 and 1490; the architectural styles show the south side was completed before the north side, and there have been a number of additions over the last 150 years, with the Victorians adding the pulpit and lectern, plus the line of mosaics on the north aisle wall. These mosaics show scenes from the lives of Abraham, Moses, David and Elijah. The south aisle wall, in contrast, is covered with memorial tablets mainly from the 18th and 19th centuries. From here there is a good view of the west window, whose glass was installed in 1961. Figures represented include the Holy Family, Queen Aethelflaeda and saints Werburgh, Chad, Aidan, Oswald and Wilfred.

Continuity and Change

Carry on to the west end where, in the northwest corner, you find the **Baptistry (3)**, located in the base of a tower which the monks never got around to building. The font was brought from Venice in 1885, and some authorities think it was originally a Roman well head. In the opposite corner of the west end is the **Consistory Court (4)**, which dates from 1636 and is the oldest complete example of an ecclesiastical courtroom in England.

Walk along to the south nave aisle to inspect the **Westminster Windows (5)**, given to the cathedral in 1992 by the sixth Duke of Westminster in memory of his parents and to mark the cathedral's ninth centenary. They have the theme of continuity and change.

At the end of the aisle, turn into massive **South Transept (6)**, which is almost as large as the nave. It dates from 1350 and acted as the parish church of St Oswald; it was partitioned off from the main church until the parishioners moved out in 1881.

There are four chapels on the east side of the transept. The first is the Chapel of St Mary Magdalene of the Ascension, also known as the Children's Chapel. The second, and most interesting, is the Chapel of St Oswald. Note the carved wooden reredos, designed by Charles Eamer Kempe (1837–1907) and carved in Oberammergau. It shows Oswald, King of Northumbria (*c*605–642), leading his soldiers in prayer before battle against King Caedwalla. Next comes the Chapel of St George, the Regimental Chapel of the Cheshire Regiment, and finally there is the Chapel of Sts Nicholas and Leonard.

On the west side of the transept is the impressive **Westminster Memorial (7)**, in remembrance of Hugh Lupus Grosvenor (1825–1899), first Duke of Westminster. The memorial is surrounded by ornate wrought-iron railings. Note the four dogs in the corners – they are of a rare old breed known as the Talbot.

Move towards the crossing and approach the **HMS *Chester* Memorial (8)**. The ensigns remind us that this was the ship on which the teenage Jack Cornwell (1900–1916) died winning the VC at the Battle of Jutland. Walk under the tower and towards the **North Transept (9)**. The view is dominated by the organ, which was moved there by Scott during the 19th-century renovations. From an architectural point of view, the north transept is one of the most fascinating parts of the cathedral. There is a large Norman arch (*c*1100) on the east side and above it, at triforium level,

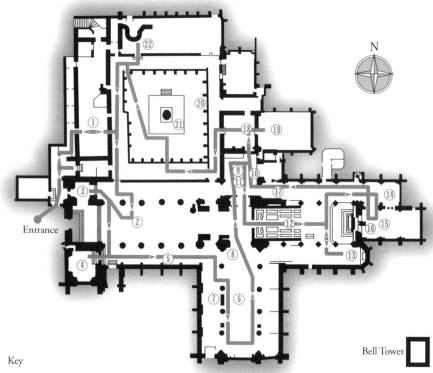

Key

1. Undercroft
2. Nave
3. Baptistry
4. Consistory Court
5. Westminster Windows
6. South Transept
7. Westminster Memorial
8. HMS *Chester* Memorial

9. North Transept
10. Cobweb Picture
11. Memorial to John Pearson
12. Quire
13. Chapel of St Erasmus
14. St Werburgh's Chapel
15. Lady Chapel
16. Shrine of St Werburgh

17. North Quire Aisle
18. Vestibule
19. Chapter House
20. Cloisters
21. Cloister Garden
22. Refectory

a line of smaller Norman arches, giving an indication of the appearance of the cathedral before the monks introduced the Gothic style. Also in this area of the transept, placed in a wall niche, is the **Cobweb Picture (10)**. It shows Our Lady and the Holy Child painted on the net of a caterpillar – a common Tyrolean artform in the 19th century. Nearby is the imposing **Memorial to John Pearson (11)**, built in the 19th century to remember Bishop Pearson of Chester (in office 1673–86), the author of a well known book on the Apostles' Creed.

From Quire to Chapter House

Walk back to the crossing and turn left into the **Quire (12)**. If you've been thinking the cathedral is so far rather dull, this impression will immediately change: the quire stalls and canopies are without doubt the best in the country. The quire itself was built 1280–1300 and is believed to have been the work of Richard of Chester, military engineer to Edward I. The stalls date from *c*1380 and are carved in Baltic Oak. The delicately carved canopies are individual in design. Immediately below is a line of corbels, while under the seats are some forty misericords treating both religious and secular topics. There are also some unusual bench ends, including a Tree of Jesse on the Dean's stall. Other carvings include a pelican, the so-called Chester Pilgrim and a variety of animals and grotesque figures. Scott's 19th-century additions to the quire fit in rather well: they include a carved wooden rood screen which matches the canopies, a superb tiled floor, the painted wooden ceiling and the Italian mosaic reredos behind the high altar. A modern altar front is based on the eucharistic symbols of bread and wine.

Leave the quire to the right of the high altar to look briefly at the **Chapel of St Erasmus (13)**, a semicircular apse at the east end of the south aisle. The chapel has Victorian glass and a painted, vaulted ceiling. It is reserved for private prayer.

Return through the quire to the north aisle. Turn right. At the end of the aisle is **St**

The Chester Pilgrim

Werburgh's Chapel (14), whose altar is believed to have been built from the remains of the original high altar, which was in the quire until 1876. Look at the floor by the altar: lines indicate the original east end of the Norman church. Werburgh (d*c*700) was the daughter of Wulfere of Mercia. About 675 she became a nun in the monastery at Ely founded by her aunt, St Etheldreda or Aethelthryth (*c*630–*c*679). Later she was made abbess of a convent in Mercia and became noted for her holy life. She was buried at Hanbury in Staffordshire, where numerous miracles occurred at her tomb. In the early 10th century her relics were brought to the Saxon minster at Chester.

Move next into the **Lady Chapel (15)**, built between 1250 and 1275 in Early English style, with some striking lancet windows. Note also the three large bosses in the roof, which show (from east to west) the Trinity, the Virgin and Child and the Martyrdom of St Thomas à Becket. The painted ceiling, the stained glass and the tiled floor are all Victorian. At the rear of the Lady Chapel is the early-14th-century **Shrine of St Werburgh (16)**. This was badly damaged at the Dissolution of the Monasteries and the relics removed, but was restored in the 19th century. On one of the corners there's a charming little carving of a dog scratching its ear.

Return to the **North Quire Aisle (17)** and walk back towards the crossing. On the left are some fragments of the 12th-century abbey church, later used for the foundations of the present quire. The remains, which came to light during the Victorian renovations, include a column, a capital and some medieval tiles. The stone screen behind is part of the pulpitum that divided quire from nave until 1875.

From the north transept, move into the **Vestibule (18)**, originally a waiting area for townspeople who wished to see the abbot, who would receive them in the chapter house. Six medieval abbots are buried here among the fine columns.

Next you come to the **Chapter House (19)**, built 1225–50 as a place for the monks to discuss daily business and hear a chapter from the Rule of St Benedict. The founder of the abbey, Hugh Lupus, is buried here. The rectangular chapter house retains its original stone vaulting (the only example in the cathedral) and has over twenty tall lancet windows.

The Cloisters

Leave the chapter house and proceed via the vestibule to the **Cloisters (20)**. Originally built in the 12th century, these were redesigned in the 16th century and restored by Sir Giles Gilbert Scott, a grandson of Sir George, in 1911–13. The cloister roofs have simple rib vaulting and bosses. The windows were added in the 1920s. Most visitors are entranced by the **Cloister Garden (21)**. In the centre is a deep-set pond, once the abbey well. It contains a sculpture entitled *Water of Life* by Stephen Broadbent, representing the story of Jesus and the Woman of Samaria. Around the pond are seats set among trees which came from the Holy Land. The south cloister has a number of slabs and tombs – one may relate to the 13th-century abbot Simon Ripley and another could be that of Richard of Bec (d1116), who came to England in 1092 as clerk to St Anselm and the following year was appointed the first abbot of the new monastery. His coffin is very large – the internal space is about 6ft 6in (2m) long – which suggests Abbot Richard was abnormally tall for the time.

The north cloister has a lavatorium, where monks washed before proceeding to the **Refectory (22)** which, appropriately, is today the cathedral restaurant. This is undoubtedly the most awe-inspiring of any cathedral eating place in the country. It was built in the 13th century and subsequently enlarged to take about forty monks and their frequent guests. While they ate in silence, one of the brothers read to them from the stone pulpit halfway up the south wall. Other features of interest for modern diners are the 17th-century tapestry on the west wall, the heraldic paintings on the north wall showing the arms of the earls of Chester and the modern (1939) hammer-beam roof.

Leave the refectory and return via the shop and the undercroft to the northwest porch, where the tour concludes.

WALKING TOUR FROM CHESTER CATHEDRAL

After you've had a look at the environs of the cathedral, the walk continues with a complete circuit of the city's walls, with short detours to view other attractions. At the end of this circuit the route moves into the city centre so that you can look at the unique double-layered shopping walks known as The Rows, set among ornate half-timbered buildings.

Start and finish: The west front of the cathedral.
Length: 3 miles (4.8km), with the circuit of the walls alone being 2 miles (3.2km).
Time: The walls walk takes up to 2hr, but allow longer for detours. Add a further 45 minutes for the walk into the city centre.

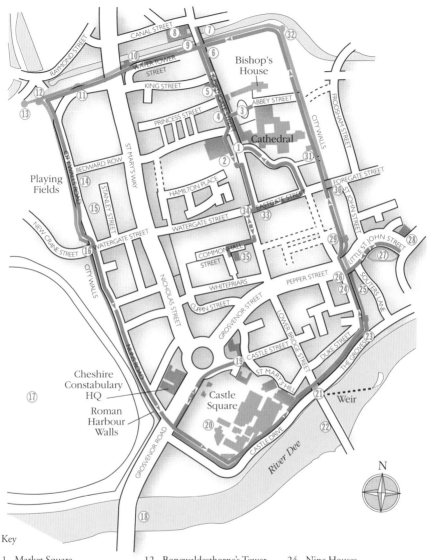

Key

1. Market Square
2. Town Hall
3. Abbey Gateway
4. Westminster Coach and Motor
   Car Works
5. Pied Bull Inn
6. Northgate
7. Shropshire Union Canal
8. Bluecoat School
9. Bridge of Sighs
10. St Morgan's Mount
11. Pemberton's Parlour
12. Bonewaldesthorne's Tower
13. Water Tower
14. Queen's School
15. Stanley Place
16. Watergate
17. Roodee Racecourse
18. Grosvenor Bridge
19. Grosvenor Museum
20. Chester Castle
21. Bridgegate
22. Old Dee Bridge
23. Recorder's Steps
24. Nine Houses
25. Roman Garden
26. Newgate
27. Roman Amphitheatre
28. Chester Visitor & Craft Centre
29. Thimbleby's Tower
30. Eastgate
31. Bell Tower
32. King Charles' Tower
33. The Rows
34. High Cross
35. Deva Roman Experience

Refreshments: The cathedral refectory can be highly recommended for its space, ambience and food. On the walls walk there is a group of excellent pubs approximately halfway round the circuit. These include the 16th-century Bear and Billet, close to the Bridgegate, the Albion in Bridge Street and the Off the Wall next to Newgate. The Pied Bull Inn in Northgate Street is an archetypal coaching inn, while in the town centre there are numerous inns with atmosphere, including many adjacent to the High Cross.

Leave the west front of the cathedral and head along St Werburgh Street to the **Market Square (1)**. In the centre of the square is an attractive modern sculpture by Stephen Broadbent, *A Celebration of Chester*, the three entwined figures represent protection, industry and thanksgiving. A few yards away to the north are other examples of stonework, in this case a group of Roman pillars and capitals. Dominating the square is the imposing **Town Hall (2)**, built 1865–9 and opened by Edward, Prince of Wales, later Edward VII. The building replaced the previous town hall, known as the Exchange, burnt down in 1862, and is constructed of bands of red and grey sandstone; its massive tower reaches 160ft (48.7m). which is higher than the cathedral tower. Spend a moment to look inside the building, because the waiting hall and staircase, just inside, are its finest features. The building's southeast corner houses the Tourist Information Centre, which incorporates a wall built of Roman masonry, possibly from the praetorium, the fortress's main building.

Cross Northgate Street to **Abbey Gateway (3)**, which was the main entrance to St Werburgh's Abbey. The gateway was built in red sandstone in the 14th century, but the upper storey was rebuilt at the end of the 18th. As you pass through the gateway look up at the sturdy vaulting and bosses.

You now arrive in Abbey Square, which was at one time surrounded by the medieval monastery's kitchens, bakery, brewery and other buildings. These have all been replaced by attractive Georgian houses, including the Bishop's House in the northeast corner. The pillar in the centre of the square is said to have come from the old Exchange. Note the cobbled surface of the square and the lines of flat stones ('wheelers') designed to make the passage of carriages more comfortable.

Return to Northgate Street. Immediately opposite is the former **Westminster Coach and Motor Car Works (4)** with its arched Edwardian façade. This elegant building has been converted into the city library. Further along on the same side of the street is the **Pied Bull Inn (5)**. As the Bull Mansion this was the residence of Chester's recorder in the 17th century. It was refronted in the 18th century and became an important coaching inn (notice the distances to major cities shown on the wall). George Borrow (1803–1881) stayed here *en route* to write his *Wild Wales* (1862).

The tour now arrives at the **Northgate (6)**, a main entrance – the Porta Decumana – to the Roman city. Until 1807 Northgate was also the city jail. Like the rest of the city's medieval gates, it was replaced in the early 19th century with an archway. Step briefly through the gateway and stand on the bridge which crosses the **Shropshire Union Canal (7)**. Cut deeply into the local sandstone, the canal was opened in 1775 and provided a link between the Cheshire salt mines and the Midlands canal system.

The building next to the canal is the **Bluecoat School (8)**, which was built as a charity school in 1717 in an attempt, it is said, to combat the debauchery of the children of the city. There is a statue of a Bluecoat schoolboy over the main door. The school closed in 1949. Linking the school to the walls on the other side of the canal is the **Bridge of Sighs (9)**, across which condemned men were led from the jail to the Bluecoat School chapel for their last rites. It once had tall railings to stop the prisoners making their bid for freedom by jumping into the canal.

Around the Walls
Return to the Northgate, turn right and climb the steps up to the walls. Our route takes us in an anticlockwise circuit. The path runs downhill, parallel with the canal, to **Morgan's Mount (10)**, a square watchtower named after the commander of a gun battery during the siege of Chester in the Civil War. The walls were first built by the Romans as turf ramparts, later faced with stone. The Saxons strengthened and extended the walls down to the River Dee, and by the Middle Ages there were many towers, bastions and spurs. After damage during the Civil War, the walls were repaired and they became a popular venue for promenading during Victorian times. Today, Chester is the only English city whose walls survive in their entirety.

The Roman walls turned left here, but the course changed when the Saxons extended the fortifications down to the river. The path now crosses the inner ring road, on the other side of which is **Pemberton's Parlour (11)**, the remains of a round tower badly damaged in the Civil War. It was named for an 18th-century mayor of the city; it is known also as Goblin Tower, after a ropemaker who worked here.

Walk on to **Bonewaldesthorne's Tower (12)**, which marks the northwest corner of the walls. The waters of the River Dee once ran beneath the walls here, but after the river silted up and changed its course it was necessary to build the **Water Tower (13)** on the end of a spur. The tower did not hold water, as the name might imply, but was built to protect shipping in the nearby quays.

The path now drops down to street level, in City Walls Road. On your left here is the **Queen's School (14)**, which occupies the site of the former city gaol, closed in 1872. Presumably the pupils make the obvious jokes about the building's former use. The area in front of the present school was used for public executions. Also on the left is **Stanley Place (15)**, a small tree-lined square of Georgian houses. Cloth was sold for many years at the Linen Hall, which used to stand at the eastern end of the square.

You now reach the **Watergate (16)**. The original narrow gate was a place where tolls were charged for goods coming into the city from the river. The old Watergate was replaced in 1788 with the present arch. The path again returns to street level in Nuns Road. The 12th-century Benedictine nunnery of St Mary's stood here, while there were also Franciscan and Dominican friaries in the vicinity. To the right there are fine views of Chester's **Roodee Racecourse (17)**, claimed to be the oldest in the country. It is on the site of the Roman harbour, and a Roman quay can be identified beneath the walls. The unusual name comes from the Saxon *rood* (cross) and *eye* (island), the whole meaning 'the island with the cross'. From the walls you can just pick out the stump of a cross in the centre of the course. The walls also afford free viewing during the flat-racing season! You can see the track is an unusual shape: it is almost perfectly oval, with no finishing straight.

Grosvenor Bridge (18) is visible through the trees to your right. It was opened in 1832 by Princess Victoria, and at that time was the largest single-span stone bridge in the world. You can make detour here, following Grosvenor Road up to the roundabout and **Grosvenor Museum (19)**. This has displays of art, archaeology and natural history. Don't miss the Charles Darwin Natural History Gallery, the award-winning Roman Stones Gallery and the mock-up of a Georgian house.

Back on the walls, you are now approaching **Chester Castle (20)**, which in medieval times guarded the port and river crossing. Between 1788 and 1822 the site was redeveloped, leaving only Agricola's Tower. Much of the rest of the area has Greek Revival buildings, such as County Hall, the Museum of the Cheshire Regiment, the law courts and the local police headquarters. The riverside area beneath the city walls at this point was where leatherworkers (skinners) plied their trade. Famed for its obnoxious smells, the industry could not be tolerated in the city. The area can be pretty smelly today when the tide is out – the mangrove-like willows contain a good collection of supermarket trolleys, beer cans and other garbage.

On the left is the impressive balustraded **Bridgegate (21)**. The medieval Bridgegate (or Welshgate, as it was sometimes called) was heavily fortified and guarded the old Dee bridge. The gateway was badly damaged during the Civil War siege and was eventually replaced with the present structure in 1782.

Walk across the road to view the **Old Dee Bridge (22)**. This was built of stone in the 14th century after a number of earlier wooden bridges had been destroyed during floods. Until the 19th century it was the only crossing into Wales, and at the far end of the bridge was another gate, complete with portcullis and drawbridge. On the upstream side of the bridge is a weir, and the head of water created once powered numerous water wheels for grinding corn and fulling cloth.

Return to the walls. A little along on the right are the **Recorder's Steps (23)**, a recorder being a local 18th-century official. The steps provide a detour down to The Groves, a shady riverside area where boats can be hired.

The main walls path now swings north, running parallel with Park Street. On the left are the **Nine Houses (24)**, half-timbered almshouses provided for the local poor and needy; only six of the nine remain. On the other side of the wall is the **Roman Garden (25)**, where, among the greenery, a collection of Roman masonry has been assembled and a hypocaust put together. Modern 'Romans' in authentic costume can be seen guiding parties of children through this aspect of their history.

You next reach **Newgate (26)**, installed in 1938 alongside the old Wolfgate, named for Hugh Lupus. A nice local story about the gate involves a 16th-century alderman's daughter. She eloped through the gate at night on horseback, and the livid alderman persuaded the city authorities thereafter to have the gate permanently closed – clearly a local version of the saying 'to lock the stable door after the horse has bolted'!

A short diversion from Newgate takes you to the **Roman Amphitheatre (27)**, discovered in 1928 and excavated during the 1960s. The excavations revealed that this was the largest stone amphitheatre the Romans built in Britain, having a seating capacity of 7000. It would have been used for military training and ceremonies plus other, doubtless more bloodthirsty, activities. Across the road from the amphitheatre is the **Chester Visitor and Craft Centre (28)**, housed in a former

Victorian school. A video show can be seen along with a life-sized reconstruction of The Rows with local craftsmen at work as in Victorian times. There is a restaurant and a Tourist Information Centre.

Return to Newgate and head north. After a short distance you come across the ruined **Thimbleby's Tower (29)**, probably named after Lady Mary Thimbleby, buried in the nearby St Michael's Church. The upper part of the tower was destroyed during the Civil War and the lower part is preserved under the wall of the walkway.

You now reach **Eastgate (30)**, capped by the highly photogenic Victorian clock. The present Eastgate was erected in 1769, replacing a medieval gate believed to have had traces of Roman arches in its stonework. Eastgate was the main Roman ceremonial entrance to the fortress, Eastgate Street being the eastern section of the Via Principalis. The clock was put up in 1897 to celebrate Queen Victoria's Diamond Jubilee. From here there are fine views into the heart of Chester's shopping area.

Continue along the walls towards the cathedral. On the left is the cathedral's modern free-standing **Bell Tower (31)**, completed in 1975 and claimed to be the first independent cathedral tower to be constructed in Europe since the 15th century. Further along on the left is the Deanery Field, where archaeologists have discovered the foundations of a Roman legion barracks.

The northeast corner of the walls circuit is marked by **King Charles' Tower (32)**, from where, it is believed, Charles I watched in 1645 as his forces were defeated by the Parliamentarians at nearby Rowton Moor.

The route now runs westwards along the walls, parallel to the Shropshire Union Canal, back to the Northgate, where you first joined the walls.

Back to the City Centre

Head along Northgate Street, past the Town Hall, into the area known as **The Rows (33)**. These are basically a series of covered galleries above street-level shops and probably date back to the 13th century. They are best seen in Watergate, Eastgate and Bridge Street, with a shorter section surviving in Northgate Street. A lot of the buildings are ornately half-timbered, with the upper floors being jettied and supported by pillars down to ground level. Many are, however, not as old as they look: the whole area received considerable renovation in Victorian times as part of the Gothic Revival. Nevertheless, the area is unique in Britain and is enjoyed by thousands of visitors annually, who come both to shop and to soak up the atmosphere.

In the centre of The Rows is the **High Cross (34)**, the battered old market cross where merchants struck bargains. Here, during the summer months, the town crier issues proclamations each day between Tuesday and Saturday at noon and 14:00.

A short detour from the High Cross along Bridge Street, Commonhall Street and Pierpoint Lane brings you to an unusual museum, the **Dewa Roman Experience (35)**. Dewa, it is claimed, is the way Deva was pronounced in Roman times. Thanks to mock-ups, you can sail back in time on a Roman Galley and walk through a typical Roman-era street experiencing some of the sounds, sights and smells of Roman Chester.

Return to the High Cross and walk along Eastgate Street. In the near distance is a fine view of Eastgate and its clock. Turn left into St Werburgh Street, which brings you back to the cathedral and the end of the walk.

Liverpool

Access: Liverpool is easily accessible by road, rail, air and sea. Road visitors arriving by car should use the motorway system leaving the M6 via the M56 or M62. National Express run coach services to Liverpool from all the major cities in UK. Virgin run regular rail services from London Euston to Liverpool Lime Street, the journey taking under three hours. Liverpool airport is at Speke, some 7 miles (11km) from the city centre. Ferry services run to Liverpool from the Isle of Man, Belfast and Dublin.

The city of Liverpool takes its name from a tidal inlet that once stretched from the present Albert Dock to what is now the entrance to the Mersey Tunnel. The 'Liver' prefix probably comes from the Danish *lithe* or inlet. In the 12th and 13th centuries the settlement consisted of the church of St Nicholas, a substantial castle built by King John and a few surrounding streets occupied by no more than 500 people.

During the Civil War (1642–1648) the castle was completely destroyed by Royalist soldiers. In the succeeding years Liverpool grew in importance, helped by the discovery of local rock salt and coal. Its influence as a port also increased as the river at Chester silted up and trade with North America developed. Liverpool was heavily involved in the notorious slave trade. A 'triangle' of trade saw manufactured goods bound for West Africa, where slaves were taken on board for the West Indies and the southern part of the United States. Sugar and rum were then brought back to Liverpool. The slave trade was abolished in 1807, but by then the port had established trading links worldwide and it grew to be the country's second largest port. The first enclosed dock appeared in 1715 and further docks quickly spread along the waterfront. This was a time of considerable wealth for Liverpool and by the end of the 18th century the town had a population of over 50,000. Fine new buildings were constructed with the profits from the cotton trade. A landmark was the opening of the world's first passenger railway line, which ran from Manchester to Liverpool's Lime Street station.

Liverpool became an important port for immigration and emigration. Thousands left for a new life in Canada, America and Australia, while many Irish people settled in the city following the potato famine in the 1840s. The huge new transatlantic liners became a common sight in the port and firms such as Cunard and White Star set up their headquarters in Liverpool.

In 1890, Liverpool gained the status of a city and became the centre of a new diocese. The first bishop used St Peter's Church as his cathedral, but it soon became clear that this was inadequate. The second bishop, Francis Chevasse, and the Earl of Derby set up a committee that invited architects to submit plans for a new cathedral. The winning design was that of Sir Giles Gilbert Scott (1880–1960), the grandson of Sir George Gilbert Scott who had carried out a massive amount of restoration work on English cathedrals during Victorian times. Only 22 at the time, Giles was also, ironically, a Roman Catholic. It became his lifetime's work and he died before the building was completed. Built of local sandstone, the cathedral took 74 years to finish and was finally dedicated in 1978 in the presence of Queen Elizabeth II. It is the largest Anglican Cathedral in the world.

Meanwhile, the city of Liverpool was experiencing mixed fortunes during the 20th century. Despite being a key port in both world wars, the city, the port and its ships suffered badly. As one of the most strategic places in the country, Liverpool was heavily bombed in 1941. The result was 4000 dead and more than 10,000 homes destroyed. Fortunately the half-finished cathedral remained unscathed. The city received further blows in the post war years. The textile industry declined in the face of cheaper competition from abroad, while Britain's entry into Europe meant that Liverpool's links with the Commonwealth were no longer so important. Liverpool found itself on the wrong side of the country to develop trade with Europe. The docks were saved from terminal decline by the development of deepwater facilities downstream at Gladstone and Royal Seaforth docks.

The end of the 20th century, however, showed a distinct revival in Liverpool's fortunes. The fields of art, entertainment and sport thrived, while the resilience and humour of its people refused to die. The Beatles phenomena put the city back on the map. The docks area was re-developed, with museums, restaurants, retails outlets and art galleries. Light industry has been attracted to the area. The two universities are popular with students. Above all, Liverpool has become the centre of a thriving tourist industry, in which its two cathedrals form important attractions.

TOUR OF THE ANGLICAN CATHEDRAL
Start and finish: The west front of the cathedral.

The cathedral is located on St James' Mount to the east of the city centre. Built almost entirely of the local pink sandstone, its statistics are impressive:

Length = 619ft (187m)
Area = 104,275 sq ft. (9687m²)
Height of tower = 331ft (101m)
Nave vault = 120ft (36.5m)
Bells = Highest and heaviest ringing peal of bells in the world
Organ = 9765 pipes, making it the largest church organ

Not surprisingly, Liverpool Cathedral is the largest in Britain and the biggest Anglican cathedral in the world. The plan of the cathedral is in the form of a double-armed cross. In other words it has four transepts, and this plan has been adopted as the logo of the cathedral. The building is aligned differently to other English cathedrals as the nave runs north–south instead of the usual east–west, so that, for instance, there is a an east and a west transept and north and south ends. To save confusion, however, the usual liturgical directions will be used here with inverted commas.

The tour begins outside the '**West' Front (1).** Note the outcrops of local sandstone to the right, while to the left is a deep gully, which was once a quarry. It later became a graveyard. When the cemetery closed in the mid-1930s, it was estimated that there were over 57,000 bodies there. Included amongst their number was William Huskisson MP, the first man to be killed by a train (at the opening of the Liverpool–Manchester railway). The ground in front of the west porch contains a

155

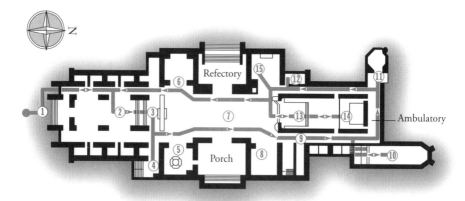

Key

1. 'West' Front
2. Nave
3. Dulverton Bridge
4. Lift to Tower
5. Baptistry

6. Visitors Centre
7. Central Space
8. 'Eastern' Transept
9. 'South' Choir Aisle
10. Lady Chapel

11. Chapter House
12. Holy Spirit Chapel
13. Choir
14. High Altar
15. War Memorial Chapel

small plaque marking the burial place of Sir Giles Gilbert Scott and his wife. Look now towards the West Front, which is dominated by *The Welcoming Christ*, a sculpture by Dame Elizabeth Frink, who died shortly after it was dedicated in 1994.

Enter the cathedral by the glass door on the left hand side of the main porch. Walk along to the reception desk. There is no entrance fee but you will be gently encouraged to make a donation. Move from here into the **Nave (2)**, where the massive dimensions of the cathedral can be appreciated. Look towards the 'West' End and the tall west window, which covers an area of 16,000 sq ft (1468m²). The stained glass commemorates those who made a contribution to the building of the cathedral. Turning in the other direction, there is a unique feature, the **Dulverton Bridge (3),** which completely spans the nave.

Turn through an arch on the 'south' side of the nave, where to every visitors' surprise is an old-fashioned red telephone box. This was also designed by Sir Giles Gilbert Scott, so we have Scott's smallest structure sitting within his largest building! This is also the point where a lift leaves on the first stage of a journey to the top of the **Tower (4)**. There are three stages to this climb. The first stage is by lift, followed by a walk along a corridor to the next lift and finally a climb of just over 100 steps to the top. There is plenty of opportunity to pause and view the massive interior of the tower, which is built not of stone, but brick and concrete. Also to be seen are the cathedral bells, the heaviest in the world. Emerging at the top of the tower, you are met by magnificent views over the city and the River Mersey. On a fine day with good visibility, Blackpool Tower and even the Lake District can be picked out. There is a small admission fee to the tower and tickets may be purchased in the bookshop.

We are now in the 'western' transept. To the 'south' is the **Baptistry (5).** The font is made from French marble and its 12 sides show figures representing the Apostles. The font's cover or baldachino is 39ft (12m) high and made of gilded oak. Note the font's surround, which represents the sea with fish swimming around. This symbolises the Israelites' passage from slavery in Egypt through the Red Sea to a new life. Move to the far side of the transept where you will find the **Visitors Centre (6).** Here is the cathedral shop which leads into the refectory. Above the shop is a hanging sculpture, the *Spirit of Liverpool*, in the form of sails meant to symbolize the seafaring traditions of the city. Note the subtle change of lighting every hour.

Walk now into the area known simply as the **Central Space (7)**, which lies directly under the tower. This huge area can accommodate several thousand people, so it can be put to a variety of uses, including concerts, plays, graduation ceremonies and festivals as well as cathedral functions. At the front of the steps of the Rankin Porch lies the Hillsborough Memorial Stone which remembers the Liverpool football fans who lost their lives at the FA Cup semi-final in 1989. On the floor in the middle of the Central Space is a circular marble memorial to Sir Giles Gilbert Scott, the architect who designed the cathedral.

The tour now reaches the '**Eastern' Transept (8).** Note the plaque in the paving, commemorating the consecration of the eastern transepts and the chancel of the unfinished cathedral in 1924 in the presence of Queen Mary and King George V. Move across the right-hand transept, where there is a monument to the Earl of Derby. The Stanley family, the Earls of Derby, have been influential in the Liverpool area since the 12th century. The famous horse race gets its name from this family and although now run at Epsom, it was originally run at Wallasey on the other side of the Mersey.

Proceed now along the **'South' Choir Aisle (9)**, where immediately on the right, set into the wall, is the Foundation Stone laid in 1904 by King Edward VII. Close to the stone is a model of one of Scott's early designs for the cathedral, which shows twin towers instead of the present single tower. As we move along the aisle, note the memorials and relief plaques to former bishops and deans, including Frederick Dwelly, the first Dean and Francis Chevasse, the second bishop. Those memorials in relief, along with many other works in the cathedral, have been carved by Liverpool's Edward Carter Preston.

On the right of the aisle, steps lead down to the **Lady Chapel (10).** This was the first part of the cathedral to be completed, being consecrated in 1910. Indeed it acted as the cathedral until the High Altar was consecrated in 1924. Take the upper steps first, which lead to a gallery giving a fine overall view of the chapel. Then take the lower steps into the chapel, where it is immediately obvious that it is far more elaborately decorated than the rest of the cathedral. Right round the chapel between the points of the arches and the triforium is a continuous text in gothic script. Many of the stained-glass windows of the Lady Chapel show women of significance from the bible and important Liverpool women who were missionaries or who worked with the poor of the city. Dominating the 'east' end of the chapel is a reredos in the form of a triptych. It was carved by G. W. Wilson to Scott's design. The side panels are fairly plain, but the central panel is elaborately carved and gilded. It shows the Nativity scene and Christ's Baptism in the Jordan. On the left of the altar is a statue of the Virgin Mary by Giovanni della Robbia, the 15th-century Italian sculptor. Before leaving the Lady Chapel, take a look at the entrance area where there is a bronze entitled *Redemption* by the Liverpool sculptor Arthur Dooley, backed by a superb modern embroidery by Ann McTavish.

Return to the 'South' Choir Aisle. At the end of the aisle by the votive candles is a maquette of Frink's *The Welcoming Christ*. Turn now into the ambulatory, where at the far end we reach the **Chapter House (11).** Compared with the size of the cathedral, the octagonal Chapter House appears tiny. It was built with donations from local lodges of Freemasons. There is a simple wooden altar backed a modern painting by Craigie Aitchison entitled *Calvary 1998*. The Chapter house is usually closed to visitors, but most of the features can be seen through the wrought iron gates.

Walk along the 'North' Choir Aisle, pausing at the **Holy Spirit Chapel (12)**, which is reserved for quiet meditation and prayer. Note to the right of the altar an aumbry, where the Sacrament is reserved. There is a superb alabaster reredos showing Christ (in relief) praying by the Sea of Galilee.

Our tour has now returned to the Eastern Crossing. Move into the **Choir (13)**, with the pulpit to the left and the lectern to the right. Behind the choir stalls are two murals by Christopher Le Brun based on the parables of the Prodigal Son and the Good Samaritan. High above the choir is the organ, which is believed to be the largest in Britain. Proceed towards the **High Altar (14)**, noting on the right the massive stone-built *cathedra* or Bishops' Throne. As there is no barrier between the choir and the nave, the High Altar is visible from the full length of the cathedral. The simple altar is backed by magnificent carved sandstone reredos full of gilt work. Immediately above the altar is a representation of the Last Supper, while higher up is a Crucifixion scene. Note also the wooden altar rail, which has 10 beautifully carved figures, each representing one of the Ten Commandants.

Leave the choir and return to the Eastern Crossing. Step into the **War Memorial Chapel (15)** There is a cenotaph with an illuminated Book of Remembrance listing over 40,000 war-dead. Included among these names is Noel Chevasse, son of the second bishop, who during World War I was awarded two V.C's and a Military Cross for his gallantry – the only member of the armed forces to have been awarded such accolades. His bust can be seen on the east side of the transept. Also on show is the ship's bell from HMS *Liverpool,* which acts as a memorial to those who lost their lives in the Battle of the Atlantic.

Return now to the north nave aisle and the west end of the cathedral, where the tour concludes.

Memorial to Bishop Chevasse

WALKING TOUR FROM THE ANGLICAN CATHEDRAL

The tour begins in the religious and academic part of the city, before moving down into the commercial area with its imposing public architecture. The Cavern area, made famous by the Beatles, is visited, before going on to the River Mersey and the revitalised port area. There are art galleries and museums *en route*, so it is worth purchasing a National Museums and Galleries on Merseyside Pass (NMGM). For the cost of visiting one museum you can visit the rest free of charge, the pass being valid for one year.

Start and finish: The tour begins at the west front of the Anglican Cathedral and ends at Lime Street Station.
Length: 4 miles (6.5km)
Time: Allow at least half a day for the tour, so that the Roman Catholic Cathedral and a selection of the museums can be visited.

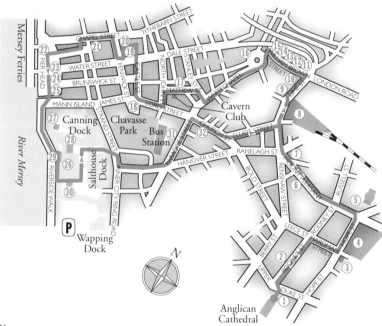

Key

1. Oratory
2. Rodney Street
3. Philharmonic Hall
4. Universities
5. R.C. Metropolitan Cathedral
6. Roscoe Memorial Garden
7. Britannia Adelphi Hotel
8. Lime Street Railway Station
9. St George's Hall
10. Wellington Column
11. Lancashire County Sessions House
12. Walker Art Gallery
13. Picton Reading Room and Hornby Library
14. Liverpool Museum
15. Mountford Building
16. Entrance to Mersey Tunnel
17. Beatles Area
18. Derby Square
19. Town Hall
20. Western Approaches Museum
21. Church of Our Lady and St Nicholas
22. Pier Head
23. Royal Liver Building
24. Cunard Building
25. Port of Liverpool Building
26. Albert Dock Area
27. Museum of Liverpool Life
28. Merseyside Maritime Museum
29. Tate Gallery
30. Beatles Story Museum
31. Paradise Street
32. Church Street

Refreshments: The refectory at the Anglican Cathedral has won Egon Ronay awards and is highly recommended. There are also a number of eating outlets in the Albert Dock area, including Taste at the Tate Gallery. There are a number of Victorian and Irish-style pubs in the city centre.

Leave the West Front of the Cathedral, noting on the right the building looking like a miniature Greek Doric temple. This is the **Oratory (1)**, which was the mortuary chapel for the nearby St James's cemetery. It was designed by John Foster junior and dates from 1829.

Notable Streets and Famous Addresses

Walk down the cathedral steps, cross Upper Duke Street and proceed along **Rodney Street (2)**. This is probably the most famous residential street in the city and many well-known figures have lived in these elegant Georgian terraced houses. The first house was built in 1783, one year after Admiral Rodney's famous naval victory. William Gladstone (1809–1898), four times Prime Minister, was born at no. 62. Lytton Strachey (1880–1932), one of the Bloomsbury Group of authors, who lectured for a while at Liverpool University, lived at no. 80. Arthur Clough (1819–1861) the poet, was born at no. 74, while no. 54 was the home of Dr. W.H. Duncan, who was Liverpool's first Medical Officer for Health in the mid-19th century. This was the first post of its kind to be set up anywhere in Britain, but made necessary by the poor health and appalling housing conditions of Liverpool's working classes. No. 11 was the birthplace of the author Nicholas Monsarrat (1910–1979), who wrote the classic *The Cruel Sea*. Few people live permanently in Rodney Street today, however. Most of the houses are used by professional firms. There is a sprinkling of architects and accountants, but the overwhelming majority are medical consultants – Liverpool's version of Harley Street.

Turn right at the traffic lights and continue to the right up Hardman Street to the next set of traffic lights. On the corner is the **Philharmonic Hall (3)**, home of the Liverpool Philharmonic Orchestra, the only orchestra in the country to own its own concert hall. The original hall on this site burnt down in 1933 and the present building dates from 1939. Its architectural style is officially 'Dutch impressionist', but there is more than a hint of Art Deco around. Opposite is the Philharmonic pub. The interior is one of the most ornate in the country and it is well worth having a quick glance inside.

We are now on Hope Street, the appropriately named road that links the two cathedrals. This area is also the academic centre of the city. Liverpool not only has two cathedrals but also boasts two **Universities (4)**, which makes for a lively atmosphere with many student bars and eating houses. Liverpool University was founded in the 19th century, while the John Moores University is of more recent origin, having developed from Liverpool Polytechnic. It also swallowed up the School of Art (where John Lennon and his wife Cynthia were students) and the Liverpool Institute (attended by Paul McCartney and George Harrison).

Ahead, and dominating the skyline, is the **Liverpool Roman Catholic Metropolitan Cathedral (5)**, which is located on the site of one of the largest workhouses which ever existed in England. The land was bought in 1930 and Sir

Edward Lutyens (1869–1944) was commissioned to design a cathedral. Had his plans been completed, the building would have been the largest cathedral in the world, but because of the intervention of the World War II only the crypt was built. It was soon clear that Lutyens scheme was far too expensive and in 1959 a competition was held to design a new, more modest cathedral. Sir Frank Gibberd (1908–1984) won the competition with a spectacular design. (It is an interesting thought that the designer of the Anglican Cathedral was a Catholic and the designer of the Roman Catholic Cathedral was a Protestant!). Work started in the early 1960s and was completed within four and a half years.

Affectionately known as 'Paddy's Wigwam', the cathedral is circular in shape and built of modern materials such as concrete and glass. It is crowned by a cylindrical lantern of glass. The cathedral is notable for the marvellous modern stained glass, causing changing shafts of colour to pierce the interior like laser beams. The visitor will also be impressed by some superb work by contemporary artists such as Elizabeth Frink, John Piper and Patrick Reyntiens.

The interior design is fascinating. The High Altar, pulpit and choir are in the centre. The main aisle runs around the outside, flanked by 12 side chapels, interspersed by bronze Stations of the Cross designed and made by Liverpool artist Sean Rice. If you wish to see Lutyens' crypt, contact an attendant.

Leave the cathedral and walk down Mount Pleasant towards the city centre. Near the bottom of the hill on the left is the **Roscoe Memorial Garden (6)**, which occupies the graveyard of an old Unitarian chapel. The Garden is named after William Roscoe (1753–1831) a well-known social reformer in the city who attended the chapel. In the centre of the garden is a monument with eight Doric columns. Look for the Spanish tiles from Seville which are a monument to Joseph Blanco White (1775–1846), a Spanish priest and political exile, who spent the last six years of his life in Liverpool. He was a noted poet, who wrote in both Spanish and English. On the opposite side of Mount Pleasant is the massive **Britannia Adelphi Hotel (7),** built in 1912 to accommodate passengers overnight before or after their transatlantic trips by liner. Once used by royalty and presidents, it was considered to be one of the most luxurious hotels in the world, but today its grandeur has somewhat faded. A rather bizarre event occurred at the Adelphi in 1954, when Roy Rogers was a guest. He rode his horse Trigger up the steps of the hotel and into the foyer, both later appearing at a first floor balcony!

A Neo-Classical Extravaganza

The tour now enters Lime Street and on the right is **Lime Street Railway Station (8)**, terminus for trains from London. Built on the site of old lime kilns, the station was also the terminus of the Liverpool and Manchester Railway which opened in 1830. Cross Lime Street by subway or at the traffic lights to **St George's Hall (9).** By any standards, this must be one of the most impressive public buildings in the country, if not the world. It was designed in neo-classical style by Harvey Lonsdale Elmes and incorporated a concert hall and the assize courts. The hall was completed in 1854. The exterior features a vast array of Corinthian columns, plus a cenotaph and equestrian statues of Queen Victoria and Prince Albert. There are further statues and monuments, this time to the great and good of Liverpool, in

St George's Gardens on the far side of the building. To the north of St George's Hall is the imposing **Wellington Column (10)**, which was inaugurated in 1863. The base of the column lists Wellington's campaigns and victories. Wellington's statue at the top of the column is cast in metal from guns captured at Waterloo. The column is 132ft (40m) high and nicely balances the modern Radio Tower in the city centre. Next to the column is a delightful fountain donated to the city by a former mayor in 1887.

Opposite the column is a string of further public buildings in matching neo-Classical style. First comes the former **Lancashire County Sessions House (11)**, which dates from 1887. Next is the **Walker Art Gallery (12)**, completed in the same year. It was sponsored by Sir Andrew Barclay Walker, a wealthy local brewer, after a disappointing public response for funds There are a number of friezes on the exterior of the building depicting Liverpool life. Look also for the Britannia look-alike in the portico – she carries a ship's propeller and is seated on a bale of cotton. The Walker Gallery is acknowledged to have one of the best collections of paintings and sculptures outside London.

The next neo-Classical building is the **Picton Reading Room and Hornby Library (13).** The circular reading room was opened in 1879 and is based on the design of the British Museum Reading Room. Alongside is the **Liverpool Museum (14)**, which was designed by Thomas Allom and opened in 1860. The displays are on three floors. The first floor deals with archaeology, concentrating on ancient Egypt and Greece. The second floor contains the Natural History section and has a comprehensive collection of geological specimens, including, inevitably, dinosaurs. The top floor appeals most of all to youngsters, concentrating on space and the universe, with a wealth of hands-on opportunities. The final building in this superb neo-Classical range is the **Mountford Building (15),** which opened in 1902 and is now part of John Moores University.

Immediately opposite the Mountford building is the entrance to the **Mersey Tunnel (16)** which links Liverpool with the Wirral on the far side of the Mersey estuary. Work started on the tunnel in 1925 and it was finally opened by King George V in 1934. It is 2.13 miles (3.4km) long and at its lowest point it is 33ft (10m) below the riverbed. The entrance to the tunnel is in Portland stone, decorated with Egyptian Art Deco designs.

Cross the busy junction via the pedestrian crossing and proceed along Whitechapel. This road follows the line of the tidal creek that was known as the Pool, long since filled in and built over. Proceed along Whitechapel until Stanley Street appears on the right. A statue of *Eleanor Rigby* sculptured by Tommy Steele used to stand on the right hand side of the road, but at the time of writing this area was being re-developed and the statue may well move to another location.

Turn left into Matthew Street, which could be described as the birthplace of the **Beatles (17)** phenomena. On the right is the Grapes pub, which was one of the 'fab four's' haunts, while on the left is the famous Cavern Club where the Beatles made their name. Other pop musicians who performed here included Gerry and the Pacemakers, the Searchers and P. J. Proby. The Cavern club was demolished in 1973 to allow an underground railway to be built, but it has been faithfully rebuilt under the Cavern Walks shopping centre. Some hotels in the city provide vouchers to visit the Cavern. Look for the statue of John Lennon which lounges in a doorway on the right hand side of the street.

At the end of Matthew Street turn left and walk to Lord Street. Turn right here and proceed to **Derby Square (18)**, which lies on the site of the Liverpool Castle that was badly damaged in the Civil War and eventually demolished in 1721. The Square is dominated by the Statue of Queen Victoria, unveiled in 1906 by her daughter Princess Louise (who apparently was not enamoured with the representation of her mother). Turn right into Castle Street. We are now entering the financial area of the city, and imposing Victorian bank frontages can be seen on either side of the street. The road plan in this area of the city has changed little since the streets were laid out in the 13th century and it is often said that 'the history of Castle Street is the history of Liverpool'.

At the end of Castle Street is the magnificent **Town Hall (19).** It was completed in 1754 and was the last work of John Wood the Elder of Bath (1704–1754). It was badly damaged by fire in 1795 and was later reconstructed by James Wyatt (1746–1813) (the same man who was responsible for some disastrous 'improvements' to cathedrals). He added an impressive dome and the two-storey Corinthian portico. The Town Hall was badly damaged during World War II, but was quickly restored.

Walk around the back of the Town Hall into the space known as Exchange Flags (just to the right was the site of the old Liverpool Stock Exchange). Dominating this area is the Nelson Monument, which was almost certainly the first outdoor public sculpture erected in the city. Walk down the other side of the Town Hall to Water Street, where imposing banks and insurance companies line the pavements. Turn almost immediately right in Rumford Street. Shortly on the right is Derby House, now the **Western Approaches Museum (20).** It was here in the basement that the Battle of the Atlantic was directed during World War II. Because of its strategic position, Liverpool received more attention from enemy bombs than any city outside London.

Now turn left and head down Chapel Street towards the river. On the left is the **Church of Our Lady and St Nicholas (21)**, which acts as Liverpool's parish church. It is often known as the 'Sailors Church' and was for centuries a landmark for ships. It dates from the 13th century, but little of

Church of Our Lady and St Nicholas, the city's parish church

the structure remains from these times. The old tower fell in 1810 and killed 25 worshippers. It was replaced five years later. The nave was destroyed during the World War II and rebuilt in the 1950s. There is an impressive metal sculpture on the Chapel Street side of the church showing *Christ Upon an Ass* by Brian Burgess.

Old Docks and New Tourism

Ahead is the road known as The Strand, which marks the course of the old Overhead Railway which ran parallel with the docks for 7½ miles (12.5km). It was pulled down in 1956. Cross the Strand by the traffic lights and head for the river. This is the area known as the **Pier Head (22)**. The original stone pier is long gone and there is now a line of floating piers, which can cope with the rise and fall of the tides. It is from here that ferries leave for various points on the far side of the River Mersey and further afield to the Isle of Man, Belfast and Dublin. There have been ferries crossing the Mersey since 1207 and for several centuries they were operated by the monks of Birkenhead Priory. The crossing was always hazardous due to the strong tides and frequent fogs. This changed when steam ferries were introduced towards the end of the 19th century. It was thought that the ferry trade would decline when the Mersey tunnel opened, but many of the ferries not only survive, but flourish with the addition of the tourist trade.

Turn to look inland at the range of superb buildings for which Liverpool is justly famous. The first is the **Royal Liver Building (23)**, the offices of the Royal Liver Friendly Society. The building, which was completed in 1911, was designed by W. Aubrey Thomas (1859–1939). Its two towers are capped by the mythical Liver Birds, which are made of copper and are 18ft (5.5m) high. The birds should have been eagles, as on the seal presented to Liverpool by King John, but the seal was lost during the Civil War. Its replacement shows a bird which resembles the cormorant, commonly found in the Mersey estuary. The next building is the **Cunard Building (24)**, which was completed in 1916 in an Italianate style. It was the headquarters of the Cunard company founded by a Canadian, Samuel Cunard. The firm was famous for its large and luxurious transatlantic liners such as *Mauretania*, *Lusitania*, *Queen Mary* and *Queen Elizabeth*, which eventually reduced the Atlantic crossing to 3½ days. The advent of air travel was the death knell for the transatlantic ships and the last Cunard liner left Liverpool in 1966.

The third building in the row is the **Port of Liverpool Building (25)**, which has the role of port administration. It was built in 1907 and designed by Arnold Thornely. It is built in Portland stone and has three fine domes. Outside the building is a monument to Sir Alfred Lewis Jones (1845–1909) who introduced bananas to Britain, pioneered refrigeration in ships and founded the Liverpool School of Tropical Medicine.

The tour now approaches the **Albert Dock (26)** complex, which was built between 1841 and 1848 and opened by Prince Albert. It was one of the first enclosed docks in the world, with a water area of 7½ acres (3ha) and surrounded by five-storey warehouses which were claimed to be fire-proof. The whole complex was designed by Jesse Hartley (1780–1860), who was the Liverpool Dock Engineer. After World War II, the warehouses were used for bonded goods such as tobacco and rum, while the dock itself gradually silted up. In the 1980s the local authority decided to revitalize the area. The dock was dredged and the warehouses converted into museums, art galleries, shops and restaurants, so that by the end of the century the Albert Dock complex had become a major tourist attraction. It is quite possible to spend a whole day here, so the visitor must decide which attractions to visit or omit on this half-day walking tour.

At the entrance to the dock is the **Museum of Liverpool Life (27)**, based largely in the old river pilots' building. The museum traces the history of Liverpool and its people and the special culture of the area. Next on the left, in the arms of the Canning half tide dock, are a number of boats and sailing craft belong to the **Merseyside Maritime Museum (28).** The main part of the museum is based in a warehouse on the north side of the dock. Its four floors contain displays on emigration, cargo handling and transatlantic slavery. Walk now along the side of Albert Dock to the **Tate Gallery (29),** home to the largest collection of contemporary art outside London. The London Tate Gallery was given to the nation by the sugar magnate Henry Tate who started his Tate and Lyall sugar business in Liverpool.

Now walk around to the far corner of the dock where the Tourist Information Centre is located. Note on the way the floating weather map in the dock. Go outside the line of old warehouses and turn right. This leads to the entrance of the **Beatles Story Museum (30)**. This traces the history of the famous Liverpool pop group and includes a mock-up of the Cavern Club. The tour concludes with an account of John Lennon's assassination (with the tune *Imagine* playing in the background) ensuring that few emerge dry-eyed into the giftshop. Continue from here anticlockwise around the dock, ending at the pub which was formerly the pumphouse operating many of the cranes using steam power.

Back into the City

Leave Albert Dock by the bridge between Canning and Salthouse Docks and cross Strand Street at the traffic lights. Turn slightly to the right and then immediately left into Canning Place. Both the dock and the street are named after George Canning (1770–1827), who was MP for Liverpool between 1812 and 1823. He was also briefly Prime Minister in 1827 but died shortly after taking office. Walk along Canning Place. At the traffic lights fork left into **Paradise Street (31).** Despite its name this road was once a notorious part of the seaport, filled with brothels, drinking dens and gambling joints. Near to the crossroads is the Eagle public house, which is one of the few survivors of those times. Many emigrants would stay here before boarding their ships.

At the end of Paradise Street turn right into **Church Street (32),** the main pedestrianized shopping street in the city. It was developed in the early 18th century and takes its name from the Church of St Peter, which has since been demolished. This busy street has branches of most of the country's 'high-street' shops and it was here that Frank Winfield Woolworth opened his first store in Britain in 1909. This is a favourite street for buskers. Look for the jovial statues of the Moores brothers, who have been important benefactors to the city in recent years. At the top of Church Street fork left into Parker Street, which leads on to Clayton Square. This was named after Sarah Clayton, a local colliery owner and coal merchant. At the end of Parker Street is Lime Street Station, where the walking tour ends.

Further Information

EXETER
Cathedral
web site: www.exeter-cathedral.org.uk
Toilets are located in the cloisters and in the refectory. **The cathedral shop**, just off the south quire aisle, sells guidebooks (in English, French and German), souvenirs and gifts. **The refectory** in the cloister room sells light meals Mon–Sat 13:00–17:00. Both shop and refectory are closed Sundays.
Underground Passages
Guided tour every half-hour preceded by a video presentation. Exhibition. Open Easter–Oct Tue–Sat 10.00–17.00, Nov–Easter Tue–Fri 14.00–17.30, Sat 10.00–17.00. Admission charge.
Royal Albert Museum
Open Tue–Sat 10.00–17.30. Admission free to Exeter residents; small charge to others.
St Nicholas' Priory
Open Easter–Oct Mon–Sat 13:00–17:00. Admission charge.
Tuckers' Hall
Open Jun–Sep Tue, Thu and Fri 10:30–12:00. For the remainder of the year Fri only 10:30–12:30.

WELLS
Cathedral
A **giftshop** and a **refectory** occupy the west cloister. It is no surprise to see that they are linear in shape! **Toilets** may be found in the Camery Gardens, with facilities for the disabled in the west cloister.
Wells Museum
Open daily 10:00–17:00 (summer) and 11:00–16:00 (winter).
Bishop's Palace
Open on a somewhat irregular basis Apr–Oct.

BATH
Abbey
The nearest **toilets** are located inside the entrance to the Roman Baths (turn left and go down the stairs). There is **wheelchair access** to most parts of the abbey, which has few interior steps. A small **bookshop** just off the south aisle sells a variety of gifts, music and books.
Abbey Vaults
Open 10:00–16:00 Mon–Sat; closed Sun. Modest entrance fee.
Museum in Sally Lunn's
Open during restaurant opening hours.
Museum in the Octagon
Open Mar–Dec 11:00–17:00 Mon–Sat; 14:00–17:00 Sun.
Postal Museum
Open Mar–Dec 11:00–17:00 Mon–Sat; 14:00–17:00 Sun.
Museum of Costume
Open 10:00–17:00 Mon–Sat; 11:00–17:00 Sun. Admission free.

Museum of East Asian Art
Open Mon–Sat 10:00–18:00 , Sun 10:00–17:00. Admission charge, with concessions.
Museum in No 1 The Royal Crescent
Open 10:30–11:00. Closed Mondays.
Roman Baths Museum
Open in summer 09:00–17:00, winter 09:00–18:00; torchlit visits on August evenings
20:00–22:00. Visitors are given easily used `wands' or autoguides, which give commentaries
in six languages. Entrance charge.

SALISBURY
Cathedral
web site: www.salisburycathedral.org.uk/pages/index.html
Open daily Apr–Sep 07:00–20:15 and Oct–Mar 07:00–18:30. **Toilets**, including those for the
disabled, may be found adjacent to the chapter house. Self-service **coffee shop** and **giftshop**
alongside the north cloister. Salisbury is a **wheelchair-friendly** cathedral, with ramps through-
out the building. For details of the **Friends of Salisbury Cathedral** tel (01722) 555120.
Salisbury and South Wiltshire Museum
Open Mon–Sat 10:00–17:00; Sun in Jul and Aug 14:00–17:00. Entry charge. Tel (01722)
332151.
Museum of the Royal Gloucestershire, Berkshire and Wiltshire Regiment
Open Apr–Oct daily 10:00–16:30; Nov, Feb and Mar Mon–Fri 10:00–16:30. Closed
Dec–Jan. Entry charge. Tel (01722) 414536.
Mompesson House
Open Apr–Oct 12:00–17:30; closed Thu and Fri. Tel (01722) 335659.

WINCHESTER
Cathedral
web site: www.win.diocese.org.uk/cathedral.html
The modern **Visitor Centre** is located in an attractive walled garden just to the southwest
of the cathedral. It includes a spacious **restaurant**, with some outside tables. Food is cooked
on the premises, and the lunches are imaginative. Next to the restaurant are **toilets**, with full
facilities for the disabled. A comprehensive **giftshop** in the Visitor Centre sells books, music
and souvenirs. There is **wheelchair access** to all parts of the ground floor of the cathedral;
use the main entrance.
Guildhall
The gallery is open daily during office hours.
City Mill
Open in summer Wed–Sun 11:00–16:45.
Winchester College
Guided tours available during the summer months, starting from the Porters' Lodge at 14:00
and 15:15.
City Museum
Open daily 10:00–19:00, Sun 14:00–17:00. Admission free.
Peninsula Barracks/Regimental Museums
Opening times vary. Free admission to all five museums.

CHICHESTER
Cathedral
There is a **refectory** in the Bishop Bell Rooms in the cloisters, where **toilets** may also be
found. The **wheelchair entrance** is in the southwest corner of the building (disabled visitors

may have to vary the route described in the text). There is a **giftshop** in the ground floor of the bell tower. For details of the **Friends of Chichester Cathedral**, contact The Royal Chantry, Cathedral Cloisters, Chichester, PO 19 1PX.

Pallant House
Open all year Tue–Sat 10:00–17:30. Closed Sun, Mon and bank holidays. Modest entry fee, with concessions.

City Museum
Open 10:00–17:30 Tue–Sat. Entrance free.

Guildhall Museum
Open Jun–Sep only, Tue–Sat 13:00–17:00. Entrance free.

OXFORD
Cathedral
web site: www.chchcath/index.html
There is no eating place at the cathedral or in the remainder of Christ Church. **Toilets** can be found on the west side of the cloisters. The **bookshop** is in the chapter house. Christ Church Cathedral is open daily 09:00–17:00, Sun 13:00–17:00 – note one peculiarity: cathedral time is five minutes behind standard time.

Christ Church Picture Gallery
Open Mon–Sat 10:30–17:30, Sun 14:30–17:30. Small entrance fee.

Botanic Gardens
Open Apr–Sep 09:00–17:00 and Oct–Mar 09:00–16:30 (greenhouse times may vary). Entrance free.

St Mary the Virgin Tower
Open 09:00–17:00 all year round. Entrance fee.

Bodleian Library
Open to the public 09:00–17:00. Entry to the Divinity School and Duke Humphrey's Library is by guided tour only during the summer months.

The Oxford Story
Open Apr–Oct 09:30–17:00; Jul and Aug 09:00–18:30; Nov–Mar 10:00–16:00. Admission charge.

Carfax Tower
Open Mar–Oct 10:00–17:30 and Nov–Feb 10:00–15:30. Admission charge.

GLOUCESTER
Cathedral
The spacious **refectory** and the **toilets** (including for the disabled) are located on the west side of the cloisters. There is a **bookshop** situated in the southwest corner of the nave and another in the Cathedral Close. There is good **wheelchair access** in the main body of the cathedral, though not for the Gloucester Cathedral Exhibition. For details of the **Friends of Gloucester Cathedral** contact the Chapter Office, tel (01452) 528095.

Folk Museum
Open Mon–Sat 10:00–17:00; Sun (Jul–Sep only) 10:00–16:00. Modest entrance fee. Wheelchair access to the ground floor only.

Soldiers of Gloucester Museum
Open Tue–Fri 10:00–17:00. Modest admission charge.

National Waterways Museum
Open daily 10:00–18:00, with reduced hours in winter. Sizeable admission charge, but with concessions.

Museum of Advertising and Packaging (Robert Opie Collection)
Open daily 10:00–18:00, with reduced hours on Sun and in the winter. Admission charge, with concessions.

East Gate Viewing Chamber
Open May–Sep 10:00–13:00 and 14:00 and 17:00, Sat only.

HEREFORD
Cathedral
The **Mappa Mundi/Chained Library** are open 10:00–16:15 in the summer and 10:00–15:15 in the winter. Closed Sun in the winter. Admission charge. The **giftshop** and **refectory** are located in the East Cloister. There are **toilets** including those for the disabled in Chapter House Yard.

City Art Gallery, Museum and Library
Open all year Tue–Sat 10:00–17:00; also Sun 10:00–16:00 during the summer. Entrance free.

Cathedral Cruises
40min river boat cruises leave hourly from 11:00 between Easter and October.

The Old House
Open Tue–Sat 10:00–17:00; also Sun during the summer. Admission free, although donation welcome.

Cider Museum
Open Apr–Oct daily 10:00–17:30; Nov–Mar Tue–Sun 11:00–15:00. Entrance charge, with concessions.

WORCESTER
Cathedral
web site: www.cofe-worcester.org.cathedral.html
Open daily 07:30–18:00. The **giftshop** is located to the west of the cloisters. There is a small **tearoom** on the east side of the cloisters. **Toilets** (including for the disabled) are on the north side of College Green. **Wheelchair access** throughout the cathedral except in the crypt. Details of the **Friends of Worcester Cathedral** from the Secretary, 10a College Green, Worcester, WR1 2LH.

Royal Worcester Porcelain Company
Open 09:00–17:00 daily, not Sun. Tours of the factory on weekdays at regular intervals starting at 10:25. Clearance shop, a seconds shop and an interesting museum.

Civil War Centre
Open daily Mon–Sat 10:00–17:00; Sun 13:30–17:30. Entrance fee, with concessions.

Museum of Local Life
Open daily 10:30–17:00, closed Thu, Sun, Bank Holidays. Wheelchair access limited.

The Greyfriars
Open Apr–Oct 14:00–17:00. Entrance fee, except for NT members.

COVENTRY
Cathedral
web site: www.coventrycathedral.org.welcome.htm
The cathedral is open daily 09:00–17:00. Note that the **Visitor Centre** and **Benedict's Coffee Shop** have restricted winter opening. There is a **giftshop** on the north side of the old cathedral. **Toilets** are available in the Visitor Centre. There is **wheelchair access** throughout.

Museum of British Road Transport
Open daily (except Christmas Eve, Christmas Day and Boxing Day) 10:00–17:00. At time of writing, entrance was free. Small restaurant and giftshop.

St Mary's Guildhall
Open only in the summer. Check current opening times with the Tourist Information Office.
Herbert Art Gallery and Museum
Open Mon–Sat 10:00–17:30; Sun 14:00–17:00. Entrance free.

LICHFIELD
Cathedral
website: www.lichfield.anglican.org.uk
No entrance fee, but donation recommended. The **cathedral cafeteria** is on the south side of the close, and has public **toilets**. There are two cathedral **giftshops**, one in the south aisle of the cathedral and the other in a house on the west side of the close. There is **wheelchair access** to most parts of the cathedral, but not to St Chad's Head Chapel. For details of the **Friends of Lichfield Cathedral**, contact the Friends' Office, 19A The Close, Lichfield, Staffs. WS13 7LD, tel (01543) 306120.
Heritage Centre
Open daily 10:00–17:00 all year round. Admission fee also covers entry to the Samuel Johnson Birthplace Museum. Concessions available.
Samuel Johnson Birthplace Museum
Open daily 10:30–16:30; closed Sun during winter. Admission fee also covers entry to the Heritage Centre. Concessions available.
Erasmus Darwin Centre
Open Tue–Sat 10:00–16:30, Sun 12:00–16:30. Closed Mon except Bank Holidays. Admission charge, with concessions.

CHESTER
Cathedral
web site: www.chestercathedral.org.uk
The **giftshop** and **toilets** are in the west cloister. There is good **wheelchair access** to most parts of the cathedral. The **Friends of Chester Cathedral** can be located at their e-mail address: friends@chestercathedral.org.uk.
Grosvenor Museum
Open Mon–Sat 10:30–17:00, Sun 14:00–17:00. Admission free. Only limited access for wheelchair users.
Chester Visitor and Craft Centre
Open Mon–Sat 09:00–17:00. Admission free.
Dewa Roman Experience
Open 09:00–17:00 daily. Admission charge.

LIVERPOOL
Anglican Cathedral
Open daily 08:00-18:00. Admission free, but donations invited. **Wheelchair access** throughout. There are **toilets** at the Vistors' Centre and also near the Chapter House. The Visitors' Centre includes a SPCK **Gift Shop** and an excellent **Refectory** that has gained Egon Ronay recommendations. The **Tower** is open to the public Mon–Sat 11:00–16:00. Tickets are available from the shop. The first tower lift also leads to the **Elizabeth Hoare Embroidery Gallery**, where there is a fine collection of Edwardian and Victorian ecclesiastical embroidery.
Metropolitan Roman Catholic Cathedral
Mount Pleasant, tel (0151) 709 9222. Open daily 08:00-18:00. Admission free, but donations welcome. **Wheelchair access** except to crypt.

Liverpool Museum and Planetarium
Open Mon-Sat 10:00-17:00, Sun 12:00-17:00. Admission fee. Extra charge for planetarium.
Merseyside Maritime Museum
Open daily 10:00-17:00. Admission fee. **Full wheelchair access.**
Museum of Liverpool Life
Open daily 10:00-17:00. Admission fee. **Full wheelchair access.**
Tate Gallery
Open Tues-Sun 10:00-18:00, closed Mon. Admission free, but charge for special exhibitions.
Wheelchair access throughout.
Walker Art Gallery
Open Mon-Sat 10:00-17:00, Sun 12:00-17:00. Admission fee. **Wheelchair access** throughout.
Western Approaches Museum
Open Mar-Oct Mon-Thu and Sat 10:30-16:30. Admission fee. No wheelchair access.
The Beatles Story Open daily Mar-Oct 10:00-17:00, Nov-Feb 10:00-17:00. Admission fee.

Bibliography

Most cathedrals have official guidebooks, usually approved by the dean and chapter, which can be obtained in cathedral shops.

Clifton-Taylor, Alec *The Cathedrals of England,* London, Thames & Hudson, 1967
A classic and very readable.

Ditchfield, R.H. *An Illustrated Guide to the Cathedrals of Great Britain,* London, J.M. Dent, 1902
Out of print, so scour the second-hand bookshops.

Howarth, Eva *Crash Course in Architecture,* Brockhampton Press, 1994

Morris, R. *Cathedrals and Abbeys of England and Wales,* J.M. Dent, 1979

Morris, Richard and Curbishley, Mike *Churches, Cathedrals and Chapels*, London, English Heritage, 1996

For teachers, but useful for younger readers.
Pitkin Guide Cathedral Architecture, Pitkin, 1992

Pictorial account of English cathedral architecture.

Pitkin Guide - Dissolution of the Monasteries, Pitkin, 1995

Smith, Edwin and Cook, Olive, *English Cathedrals,* The Herbert Press, 1989
Fascinating largely photographic volume.

Cook, G.H., *The English Cathedral Through the Centuries,* The Herbert Press, 1961
Out of print, but can often be found in second hand bookshops.

Tatton-Brown, T. *Great Cathedrals of Britain,* BBC Books, 1989

Wilson, C. *The Gothic Cathedral,* Thames and Hudson, 1990

Index